THE RULES OF THE TUNNEL

THE
RULES OF THE
TUNNEL

MY BRIEF PERIOD OF MADNESS

NED ZEMAN

GOTHAM BOOKS

GOTHAM BOOKS
Published by Penguin Group (USA) Inc.
375 Hudson Street, New York, New York 10014, U.S.A.

Penguin Group (Canada), 90 Eglinton Avenue East, Suite 700, Toronto, Ontario M4P 2Y3, Canada
(a division of Pearson Penguin Canada Inc.) · Penguin Books Ltd, 80 Strand, London WC2R 0RL,
England · Penguin Ireland, 25 St Stephen's Green, Dublin 2, Ireland (a division of Penguin Books
Ltd) · Penguin Group (Australia), 250 Camberwell Road, Camberwell, Victoria 3124, Australia (a
division of Pearson Australia Group Pty Ltd) · Penguin Books India Pvt Ltd, 11 Community
Centre, Panchsheel Park, New Delhi–110 017, India · Penguin Group (NZ), 67 Apollo Drive,
Rosedale, Auckland 0632, New Zealand (a division of Pearson New Zealand Ltd) · Penguin
Books (South Africa) (Pty) Ltd, 24 Sturdee Avenue, Rosebank, Johannesburg 2196, South Africa

Penguin Books Ltd, Registered Offices: 80 Strand, London WC2R 0RL, England

Published by Gotham Books, a member of Penguin Group (USA) Inc.

First printing, August 2011
1   3   5   7   9   10   8   6   4   2

Gotham Books and the skyscraper logo are trademarks of Penguin Group (USA) Inc.

LIBRARY OF CONGRESS CATALOGING-IN-PUBLICATION DATA
has been applied for

ISBN 978-1-592-40598-5

Printed in the United States of America
Set in Apollo MT   ·   Designed by Elke Sigal

Some names and identifying characteristics have been changed to protect the privacy of the
individuals involved.

While the author has made every effort to provide accurate telephone numbers and Internet
addresses at the time of publication, neither the publisher nor the author assumes any responsibility for errors, or for changes that occur after publication. Further, the publisher does not
have any control over and does not assume any responsibility for author or third-party websites or their content.

*Penguin is committed to publishing works of quality and integrity.
In that spirit, we are proud to offer this book to our readers;
however, the story, the experiences, and the words
are the author's alone.*

For my parents, for everything

THE RULES OF THE TUNNEL

Not so long ago, in the heyday of your idiocy, you made yourself a promise. That you can no longer remember making this promise, nor anything about it—aside from a yellow sticky-note reading "Remember Promise!"—fills you with the warm glow of achievement. You lived, if only briefly, among The Great Amnesiacs. And you did live well. Reportedly.

Every second was, in addition to your first second, a small revelation. That strawberry wasn't just a strawberry; it was The Dawn of Strawberry. That gorgeous woman you just met (for the sixth time)? The Eve to your Adam. *The Wire* was the best new show on television, in perpetuity. The best day of an amnesiac's life is always today.

The mind uncluttered by memory bears no preconceptions, no baggage. You, for example, were up for anything. A seeker. A student of life at the College of Now. To question others was not to question *them;* you were just really excited to hear their answers. That you asked the same questions day after day, each time evincing the same bushy-tailed curiosity ("So what's your baby's name?") underscored a commitment to higher education.

A common fallacy, perpetuated by civilians: The amnesiac forgets *everything.* His surname. Toilet training. Civilians believe this because, for all their accumulated knowledge, they don't know shit. *Amnesiac* is not a synonym for *retarded*. It's a kind of power-cleaning of the body, mind, spirit. A suctioning of accumulated dirt and detritus that leaves appliances looking like new. This lifestyle has been practiced by Hindus, Buddhists, and Taoists—all the best -ists, with the possible exception of Methodists—for god only knows how long. And yet somehow they manage to not shit their sandals.

Let go.

Be here now.

Faith. Also a biggie. The amnesiac ventures forth, ineluctably, because the man who remembers nothing has nothing to fear. Friends confiscating your car key? Find the other key and burn rubber. Ex doesn't want to see you anymore? Yeah? Says who? Forward. Always forward. The amnesiac is about making things happen, in the here and now; his best days are forever ahead of him—the gold Rolex, to an amnesiac, means "welcome aboard."

Where once you had been a weasel—and there were reasons why the girlfriend called you "a seven-year-old in a man's body"—now you were the un-weasel. Amnesia was god's reset button. A perpetual baptism. Here you struggle to recall personal examples, because the do-overs came and went so rapidly, and because that was the nature of the beast—the amnesiac being, above all else, an amnesiac.

So let's just imagine, in purely hypothetical terms, you're an amnesiac whose girlfriend—oh, let's call her "Caitlin"—happens upon inappropriate emails you've written to unsuitable young ladies you hardly know and an ex you know too well.

Let's say you deceive, undermine, and berate friends who for months had ministered to all your needs and whims, among them transportation, security, bookkeeping, and wet-nursing. Let's say you go AWOL on your doting parents, at a time when they could really use a hand.

Or let's just say you spend a month as a maniac.

Any of these developments would be a problematic one, in that you would have inflicted pain and suffering and would henceforward feel like an asshole.

Unless you're an amnesiac.

And there it is. The beauty part.

Total number of amnesiac support groups: zero.

Total number of amnesia-related suicides: zero.

Good luck finding a miserable amnesiac. The hunt will be long and perilous, through a godless land far, far away. Bring warm boots and a Bible. Bring a blowtorch.

And yet.

A certain bittersweetness must be acknowledged. That's partly because the amnesiac is naturally uncomfortable with nostalgia. It wastes time and energy. Promotes sloth and hubris. The amnesiac never rests on his laurels, because none exist, because he forgot them. But that's a given.

Amnesia, thy fickle mistress. A life of full and perpetual memory loss—as in total blank, dating back to the womb—is virtually unheard of, except among those too old or enfeebled to reap the benefits. And nobody wants to be Harrison Ford, drooling through *Regarding Henry*. Virtually everyone else who experiences amnesia eventually succumbs to memory, to some degree or another, and therefore comes to confront that which they once forgot so dearly.

Picture a PC hard drive fresh out of the box, prior to the coming incursions by Ukrainian cybercriminals—except, in this case, the worm-viruses and porno-spam arrive in the form of anxiety and depression. They are *acquired*. They are usage fees. The more data you access, the faster they come, often in tandem; they exploit your every vulnerability and misstep. Dirty mind, dirty pop-ups. Infections can be combated, rolled back. But once the firewall is breached, let's face it: The machine never quite works the same.

This much you remember.

They say the day you identify yourself as an amnesiac is the day you cease to be one. But that's cruel. Also imprecise. Memory gain, as you experienced it, was a gradual and fitful devolution. A fog of war. Suddenly, amid yet another fruitless search for your socks, the bell would go off and you'd find yourself thinking *Holy shit, I'm an amnes—*

But then, just as swiftly, you'd forget that, too. You spent weeks forgetting that you couldn't remember, then vice versa. So where did that leave you? In purgatory. That's where. Finally you'd throw up your hands, retreat to the TV room, and sit wondering why the series premiere of *The Wire* seemed so damned predictable. The strain took a toll. Your cats' weight ballooned. You'd stand there, in the kitchen, thinking, *Oh, Christ, I'm gonna forget to feed them*. So you'd fill their bowls, then return twenty minutes later, thinking *Oh, Christ . . .*

Civilians, whenever you describe the Metamorphosis period to them, always crinkle their faces and lean close and say things like "I'm *so sorry*" and "I'm *so glad* the clouds have lifted." Which always feels awkward, since amnesiacs have no words for *sorry* and *past*, and since civilians fail to grasp the fundamental point.

More memory. More problems.

And the only thing worse than remembering everything is remembering everything except the worst part. You learned this the hard way. It was like waking in an empty cineplex, having missed the final ten minutes of an M. Night Shyamalan movie about you. You assumed there had been a Big Reveal; that it had strained credulity and logic; and that it had been very, very dark. But the rest was a smoking crater. Everyone knew what happened to you. Except you. It was torture, the not knowing—memory owned you now, and wanted your last reserve of amnesia. The only amnesiac who could remain immune, at this point, would have to be living alone in the wilderness. And what kind of maniac does that?

You succumbed. It was inevitable. For more than a decade, as a writer for *Vanity Fair* magazine, you had debriefed and profiled a multitude of treacherous characters: spies, serial killers, Jennifer Lopez. But you had at your disposal, in this instance, everything a reporter could hope for. Your desk overflowed with research materials: emails, journals, medical records. Live sources—friends, relatives, doctors—were many and impeccable. Unlimited access. Nothing off-limits.

The facts as you knew them:

Everything revolved around The Procedure.

The Procedure was also known as ECT, which was an acronym for *electroconvulsive therapy,* which was a polite way of saying *electroshock,* which totally freaks people out. The Procedure, notwithstanding its dark history and eternally controversial status—thanks, in part, to crackerjack performances by Jack Nicholson and Russell Crowe—remained a treatment for depression.

Your old friend.

Depression—that was the nut of the story.

Somewhere along the way, it seemed, you had transitioned from softcore to hardcore. The distinction was a subtle but important one. It was a given that pretty much everyone falls into the wormhole, more or less—that everyone has those days when getting out of bed is a Homeric journey; when an episode of *Supernanny* makes them burst into tears; when peeling off the boss's face and drinking his blood seems like a viable career move. But when softies finally shake off the blues and embrace the day, hardcores are getting warmed up. They have the training, the tools, the will. Depression isn't a sprint. It's a marathon. Each step hurts worse than the last. But they do it anyway. They go all the way.

If hardcore teaches you anything, it's that no matter how bad the depression gets, it will get worse, fast, and in ways you haven't even imagined yet. Depression fucks anything that moves, then fucks it again. Despair. Fatigue. Oversleeping. Undersleeping. Can't think. Can't stop thinking. Can't see straight. Can't read. Can't write. Can't eat. Can't move. Depression is the greatest weight in the universe. Greater than weight. Greater than love. Love, to the low-down depressive, is an abstraction. It's something they talk about on *The View*.

If the currency of depression is loneliness—and it is—we are a wealthy people. We are a legion. One out of every seven Americans has a "mood disorder"—an umbrella term covering various depressive disorders, in addition to the doppelganger: manic depression, a.k.a. bipolar disorder. Mood disorders are the world's cause of disability and a driving force behind most suicide attempts—along with substance abuse and anxiety disorders. This only makes sense, since nothing complements mood swings like cocaine, whiskey, and fear. Roughly 30 percent of all moodies develop substance-abuse problems, and at least half the total population is of Nervous-American descent. Oftentimes, as in the case of yours truly, depression and anxiety are so incestuous that it's damn near impossible to tell which one's driving the bus.

Which is depressing.

Which is why you had The Procedure.

Which you can't remember.

All you knew about the most recent bout was that it must have been an especially pesky one, given shock's reputation as The Treatment of Last Resort. The reputation stemmed not from mortal dangers. A shock patient runs no risk of electrocution. He won't wake up as a potato. Chances are he'll feel better. He just won't know where the fuck he is. Or how to get home. Or why.

Amnesia. The big-ticket item. Short-term memory loss was almost guaranteed, but things would return to normal in a month or so. Longer-term losses were probable. Some memories might return after six months or so. Or return partially. Or in fragments. Or not. The Procedure had really been a series of Procedures, administered over a period of some weeks. Or months. But that period was over now. This much you remembered (although possibly the note taped to your fridge—"Remember ECT/Amnesia!"—proved helpful).

Surroundings were established. This was your home office. This was your desk. These were your keepsakes:

Three one-inch-tall ceramic penguins. Clustered together. Because penguins mate for life.

One six-by-ten-inch photograph of a giant grizzly bear (a.k.a. brown bear, a.k.a. Kodiak bear) retreating from view. Because bears don't hunt people; people hunt bears.

Treasures. From treasured friends.

The larger cast, too, remained crystal clear. Parents. Brothers. Friends. Girlfriend.

Girlfriend.

And fog gathered.

Caitlin. Lovely Caitlin.

And darkness fell.

The void stretched back for months, maybe a year, save for random bits (JetBlue potato chips) and pieces (tiny pink shoes) signifying nothing. The rest of the story would have to come by way of shoe leather and notepads. Which made you, in addition to the world's first amnesiac reporter, appreciative of why monkeys don't become airline pilots. You were the worst subject you'd ever interviewed (and the feeling was mutual). You felt deceived, stonewalled; you felt ambushed, persecuted. You wanted to sue yourself for libel.

Q: So why'd the girlfriend leave?
A: Like I said before. I don't recall.
Q: Don't or don't want to?
A: So you're calling me a liar?
Q: I'm just asking.

A: Ask something else.

Q: Fine. Tell me about your parents.

A: The best. Love 'em to death.

Q: How's your dad doing?

A: Fine. Why?

Q: Um . . .

A: This interview is over.

The reporter won. (The reporter always wins.) In the end, memory loss, no matter how complete and irreversible it may be—and, in your case, it certainly was both—is a sucker's bet. Amnesia can delete every last megabyte of neural data—literally wipe the hard drive clean. But there's a catch. (There's always a catch.) Once or twice a day, for the rest of his life, the amnesiac will find himself pausing midsentence or dropping his fork. *What? Shit.* He will experience a heaviness of chest and skin. The weight of absence. The phantom limb. *Something happened. Something I did.* And he will be powerless to stop this, because, for better and worse, it's the fatal flaw of every amnesiac.

The heart remembers what the mind forgets.

PART ONE

You arrived at the gates of Xanadu on a sharp blue morning in April 1997. You were thirty-two.

The kingdom stood at the center of the universe, at 350 Madison Avenue, in Midtown Manhattan. But it was visible only to a rare few, due in part to its relatively modest scale, turdish coloring, and lunky 1920s-era architecture; it would have been the crown jewel of Warsaw. But that was the beauty part. If everyone could see Xanadu, it wouldn't be Xanadu.

You had traveled far. Across a vast continent. Alone. Carrying only a suitcase and a dream. Just three weeks earlier, you had enjoyed a life of quiet domestication, in a sunny house in Los Angeles, replete with a girlfriend, two cats, and the mantle of unfulfilled potential. You wore it well. The romance was on life support, indefinitely; you held a mediocre editing job at a middling city magazine perpetually on the brink of collapse. Freelance contributors, tired of waiting for checks that would never come, would soon begin mailing bricks on the company's FedEx account.

But acquiescence had its benefits, once you really committed to packing it in. It was a *lifestyle:* enjoy brunch, sleep well. There were, in the whole of Los Angeles, upwards of six magazine writers, half of whom would be out the instant Paramount optioned their spec scripts.

Any chimp with a notepad could muddle through in the city where journalism goes to die.

New York was the last place on your mind. Already you had done a six-year stretch there, subsisting in a series of god-awful studio apartments with clanging radiators and nocturnal neighbors heard but never seen. But back then, at least, you were a Promising Young Writer for two Important Magazines Of The Day. You had, if not wealth or comfort, promise. Zing. But in the years thereafter, and throughout the bloom of your mediocrity, you retreated further and further from New York. Because that's where the talent lived, and because you were a cautionary tale.

Were.

The building at 350 Madison Avenue was home to Condé Nast Publications, which was home to the world's shiniest, swankiest magazines, among them *The New Yorker, Vogue, GQ, Wired, W, Details, Gourmet, House & Garden, Architectural Digest, Condé Nast Traveler*—and, not least, *Vanity Fair*. The braying alpha dog. The perpetrator of "buzz." The slick, fat monthly variously loved, hated, envied, resented, mocked, and/or feared in all corners of The Media-Industrial Complex, but especially in the world of print journalism.

You had read all the best stuff about the worst people—the Menendez brothers, Greta Van Susteren—by way of Dominick Dunne, *VF*'s most celebrated and indefensible writer. *VF*, in one issue, had published definitive articles on Iraq and the LAPD scandal. But of course the thing that stuck with you, in the end, was the Annie Leibowitz photo of Demi Moore's swollen, naked pregnant-ness. How was it that a single magazine could so deftly pander ("Tom Cruise On Fire") and soar (William Styron on depression, Marie Brenner on Big Tobacco)? *VF*, having dared to blend highbrow and low, bite and blow, refinement and excess, was everything that was right and wrong with journalism at the time.

Unless or until it hired you. In which case, it was just everything that was right.

You had accepted the job without hesitation or negotiation. Which seemed wise at the time, since neither option was available; your leverage was compromised, from the start, by its absence. *VF*'s editor, Graydon Carter, had seized the upper hand eight years earlier, when he was at *Spy* magazine, the elegantly cruel satirical monthly he founded with Kurt Andersen, the magazine's co-editor. They hired you straight out of grad school at Columbia, after you'd sent them an article written in Magazine 101; it was a profile of a man named Hank Schmidt, who was, in addition to New York's most decorated Ku Klux Klansman, its only one.

Graydon and Kurt published the article and hired you as a staff writer. But you weaseled out of the job, having accepted a similar position at *Newsweek*. You thought of yourself as a Serious Journalist, destined to thunder about, saying things like "truth wants to be free" and "I'm a reporter, dammit." Ideally, you would be chased through wherever the hell Mel Gibson was in *The Year of Living Dangerously*. Or tortured in Burma. Carl Bernstein and Sydney Schanberg were just two more Screaming Jew Reporters until they became Dustin Hoffman and Sam Waterston. And they were all your journalistic deities.

In later years, after Graydon's enthronement at *VF* and your free-fall into obscurity, the power dynamic trended unfavorably. He threw you occasional writing assignments but otherwise kept you at arm's length. When he finally summoned you, by phone, the power dynamic was firmly established.

"I need you to start three weeks from today," he said.

"Great," you said.

"Great."

"The only thing is, I need to quit my job, pack, move."

"Agreed."

"Cross-country. Three weeks."

"Yes. They have these things called *airplanes.*"

"Right."

"Three weeks," he said. "Enjoy the flight."

The frantic cross-country rally left little time for dithering or doubt. This evoked a feeling of nakedness. There was also the matter of your crawly skin—but the ill effects were small potatoes, considering your baseline state of emotional impairment, and given the healing power of There. The farther you got from Here, the better it felt.

You faced one last obstacle. Your face. Those damned glass doors as you entered 350 Madison were, in the sharp morning light, basically giant mirrors. This seemed inconsiderate of a guest who had spent decades avoiding the perils of reflection; your list of Things To Be Avoided At All Costs, though infinite and ever changing, included only one bona fide phobia. Mirrors brought nothing but bad news, then embellished it.

You'd always viewed yourself (in your mind's eye) as flawed but halfway presentable in appearance. Sufficient. A lanky huncher, a shade under six feet tall; brown hair, eyes; fair skin; casual in looks and manner—more Midwestern than Jewish. Inevitably, after meeting a girlfriend's mother, the latter would tell the former, "Well, he looked like a nice young man."

Now, at the doorstep of history, sufficient felt like gangbusters. You were clean-cut, freshly shaven, and dressed as if you'd stepped out of a catalogue for The Journalist's Wearhouse: dark blazer, white button-down, blue-patterned tie, and khakis. The ensemble was designed to address the unique challenges you faced; it would project an air of authority, of *gravitas,* while preventing others from mistaking you for the intern from Oberlin. You'd gone the extra mile, in consultation with the fashion experts at Desert Hills Premium Outlets, located just minutes from The Banning Municipal Airport.

But then came the glass doors. A funhouse-mirror effect lent your worst features (sunken eyes, long face) into Spitting Image proportions; the blazer, now hopelessly ill fitting, suggested a teenage usher. Shutting your eyes only made things worse, because mental images projected better in the dark, and because you looked like a disabled person, and because that didn't make for an ideal first impression.

Onward through a lobby the color of canned salmon. Into an elevator. Flanked by two nerd-chic waifs of the sort that frequently made kindling of you. Alighting on the fourth floor, you checked in with the receptionist, pushed through the glass door, and entered the inner sanctum. You experienced, initially, a twinge of disappointment; *VF*, in your imagination, was a pleasure dome for the literate and heartless. There would be skylights and koi ponds. There would be a spinning cube at the center of a stark white room.

The place, in reality, was a study in institutional gray, from the carpeting to the prefab cubicles and desks. The main corridor seemed too narrow; the fluorescent lighting, a shade dim. Thick walls and shuttered doors concealed the few people who seemed to be in attendance. The total effect was one of hushed intrigue. OfficeMax noir.

"Abandon hope, all ye who enter here."

Doug was a slender, suspiciously fit character with wire-rim glasses and thick brown hair cut short. He was forty-four, with a mien somewhere between bookish and puckish.

"Relax," he said. Then he cackled. "Just fucking with you. It's actually pretty cool here."

Doug was one of the few staffers you'd met previously. He had edited the latest of three freelance articles you had written for the magazine (Ivy League football) and had proven surprisingly un-prickish. Condé Nast, a company that trafficked in entitlement and privilege, favored editors who exuded same, most notably *Vogue*'s current editor, Anna Wintour, and *VF*'s previous one, Tina Brown. You'd once interviewed Brown for a story in *Newsweek*. She swanned into the room, flanked by a mirthless assistant dressed like James Mason, and sat at the far end of a vast table. Her gaze turned your palms into oysters. You begged off a handshake. Muttering something about a broken thumb.

"Guess I'm the welcoming party," Doug said.

"Where is everyone?" you asked.

"They don't get here till ten."

"I was told eight thirty at the latest."

He loosed another quick, high-pitched cackle.

"Even the assistants don't get here before nine," he said.

"So why are you here?"

"Because I'm an idiot."

He sighed. "California," he said. "Why would you ever leave California?"

"Because I'm an idiot."

"Did your girlfriend move with you?"

"No."

"That good or bad?"

"I don't know—"

"Because you're looking a little pale."

"Really?"

He shrugged, then said he had to get some work done. He invited you to wait things out in his office.

"Thanks," you said. "But maybe I should get my bearings. Check in with Graydon."

"He's not here yet," he said.

"How can you tell?" you asked.

"The whole place would be different." He swirled his finger in the air. "But he'll be here soon. So don't wander too far. Trust me."

A tilt of your head.

"Because that's when he'll call for you," Doug said. "Or come looking for you. He just knows. Don't ask how. It's unexplainable."

"What happens if I'm not here?"

He just laughed.

Over the next few minutes, as you shuffled about pointlessly, things changed. The hush became a hum. Lights brightened. Outside each office sat a crisp young assistant, midtwenties, strong of bone, breeding, and eye contact:

"Morning!"

"Good morning!"

"Good morning, sir!"

The assistants were better groomed and dressed than you would ever be. The males favored slim three-button suits of the sort worn by boutique hoteliers. The metrosexual ones—the *especially* metrosexual ones—wore foppish tweeds; seersucker and bow ties were also in evidence. The female assistants hewed to The Condé Nast Stylebook ("colors may range from black to black, except for the heels, which must be sparkly, spiky, strappy, and, to be frank, a little porny") while maintaining a dewy, fresh-faced appeal, as if they'd spent the weekend show-jumping in Coventry.

"Morning!"

"Good morning to you!"

Figures materialized out of nowhere, forming a natural ecosystem. At the center of the system were platoons of copy editors ("it's *composed*, not *comprised*") and fact checkers ("Camilla used brands other than Tampax") in hot, futile pursuit of the top-shelf editors. The latter were too busy talking their writers off the ceiling ("I'm aware you drank with Hemingway, but this paragraph still needs to go"). The floor seems tilted toward the far corner office, where a flurry of activity had commenced.

It was 9:30 A.M. And the boss was in.

Finally, one of the assistants led you to another assistant, who led you straight back down the hall, to the office next to Doug's. "Welcome home," she said.

At the door hovered two throbbing blue orbs. "This is your assistant," the assistant said. "Evglemniana."

Or some such. Your assistant's name (whatever it was) was marginally less daunting than her presence. Never had someone so tiny possessed eyes so large. Her giant blue gaze, set off by her Russian cheekbones and porcelain skin, was to be admired and feared.

"Nice to meet you," she said.

"Likewise, Evglemuh—"

"Evgenia."

"Right. Of course."

She smiled evenly, in that well-bred way—just polite enough to conceal what you deemed to be either indifference or contempt (or both). Evgenia was different than the others. Cooler. Formidable. But you reserved judgment, given that you were (1) new to the master-servant dynamic, (2) a superpowerful young professional, and (3) a paranoid person.

"Well," she said, before returning to her desk. "Call if you need anything."

At which point another assistant led you away, while explaining that the editor you were replacing had yet to vacate the premises. In the meantime, she said, you would be working out of an office/storage room located in a separate department, among the magazine's stylists and party planners. Evian, everywhere.

There you spent three hours, alone, waiting for further instructions. An effort at mingling went nowhere. The stylists and party planners were loud and tan people, endlessly barking about "Donatella" and "Annie" and the perils of seating Lord Goatsquabble next to Duchess von Schnurz at something called "The Serpent," or "Serpentine," or whatever. It was safer to just sit quietly, sniffing samples of Revlon Age Defying Makeup and Almay Time-Off Revitalizer.

Finally, Evgenia materialized at the door. "George needs you," she said.

"Okay," you replied. "One question."

"Yes?"

"Who's George?"

One of the other editors, evidently.

"What's this about?" you asked.

"I don't know," she said.

"Okay. But I was told to sit tight for Graydon."

"Oh." She trailed off. She seemed anxious to return to her real boss. Which made you anxious. Also covetous and ashamed.

"I'm sure it's fine," she said. "I'll tell Graydon's office where to find you."

George, a high-strung sort in wonk-chic glasses, could be found yammering on his cell phone and awash in copy. "Graydon wants you to shadow me for a few weeks," he said, between conversations. "I'm swamped right now. So I'm gonna transition a writer to you, okay?"

"Absolutely," you said. "Who?"

His assistant appeared. "He's here," she said.

George rose to greet a silver bull of a man in a pinstripe suit. "Come meet the newest member of the team," George told the writer, before introducing you.

"Carl Bernstein," the man said.

"Guh," you said.

He shed his suitcoat and settled in.

"It's an honor," you said. "Really."

"Well, thank you," he said, warmly.

"Just here to help."

"Great."

George raised the subject of Bernstein's current story assignment, about a blowhard Washington lobbyist named Tommy Boggs. Themes and plot points were discussed. Then, midsentence, Bernstein turned to you.

"Here's something," he said. "Any chance I can get my hands on a Diet Coke?"

George cried out for his assistant, who was AWOL. Things got uncomfortable.

"No problem," you said.

"Great," Bernstein replied. "Thanks, Ted."

Evgenia was on the phone. So you went for it, scrambling down the elevator, through the lobby, and into a newsstand. Your wallet, however, remained upstairs. Back up you went, only to discover that the wallet contained no cash. This precipitated a sprint out into the street, followed by an ATM withdrawal, then the purchase of two Diet Cokes, then a triumphant ascent to pay dirt. By then, however, both Bernstein and George had left the building, whereas Evgenia stood astride her desk, ramrod-straight, at mock-ten.

"There you are," she said.

"Huh?"

"You didn't get my voicemail?"

"What?"

"Graydon called for you."

"When?"

"Ten minutes ago. I left you a voicemail."

"But—"

She hurried you to Graydon's assistant, Patricia, whose parents owned Venezuela. She guided you into an airy corner office with an off-white sofa, a private bathroom, and a crescent-shaped desk of the blond retro-minimalist variety. The desk was custom-designed, in keeping with the man's stature, now in full effect. He stood six feet two, with a longshoreman's chest and forearms. He had a ruddy tan, perfect teeth, and his trademark hairstyle: wispy salt-and-pepper clouds, jutting to the east and west. He topped things off with bespoke black suit, a black tie, a crisp white dress shirt, and cufflinks fashioned out of old fishing lures; his wristwatch, also antique, was worth more than your Nissan Altima.

"No rush," he said.

"Just getting acclimated."

"Wait," he said. "You thought I was *serious*?"

He paused a moment before offering a handshake and a thick, jaunty laugh.

"Glad to be here," you said.

"Sure? You look a little pale."

"Totally sure."

"Good thing. Los Angeles would have fried your brain. I love visiting the place. And I love leaving it."

"Yep. It was time for me to go."

"What's your girlfriend think?"

"That it was time for me to go."

"Any luck finding an apartment?"

"Found one."

"Where?"

"Brooklyn Heights."

There was a pause.

"Brooklyn," he said. "You know there's a big island here we call *Manhattan*?"

Another pause.

"So you're clear about everything you'll be doing," he said.

"Um," you said.

"Writers write. Editors edit them."

"Right."

"I did hire an editor, right?"

"Right."

"As opposed to a writer."

"Right."

"Show ponies and workhorses," he said. "You've heard that expression?"

"Um," you said.

"Two kinds of editors. The ponies swan around being fabulous. The horses keep their heads down and do the work. Guess which kind I hired you to be?"

"I love horses."

He explained the magazine's basic editing structure, which was singular in its simplicity. *VF* shunned the "tiered" editing process favored by many magazines, largely because multiple editors tended to dilute a writer's voice, but also because simplicity insured accountability. You would preside over a specific stable of writers. "And you're the only one standing between them and me," he said. "It's your responsibility to keep them productive, happy, and in line. We treat writers the way they should be treated. When a writer hands in a story, he gets feedback within twenty-four hours. Calls gets returned that day. You're also part manager, part nurse. Some writers you'll find more challenging than others." He smiled. "But it rarely gets physical."

He was alluding, perhaps, to an incident involving a writer known for his Olympian alcohol consumption and expense-account abuses. He ended up biting his editor on the elbow.

Graydon handed you a typewritten list of names. These were your writers, among them nine "contributing editors"—writers officially affiliated with *VF*—and a half dozen freelancers currently on assignment. Among the latter, one named popped.

"Sydney Schanberg," you said.

"Back to *The Killing Fields*," he said. "Sam Waterston wasn't available."

"Wow. Add Mel Gibson to Schanberg and Bernstein, and it's my supertrifecta."

"*The Year of Living Dangerously*? You've got a little Mel Gibson in you."

"Really?"

He just laughed and laughed.

Finally he displayed a hardcover book. A preview copy of the sort reserved for critics and swells.

"Heard of it?" he asked.

In no way.

"Rings a bell," you said.

"It's incredible," he said.

"I'll start reading tonight."

"Then go get the writer. I want him on contract with us."

"I'm on it."

"There's no maybe on this," he said, poker-faced. "But, hey, no pressure."

"I love pressure," you said.

You lay awake all night, amid unpacked boxes and duffels, reading the boss's copy of *The Perfect Storm*.

Home was a one-bedroom apartment in a two-story walk-up in Brooklyn Heights; its rooms, though large, had evidently housed the local chain-smoking society. The walls were Marlboro White; the wood floors, sticky; the '70s-era fridge stocked with a spilled bottle of Strawberry Yoo-hoo and an ossified plate of kung pao something. The apartment in Los Angeles had been half as expensive and five times nicer.

But, hey. The road to glory and plunder would be paved with setbacks and sacrifices, because they wouldn't be glory and plunder if any clown could find them, and because that's how it worked in Viking times. Nose, grindstone; eyes, prize.

The book, by Sebastian Junger, was certainly a page-turner—all the dropped r's and Men Against The Sea stuff evoked *Jaws*. Which also happened to be among your favorite movies. You were, like all cowards of a certain age, a sucker for any story involving guys who went Up The River. *Midnight Express, The Deer Hunter, Apocalypse Now*—all had to be watched without interruption (and with a bong).

But a sleepless night was a bridge too far; even in college, even when faced with finals or the remote possibility of sex, you were the guy who crashed at midnight. Then would follow ten unbroken hours of motionless, soundless, ursine slumber. Roommates treasured your ability to sleep through their crimes against nature. Sleep was a way of life. And it was a good life.

And now, suddenly and henceforward, sleep was the *Andrea Gail*. The early returns were surprising. With insomnia came a kind of energy distinct from your endless supply of nervous energy, in that it produced vitality rather than bile. An enduring rev saw you through the coming weeks—the make-or-break period, when a single lapse would have forever doomed you to the loser's lunch table.

Ultimately, it seemed, your energies were best spent trying to make your assistant like you. Investigation revealed that this was her third year as an assistant; that she was ticketed for a promotion; and that she was ten times smarter than you—a Harvard gal. Crimson had been a pox on the magazine world since your earliest days as a writer, at *Spy* and *Newsweek*. They said, rather than "I'm writing a caption," "I'm working on a piece about . . ." You'd started at the bottom, as an unpaid summer intern at *The Oakland Press*, a newspaper in Pontiac, Michigan. Harvard twerps just showed up wherever they wanted to work. They expected.

It was only a matter of time before Evgenia had your job. "Um, would you do me a favor and FedEx this?" you would stammer. "I mean, if you don't mind—"

She'd pause briefly, as if surprised to learn that you were still employed there. She'd look at you, *regard* you, without turning her body—the way an owl does when sensing threats in the night.

"Sure," she'd say.

The futility continued until the morning you "overheard" Evgenia breaking up with her stoner boyfriend, whom you didn't know but resented on principle. The doomed fool was calling from the downstairs lobby, issuing threats just wild enough to rattle the unbreakable assistant. Sensing an opening, you waved her into the office. There, after issuing a few empty offers to chase the guy away, and after recalling a few of your most regrettable Breakup Moments, you flipped her.

"I *like* you," she said.

"Sound surprised," you said.

"I always thought you were *nice*."

"Oh, god."

"No, I didn't think *you* liked *me*."

"You're terrifying."

"This can't be serious."

"And yet here we are."

"I don't think *you're* supposed to be terrified of *me*."

"So where'd I go wrong? Assist me."

She proceeded carefully. Tried not to laugh.

"Well, the apologizing," she said. "You'd go, 'Um, please, if you don't mind, can you do me a favor and FedEx this?'"

"So that's bad?"

"You're the boss. I'm the assistant. You tell me what you need."

"I need your approval."

Evgenia, it turned out, defied the mold in which you had cast her. She was a female version of you, only cooler. She shared your insanities, while somehow remaining insanely well-adjusted. She used gentle force to rein you in, starting with the khakis.

"Pleats," she said. "No."

As Evgenia went, it seemed, so went the office. The other editors seemed to find you agreeable, in a shaggy-dog sort of way. Doug always let you tag along at lunch; the fashion editor, Elizabeth, wrangled you a Prada suit, lest you arrive underdressed to a party. You had novelty value. You were the editor who could be found in Brooklyn, guzzling Budweiser and ironing his ties.

This added to the thrill. There was a sense of being, for once, at the center of something big. Magazines, at the time, were booming. The classics (*Esquire, GQ*) had been born again, after years of moldering; new ones popped up every ten minutes, because there was always another emerging niche market to exploit (*Wired*) or another mogul angling to raise his profile (Harvey Weinstein, *Talk*). And if you were pitching a new magazine to prospective investors or readers, the conversation always began with the words: "It's the *Vanity Fair* of boating/city/cat magazines." Your most recent employer, in Los Angeles, was called *Buzz*.

VF was predicated on one thing above all else. Access. *VF* was at the center of the Media-Industrial Complex because it *owned* the complex. Everyone else was a tenant. If you wanted in on the real action—to be in "the room within the room," as Graydon would say—you had to be in *VF*. If you weren't on the cover, half naked, you weren't a real movie star. If you weren't on The Power List, ideally somewhere between Al Gore and Steve Jobs, you were just another schmuck with a Gulfstream. In Washington, the only thing scarier than being profiled in *VF* was not being profiled.

And, oh, the perks. *VF* seemed to have fifty staffers dedicated solely to the acquisition of prime reservations at restaurants with silly one-word names: Babbo, Moomba. All restaurants were fair game; writers, when treated to a meal, expected to join the swells at Michael's, Elaine's, or the Four Seasons Restaurant; one writer, upon meeting you at the Palm, said the choice made him feel "disrespected." Hotels were five-star or bust; concierges, noting *VF* on a reservation, automatically upgraded you to The Shameless Asshole Suite.

It beat eating cereal for dinner.

It nurtured your feeble ego.

It was the life you *deserved*.

There was a sense of momentum. Velocity. You traversed the entire office several times a day, pretending to be in search of something. Just because it felt good. Sometimes, after work, you walked the five miles home from Midtown: down to SoHo, through Chinatown, over the Brooklyn Bridge.

Brooklyn Heights was hardly an outpost. Located just across the East River from Lower Manhattan, it was famed for its unrivaled views of the City, its historic brownstones, and its cross section of blue bloods, househusbands, and half-mad writers. The two books that had tricked you into pursuing journalism as a career—Truman Capote's *In Cold Blood* and Norman Mailer's *The Executioner's Song*—were written in Brooklyn Heights.

The apartment became, if not homey, homely. To your original furnishings—green bed frame, two wooden tables, an old TV—were added a few chairs and doodads, in consultation with the expert design specialists at Crate & Barrel. While finally unpacking the duffels, you discovered a handwritten note:

> *You will be missed. But I'm so proud.*
>   *Love, Lizz*

Lizz. The girlfriend you'd lived with for the past four years. The one everyone, including yourself, had deemed your future spouse. The bright-eyed gal's gal who had also served as best friend, confidante, consigliere, gatekeeper, nursemaid, and shrink. The girlfriend who was now your *ex*-girlfriend.

Or something. You'd left things vague, in part because that's what you did with everything, in part because neither one of you fully accepted that the end was nigh. The relationship remained as warm as ever. No fights. No tension. No tortured silences. You were, compared to many couples in your greater circles, a model of enduring love. Less evident was the fact that you and she had become like siblings.

Meantime, though, you determined to put the issue behind you by putting it behind you. Problems, when viewed from airplanes, always seemed so much smaller.

Junger proved amenable to a writing contract, and work proceeded apace with Schanberg, Bernstein, and a third decorated warhorse from the golden age of print journalism. But the latter proved less nervous-making, because there weren't any major motion pictures about him.

For days you edited Schanberg's story, a sprawling return to The Shit; his first draft, though polished, came in at something like ten thousand words long—lengthy even for *VF*. It occurred to you then that his was the first substantial piece of journalism you'd ever edited—back in Los Angeles, you'd seen nothing but glorified Crayola scribblings. Questions arose. Were you supposed to just flail away, as if editing your own copy? Or was it really about moving commas around before going to lunch? Did you have to ask the writer's permission before doing anything? How could you know what Graydon wanted before you knew what he wanted? And, most important, which strategy reduced the likelihood that someone would berate you in public?

You aimed for the middle, reasoning that it was better to risk disappointing everyone a little than one person a lot. Schanberg, having reviewed the edited version of his article, cut straight to the point. "So," he said, "did you *really* like it, or are you just being kind?"

Bernstein's story moved along smoothly until space constraints demanded some last-minute cuts. Bernstein was traveling and couldn't be reached. So you slashed away, and prayed for a merciful god.

"Carl's on the phone," Evgenia said, first thing the next morning. "He sounds anxious."

"Carl," you said, after picking up. "Thanks for calling."

"Help me understand something," he said.

"So I guess you had time to look over the cuts I sent you."

"I did."

"So, as you know, time was really tight—"

"I'm sure."

"So, listen, if there's anything—"

"Do contributing editors get gym discounts?"

"Sorry?"

"Corporate discounts? Condé Nast?"

"Um. I'd have to ask."

"Okay."

"But, um, the edit?"

"It's fine."

"Oh. Um, great."

"So you'll get back to me? About the gym?"

"Absolutely."

You celebrated the twin triumphs with a woman you'd once dated, at a bar called the Brooklyn Inn. Your cell phone rang. The caller's voice was audible well before you put the phone to your ear:

"WHO THE FUCK DO YOU THINK YOU ARE! I OUGHTA COME OVER THERE AND KICK YOUR BONEY ASS!"

The third warhorse. Didn't care for the edit.

"YOU GUTTED IT LIKE A TROUT! DO YOU EDIT WITH MIT-TENS ON? I WON'T STAND FOR THIS SHIT!"

"Slow down," you said.

He hung up.

Before you could form a sentence, the phone rang again. "THIS BET-TER GET UN-FUCKED!" he said. "I OUGHTA RIP YOUR BALLS OFF!"

Click.

"What happened?" the woman said.

"It's fine," you said.

"Doesn't look fine."

"It's fine."

"Dude, you look really pale."

All night you paced the apartment, half in the bag, churning out worst-case scenarios. You couldn't go tattle to Graydon, because that would make you the pussy who couldn't handle his writers. The War-horse would take his case straight to Graydon, exposing you for the fraud you were, and by lunchtime you'd be the latest addition to *Modern Bride*. Or perhaps the Warhorse would take matters into his own hands—he'd been through Nam, for crissake. The latter scenario seemed the way to go. Better to die violently than to fail publicly.

The next morning, you returned to the office well before 10:00 A.M., in an effort to avoid (or at least minimize) the public-spectacle aspect of the train wreck to come. By now, though, your fingers had gone from tingly to numb; your voice, from crackly to cracked. Again and again, you dialed the Warhorse's number, only to hang up midway. You started dialing Lizz's number, before realizing it was the middle of the night in California.

Bzzzing!

Long ago, during your lone visit to a child psychiatrist, the doctor had noted in you a "heightened sensitivity" to, among many other things, "external stimuli." Bright light. Loud noise. In recent years, however, only one thing had proved consistently problematic.

Bzzzing!

The best defense, when ducking phone calls, was a good offense. Turn down the ringer. Or yank the plug out. Let the voicemail know who's in charge.

"Hello!" came Evgenia's voice, from beyond the door. "It's you-know-who."

Or kill your assistant.

"Tell him I'm on another call," you said.

"Are you ducking him?"

"No."

"You're ducking."

"I'm very busy."

"With what?"

"Things!"

The phone's call light dimmed.

"Might as well get it over with," Evgenia said. "It's not like you can avoid him forever."

She underestimated you. The cat and mouse continued for days. You left a voicemail on his home phone when he was on his cell, then vice versa. Finally he just gave up. You broke him in a way the VC never could.

But the celebration was restrained, because you were too busy dissolving. The Siege at Warhorse, though glorious in its way, proved a Pyrrhic victory—battles, wars, and whatnot. You could only avoid so much confrontation and ridicule before insomnia came a cropper. Same time every night. *Only a matter of time before Warhorse calls again.* Three fifteen A.M., sharp. *Did I double-check those captions?* Every night. *Everyone smells my failure.* Clockwork. *Graydon's reading the captions right now, quaking with outrage.* Hourly updates. *Whatever you do, don't look at the alarm clock.* Till sunrise. *Better to stay awake, get a jump on the day.*

BLEET! BLEET! BLEET!

Because nobody sleeps as deeply as the guy who crashes ten minutes before the alarm goes off, response times varied. Sometimes ten minutes elapsed before the noise penetrated your woolen brain; other times, *bam,* you ejected. The bleeting continued, regardless.

Falling, falling. At the office, while pressing a hot cup of coffee against your swollen eyelids, you heard the dreaded words:

"Graydon wants to see you."

The corridor leading to Graydon's office had, in recent days, narrowed and lengthened. Heads weasel-popped out of offices and cubicles, taking in the spectacle. Graydon's assistant, Patricia, mustered the sort of smile reserved for retarded buskers. "Go right in," she said.

Graydon sat staring at a series of photo captions you'd written a day earlier, to accompany an article about Matt Drudge, the internet drone. He handed you the first caption, which read as you'd written it: "Matt Drudge outside his office in Los Angeles last year." Except for the thick black line he'd drawn through it.

He pointed to the photo, which had obviously been taken in Washington. He pointed out the date provided by the photo department: last month, not last year.

"Two errors in a one-sentence caption," he said. "Impressive work. Some editors take years to get this far."

"Oh," you said. "I—"

"It's completely unacceptable."

"I know. I'm so sorry."

"Don't be sorry. Just don't do it again."

"Never again. I swear I'll never—"

Already he was out the door and halfway to lunch with Bono or David Geffen or whomever. Doug tried his best. "He reads every little word," Doug said.

Retreating into the office. Killing the lights. Head squarely on desktop.

"Everything okay in there?" Evgenia said, from afar.

"I'm fine," you said.

"Anything I can do before I go?"

"I'm fine."

"You can't just sit sulking all night."

"I'm *fine*."

By the time you sat upright, it was nighttime. You lurched around in the dark—the prospect of light was offensive—and pressed an ear to the door. Coast was clear. Everything was quiet: the office, the street. Friday nights were like that in Midtown. Arriving home, you climbed into bed, still dressed. And there you stayed for eighteen hours. Wide awake in your pants. Beneath a five-foot-long plaque your brother Pete had acquired long ago, under mysterious circumstances:

GREAT APE EXHIBIT AND AMPHITHEATRE

A GIFT TO THE PEOPLE OF DETROIT

ALFRED E. COBO, MAYOR—1955

Everything, at this point, was an anvil on top of a piano. Utility bills sat on the kitchen table for weeks, unpaid. Not because of money concerns. Because who had the strength to find postage stamps? Meals went uneaten; suits, baggy; calls, unreturned. Writers grew restive; parents left long voicemails, asking if you'd forgotten about them.

By month six, your hands were trembling round the clock. The subway was a potential powder keg—The Taking of Brooklyn One Two Three. You kept up appearances as best you could—you were gifted that way. You were homesick. You missed Lizz. You wanted out. *Needed* it.

And that's when it happened. You glimpsed a newspaper clipping fluttering atop your overstuffed inbox. The article, frayed at the edges and torn from *The New York Times*, featured two photographs. In the first photo were two penguins; in the second, a beaming man. The headline read:

BRUNO ZEHNDER, PHOTOGRAPHER, 52, IS DEAD

CHAPTER TWO

Bruno Penguin Zehnder. That's what he called himself. The guy believed he was half penguin. He photographed penguins largely to the exclusion of all other creatures. He chased them like a schoolboy. He talked to penguins.

"*Gewt aftahnoon,*" he would say, in his weird Euro accent.

"*Glark,*" the penguins would say.

Because that's all penguins ever say. Because they're flightless birds with brains the size of walnuts.

The guy didn't just *happen* to die among them, in some freak penguin-related mishap. This Swiss-German guy, this grinning Nordic boob, chose to venture out—alone—during the South Pole's meanest season. As in fifty-five-below mean. As in hurricane force. As in the frozen hell that turned back Shackleton and entombed Scott. "Modern Antarctica" remained unsettled by humans (except for a few small research outposts) and off-limits to other animals. Not even *polar bears* were dumb enough to live there. Antarctica, by land, had only two permanent populations: seals (carnivores smart enough to do beach ball tricks and dance the conga) and penguins (toothless stumblebums).

Bruno followed the latter. Into a blizzard. And guess what? He died an ice cube. Literally. Cubed.

Bruno looked, in the photograph, like a kid playing grown-up.

While giving some sort of lecture—an image of romping penguins loomed behind him—he wore a reddish bow tie and a helmet of shoulder-length hair, as if in a late-'70s ad for Breck shampoo. His "wacky" style, coupled with his toothsome smile and Nordic features, were consistent with the sort of jackass who wears sneakers with a tuxedo. Plus, all that Swiss-ness.

People wondered. Had he known then how his story would end, maybe he would have chosen a different niche, photographing real subjects. Maybe he would have thought twice about ditching his wife—and pretty much everyone else, except those with beaks—so he could drift about like a teenager during his semester abroad.

Bruno Pinhead Zehnder. Born: September 8, 1945, in Bad Ragaz, Switzerland. Died: July 7, 1997, in frozen obscurity.

The article about Bruno's death had arrived on your desk accompanied by a handwritten note, rendered in the precise, old-school pencil-ship unique to one man:

> *Let's discuss for Sebastian.*
> —*G*

Clippings arrived almost daily, in a steady stream. Graydon read newspapers the way panthers read the jungle, only faster, and matched stories to writers with equal speed. He sensed, in Bruno's calamity, the makings of a polar adventure story. And he had only one writer in mind.

But Junger, being Junger, was presently on assignment in some godforsaken Balkan warzone or another, ducking artillery fire or freeing babies from white-slavery. Bruno, in the meantime, was relegated to the "Futures" file, which was actually the "Nevers" file, which was actually a slag heap of old clippings and manuscripts you were too lazy to throw out. But Bruno, unlike all the other doomed losers, would not go quietly. Every day he poked out from the pile. Established eye contact. Beamed.

Finally, in a moment of weakness, and because you needed something to read on the subway, you carried him home.

Zehnder was a freelance photographer whose pictures appeared in many magazines in Europe and the United States. His frequent sojourns in Antarctica resulted in photographs that won several prizes; one of his most widely published pictures was of a pair of emperor penguins in tender embrace with a chick between them.

How precious. Good for him.

Zehnder was born [in] a Swiss mountain village near the border of Liechtenstein, the youngest of six children . . . "I persuaded him to join me abroad," his brother Guido said. "There's something very depressing about being closed in by mountains."

Or by a subway car beneath the East River. Stand up. Deep breaths.

Bruno Zehnder, Photographer, 52, Is Dead.

You pinned the article to a small bulletin board above the desk. It was just something to do. A nervous tic.

So now the dead dummy and his dummy-birds faced you eight hours a day, at eye level. You would look into their goofy little eyes, and they would look into your depleted soul. The nerves were back, in a sneaky way. Like a low-grade fever that comes out of nowhere, hangs around forever, and spikes every now and again. You just had to ride it out. Shut the door. Tell Evgenia to take messages. Calls were to be avoided at all costs, because phones were the means by which an angry universe conveyed its disappointment. Writers and bosses never called to say "Just thinkin' of you." A woman who called to say "just thinkin' of you" was a woman with problems.

Penguins, you thought.

Likeable enough, as birds went. Obvious why kids took to them. All that pogoing and belly flopping, like drunken maître d's or old Jewish men. The "penguinarium" had been the hit of every field trip to the Detroit Zoo. Definitely "up" birds. A man in the midst of psychic meltdown could do a lot worse than penguins.

Several weeks after the penguins went up on the wall, a figure materialized in the office, smelling of courage. He was unshaven, chiseled, and dressed like a logger—he looked like Jason Patric gone survivalist.

"So," Junger said. "Story ideas."

"Read my mind," you said. "Got one right here."

Reaching for the Bruno article. Stopping cold. Unwilling to see Penguin Guy in the hands of another.

Because your love for him was boundless.

"What?" Junger said.

Hemming. Hawing.

"Apologies," you said. "I should let you go first."

"I've got a couple ideas, but feel free to—"

He eyed the article, which by now had yellowed considerably.

"Oh, this thing?" you said, handing it over. He scanned the few paragraphs. A chin tilt. A scratching of stubble.

"Penguins," he said.

"Penguins," you said.

He read on.

"Antarctica," he said. "Blizzard."

"Exactly," you said, nodding. "I'm just thinking, jeez, does he really wanna cover *another killer storm*—"

"Well—"

"Plus, you seem really excited to discuss *your* ideas. And we *love* fresh, new ideas."

He shrugged.

"Kosovo," he said. "Families massacred by Serbs—"

"Wow," you said. "Home run."

That you and you alone were fated to write Bruno's story was a lightning bolt. There would be naysayers. Philistines. But so be it.

"Penguins," Evgenia said.

"Not just any penguins," you said. "Emperor penguins. Three feet tall."

"Oh," she said.

But the bigger challenge would be Doug, who still held domain over anything you wrote, and who therefore could single-handedly crush the crusade. He was quick to spot false prophets, having spent more than two decades editing half-mad writers with delusions of grandeur; most were bigger or better talents than you would ever be. Doug handled *VF*'s largest stable of writers. Before that, he'd been a big-shot book editor. And now here came you, with your pleats and penguins.

The setting was Orso, a tranquil Italian restaurant popular among media types who preferred to eat, rather than do, lunch.

"Penguins," Doug said.

He put down his menu and loosed the half-silent laugh—*hee-hee-hee*—he reserved for stupid or lurid topics.

Not just any. Three feet tall.

"I know what they are," he said.

"I have to write it."

"Seriously, though."

"It's a sweeping wildlife adventure story."

Polished that one for days.

"Ever written an adventure story?" Doug asked.

"No."

"Ever been outdoors?"

"I wrote for *Outside* magazine."

"About what?"

"Auto racing."

He ran a finger down the list of entrées.

"Don't you think it's more of a Sebastian-type story?" he asked, rhetorically.

"Why?" you replied. "Because Sebastian's the only one in the world allowed to write about guys dying in storms?"

"Because Graydon's note said 'Let's discuss for Sebastian.'"

"Well, Sebastian doesn't want it."

Doug tried to be gentle.

"You'd get killed in Antarctica," he said. "You'd fall off a glacier."

"You do realize Sebastian wasn't actually on the swordfish boat. He went to *Wesleyan*."

"But he's Sebastian."

Antarctica, you explained, could be avoided. All the major players had since returned home to Russia.

"And I'm Russian," you said.

Russian-Polish. Whatever.

"From which part?" he asked.

Um. "The North."

"But where exactly?"

Er. "Various. There was a lot of chasing."

"Where were your parents born?"

"Detroit."

He smiled. "Have you ever been to Russia? Speak any Russian?"

"Oh, who the hell speaks Russian."

"I do."

"Fine. But give me one good reason why I can't write it."

"Because you're not a writer."

"I'm a writer-editor."

"And Graydon's aware of that?"

"He will be."

"No. Not yet. It's only been six months."

You died a little. He loosed a long sigh.

For two weeks, Doug helped you craft a one-page sales pitch to Graydon; the memo explained why, absent Sebastian ("showed no interest"), you were the best man for the job ("given my experience writing about outdoor sports"); why the story was even more compelling than he'd imagined ("Bruno was an international man of mystery"); and why the assignment would in no way detract from your primary editorial duties ("I'll use vacation days"). You attached to the memo color photographs of Shackleton's ice-bound ship, a fleet of emperors marching single file through a blizzard, and a lone emperor balancing an egg atop his feet. Ultimately, you felt, the penguins would sell themselves.

The proposal was greeted with silence. A week passed. Graydon, when in your presence, commented on memos you'd sent postpenguin.

"He hates me," you said to Doug. "I'm fucked."

"Relax," he said. "You don't know that."

"I can sense things."

"What do you sense from me?"

"Exasperation. And pity."

He cackled. "Not bad."

By the tenth day, a bunker mentality had set in. You spent the weekend under the covers, in the Great Ape Exhibit and Amphitheatre Room. You called Lizz in Los Angeles, because she was the only one who Understood Your Pain, and because what was misery if you couldn't share it? Plus, she worked as a reporter for *People* magazine, so it was only natural.

You met Lizz in 1989, when the both of you were wide-eyed rookies at *Newsweek*. She was a fact checker, fresh out of Bowdoin College; you were the greenest of writers, tasked with revivifying the "front of the book," specifically a section called Periscope, which had become a grave-yard of news briefs about dead Soviet cabinet ministers. The editors, flailing for the teats of *Spy* and *VF,* wanted "snark" and "buzz." They wanted to believe that newsweeklies had relevance, outside of dental offices.

Lizz was among a minority of colleagues who remained ambula-tory. There was a sparkliness to her—a playful, slightly wacky appeal punctuated by a broad, sharp laugh: "HA-ha-ha!" She was a guy's gal who ate and drank with the best of them, despite her lean frame. She indulged anyone, even the idiots. People always thought she was from a prairie town in Wisconsin, owing to her Patagonia-girl appearance: blue eyes, Scotch-Irish skin, high cheekbones. Her auburn hair was long, curly, and windblown, as if she'd spent the day speed skating. In fact, she was raised on West Eighteenth Street in Manhattan and schooled in the Bronx.

You began as friends, united against the tedium of newsweekly life. By year three, you had chased off her boyfriend, having finally found a woman you both loved and liked. Lizz was a healthier, livelier, and altogether more agreeable version of you; she made crippling self-awareness seem wholesome. "I'm one hundred percent sure I'm a moron for not knowing the answer," she would say, before posing a question. "But I'm asking anyway."

Lizz, though partial to guys who played lacrosse and wore fisherman sweaters, had a weakness for your weaknesses. She'd sit for hours, pa-tiently absorbing your latest series of petty grievances against the world. "Riveting," she'd say, nodding. The complaints, taken on their merits, were incidental to her (because they had no merits). She just appreciated your commitment to anxiety; she found the torment endearing.

Just as important, she shared your desire to get the hell out of

both the magazine and the city, neither of which suited your tempera-
ments. Together you would spend a year or so elsewhere. She missed
the idyll of New England; you missed anyplace that wasn't filled with
windbag editors and sweaty Sabrett vendors. You arranged to follow
Lizz anywhere, having wangled a writing job at *Sports Illustrated*. The
job paid well—especially for someone living in Vermont, where people
lived on chickens and butter—and demanded less. Writers at *SI* lived
anywhere they pleased, as long as they got to the games on time.

Lizz found employment at a publication whose readership was a
few rungs smaller than *Newsweek*'s: *Barre-Montpelier Times Argus,* a
daily paper in Vermont. Montpelier, the state capital, was large by
Vermont standards—which is to say, it was not large. A plus-size village, population 8,035.

That you moved there on a flyer, without ever having seen the
place, made the arrival all the more satisfying. Montpelier was literally
a golden place. There was the dome atop the capitol. There were the
maple leaves of springtime and the sunbeams over the Green Mountains, both of which illuminated the town itself: some two dozen small,
wood-and-brick shops and restaurants, all looking much as they had a
hundred years earlier. Except with air-conditioning and espresso.
Montpelier was Vermont, rather than Vermonty. Blessed few Alpine
motifs and Cheddar wheels.

You rented a modest but warm two-bedroom town house–like
place set high on a hillside; from there you could see the town below
and the Green Mountains beyond, stretching infinitely. The view of
views. Montpelier suited both of you, instantly. Friends came fast,
because Lizz could befriend the dead. Your lifestyle gamble had paid
off, logistically and romantically. Finally, shockingly, you had grown
up and settled down.

Until Allen Iverson fucked everything up. This was in the fall of
1993, when the future NBA star was in high school, in Hampton, Virginia. He was an all-state basketball player. But earlier that year, at a

bowling alley, Iverson and his buddies had gotten into a wild brawl with another group of guys. Fists, tables, and chairs flew; a woman was knocked cold; two men suffered broken bones. As a result, Iverson and three friends were charged with felonious "maiming by mob," a statute originally enacted in order to prosecute lynch mobs. The second group went unpunished. The second group also happened to be all white.

Jesse Jackson was displeased.

The Iverson mess was the subject of your second story for *SI*. The first one had been a goofy profile of an idiot Lithuanian hockey player who'd once punched his own goalie. So Iverson seemed more in keeping with your status as an Investigative Journalist, even though you'd never been one. It had all the elements: violence, race, celebrity, conflict. And everything about the case reeked of Southern gothic. Creepy white prosecutors. Creepy backwater. Poor seventeen-year-old black kid, tried as an adult, gets twenty years (fifteen suspended) for bar brawl with a pack of rednecks. A brawl sparked, allegedly, by a word beginning with the letter *n*.

You had one week. That was the catch. The editors had a "window," whatever that meant. So, in a mad dash, you talked to everyone who would talk back. Iverson, while on lunch break at his dinky minimum-security prison, confirmed something you'd heard from one of his co-defendants. When they'd first arrived at the bowling alley, they said, the woman at the counter banished them to lanes at the farthest end of the place. As in: "You boys, over there." As in: Back of the bus, Rosa.

The other side was tight-lipped. It was a whiteout. So, sweating the deadline, you raced back to Vermont. There, in the cradle of white guilt, a thousand miles from the nearest person of color, you crafted the story's first line:

To the people of Hampton, Va., the case of Allen Iverson—one of the greatest high school basketball stars the state has produced—comes down to one odious word: Nigger.

Well, that got everyone's attention.

The editors loved it. Then they loved it less, after the good white people of southeastern Virginia began tearing you to shreds. For one thing, a person mentioned in the article filed suit against the magazine, alleging that the article had branded her a racist. You would have taken the suit in stride, had you not otherwise been such an imbecile.

The article had been, as your attorney put it, "imperfect." It had contained Errors Of Fact. Plural. The exact number was disputed. A colleague picked apart your reporting; then you went at his. Editors quibbled with lawyers.

You spent the first week seated on the living room sofa, staring blankly and saying little, while Lizz coaxed you to try a bite or two of spaghetti. The absence of cognitive activity, the static void, was almost pleasant. A form of spiritual time travel. You'd be sitting there, in the morning, in your sweats and T-shirt, and then, boom, it was bedtime.

The fear arrived during week two, when the white noise ceded to bleating. Had telephones always been so loud, so confrontational? It was Mom and Dad. Just seeing how you're doing. It was one of your brothers. Just checking in. Friends fumbled for words. Hang in there. Just call if you like.

Failure was bad enough. But to fail publicly? At the one thing that gave you a measure of respectability? Deep down, despite all appearances, your parents had to be at least a little ashamed. And Lizz? Christ. She'd moved here with a Promising Young Journalist; now she was stuck with a loser who'd be lucky if anyone ever let him write with crayons.

"Fine," you'd say. "I'm fine."

Reporters called. That was the nadir. Howard Kurtz, a media columnist for *The Washington Post,* somehow got you on the phone. You muttered something about it being A Difficult Time. Kurtz, in the next day's paper, wrote that your article had set "an indoor record for lengthy corrections." Which was particularly embarrassing, given your pending job application at *The Washington Post*.

Fucking reporters. The things they do to people.

Only two options remained: run or hide. You could disappear in the wilds of Vermont, pull a Chris McCandless, become a folk hero. But that would be a hard sell with Lizz.

Your sole focus was to duck as many calls as possible. Lizz ran interference—you were forever Out Running Errands. In fact, you'd never spent more time in one place: the twenty-square-foot area stretching between the sofa and the bed. Day after day, while Lizz was at work, you'd watch game shows. News shows were verboten; magazines and newspapers, discarded. You ate only apples. Which made you constipated. Which made you spend hours in bed, trying in vain to sleep. At night, you awakened repeatedly, hands tingling, mind rehashing every cruel word written about you. You imagined what ex-colleagues were thinking. The glee.

"It's a total nightmare," Lizz said. "But it will pass."

"It won't," you said. "I'm done."

"No. It wasn't all on you. *SI* said so."

Silence. She proceeded gently.

"How much was on you?" she asked.

Plenty.

"Hard to say," you said.

"Just tell me. It's okay."

The look in her eyes.

You couldn't say it.

"Bastards," you said.

Came out of nowhere. Felt good.

You had offered to quit. The editors had talked you out of it. The failure had been a systemic one. Everyone rushed it. The article, after you emailed it from Vermont, had somehow been mangled by the magazine's computers. You had to rewrite sections of it on deadline. One of your editors had rushed the article along. And the fact checker, when questioned by superiors, quit, taking his "research materials" with him.

You were a victim. A patsy.

That was your story. You were sticking with it.

That you had been first among equals, bonehead-wise, was academic. You quit *SI* the instant the libel suit was dismissed, then went on the PR offensive. It allowed you to look everyone in the eye; it allowed you a shot at a future.

Employment prospects were slim. Magazine editors who'd once solicited you now ignored your calls; one rescinded a story assignment, saying he was "concerned" about "that thing that happened." One of the few who stuck by you was Graydon Carter, who sent writing assignments your way.

When you and Lizz moved to California, in 1996, you left the whole mess behind you. That's what you called it. A mess. The word *depression* never came up. Hadn't occurred to you.

"I can't sleep," you said.

"Damn," Lizz said. "Still too anxious?"

"I hate my apartment. It's a hovel."

"It's actually a nice apartment."

"The city's a zoo. I need to leave."

"First things first," she said. "Are you taking care of yourself physically?"

"No."

"Did you eat today?"

"No."

"Promise me you'll eat something now."

"Okay."

"Swear on the cats."

Silence.

"Damn Graydon," you said.

"Why?"

"He won't let me write the story."

"The penguins?"

"Why would he do that to me?"

"I'm not sure what he's *doing* to you?"

"So you're taking his side?"

"No, I'm . . ." Pause. "What did he say?"

"Nothing."

"So how do you know?"

"I just *do*."

"Maybe you should wait till you hear something."

"You don't understand."

"Actually, I do."

"Whatever."

The goal now was straightforward: Avoid all direct contact with Graydon. The natives had a sophisticated system for detecting the comings and goings of the tribal leader: part sign language, part sensory. You modernized the process, developing a sophisticated maze system. Cubicles were used as foxholes. To be in any non-secure area (lobby, elevator) was to be in heated cell phone conversation with yourself. You positioned your computer in a way that made you undetectable from the hallway.

Then, at long last, Graydon left town on business. The relief goosed your appetite, which prompted a lengthy binge lunch across town, which produced a kind of logy stupor, which would have been fine had you not retrieved a certain voicemail message on your cell phone.

"Graydon wants to see you now."

The sprint across town, with a belly full of lobster ravioli and cheesecake, was problematic in its own right. But you held the cargo at bay until you reached the office bathroom. Five minutes later, having returned to the standing position, you wobbled toward Graydon's office.

Patricia, his assistant, was sympathetic.

"Thought he was gone," you said.

She just shrugged and pointed.

"No rush," Graydon said.

"Sorry," you said. "I was with a writer—"

"Glad to see you're still editing."

There was a pause.

"I read the penguin manifesto," he said.

"Oh, well, I understand if—"

"I need editors here. Editing."

"Understood."

He returned the manifesto. Rolled his eyes.

"On your time," he said. "Don't make me regret this."

"Oh, god, thank you—"

"Thank Doug, too. He put in a good word."

"Really?"

He pointed to the penguin photos. "That balancing thing they do with the eggs," he said. "Fucking amazing."

Bruno took it from there, leading you on a six-month escape from the Isle of Woe. He was the escapist's escapist, practically from birth. He spent his childhood dreaming of penguins, then recounting the best parts—the sing-alongs, the dance numbers—to his siblings. "*Elaborately*," recalled his brother Guido. They indulged Bruno. He was, after all, the baby of the family.

The little Alpine town of Bad Ragaz, though idyllic in many ways, ultimately proved suffocating. Bruno bolted early and often. By 1968, when he was twenty-three, he and Guido had decamped to Paris. He'd heard it was a good place to find women. The *liberated* kind. The ones without *expectations*. "He never wanted any lasting relationships," Guido said. "He never got very serious. He just wanted to get the kick out of conquering. Thrill of the chase."

Bruno the awkward teenager had morphed into Björn Borg. He made up for lost time. By day, he worked for an oil company; by night, he banged his way through Paris with breathtaking speed and energy. But that summer, during the violent student uprisings, the swingin' Zehnders were in a cab that was stopped by riot police. Guido ordered Bruno to lock the doors. "He opened the doors, and they beat him badly." Guido recalled. "He did things like that. Impulsive things."

Once doctors stitched Bruno's wounds and repaired his broken finger, Bruno turned to Guido. "I've had it with Paris," he said, and left.

For the next eight years, Bruno journeyed farther and farther afield, chasing adventure through Russia, India, Argentina, Japan. He *modeled*. Glossies from that period reveal a Nordic bohunk wearing tight slacks and a shag. He loved extreme beauties, both human (geishas, samurais, tattoo artists) and otherwise. So he thought, Hey, photography. He was bored, stir crazy, drifting from corner to corner, woman to woman; his photographs reflected his lack of focus; they tended to be stilted, random.

In 1975, Bruno talked his way into a steward's job aboard a Danish cargo ship carrying Australian scientists to, of all places, Antarctica. He knew little about the white continent, other than that it was frozen, largely devoid of human life, and far, far away. The trip was a whim. In Antarctica, Bruno figured, he could take some photographs and "get away from things for a while."

As the ship approached the Antarctic shore, it was greeted by a honking, rollicking welcome wagon of penguins. The scientists deemed them "polar pigeons." Bruno deemed the moment a "religious experience."

Penguins were his leitmotif. The little fuckers just kept pogo-ing in his life, in that penguin way. Harbingers. Welcoming. Lifting. Now, in his early thirties, Bruno suddenly focused. His career took off; his "calling," as he put it, motivated pretty much every move he made. He moved to New York because that's where the big-ticket magazines were, and where he could chase both skirts *and* career advancement with equal zeal. Throughout the 1980s, when not dancing till dawn at Limelight, Bruno chased penguins in Chile, New Zealand, Antarctica. But he much preferred the latter, because that's where all the best penguins lived and loved. Bruno, like most kids, was a sucker for the penguin shtick. But he deemed emperors first among equals. They didn't just resemble humans. They transcended them.

The world, at the time, pre–*Happy Feet,* pre–*March of the Penguins,* remained largely unaware of nature's Greatest Story Ever Told: Emperors, having summered at sea, and gorged like tourists on all-inclusive meal packages, take the first sign of winter as their cue to get up and *go.* Single file. For weeks. Directed only by the heavens. Finally, having reached the coast, the female lays a baseball-size egg and cradles it atop her feet. The real work begins when she transfers the egg—carefully, carefully—to her mate. She heads off for food. He stands there, balancing the egg atop his feet, for *nine weeks.*

If the poor guy drops the egg, it's curtains. So, given the constant blizzards and whiteouts and so forth, the males form insular huddles, shielding one another from the cruel world. They hatch the eggs and feed the chicks until the mothers return. "And the cycle of life continues," as Bruno liked to say. Endlessly.

Shot by shot, winter after winter, Bruno endlessly told (and sold) the story. New York's Museum of Modern Art purchased some of his shots, which were now appearing widely, from the covers of *Life* and *National Geographic* to greeting cards and calendars to the face of a Visa card. He hit the mother lode in 1990, when one of his shots landed on the cover of *Time,* accompanying a story about the spoiling of Antarctica. When a magazine wanted emperors, it called Bruno. Some paid him more than ten thousand dollars for a single shot. The emperors typically earned him more than seventy-five thousand dollars a year.

In Antarctica, on the Russian base, Bruno accomplished the unlikeliest feat of all. Parts of the base were small riots of rusting barrels, cigarette butts, old skin magazines, and empty vodka bottles. The cleanup, in addition to several other green projects, earned Bruno a fancy United Nations environmental achievement award, along with Robert Redford and two of the century's iconic adventurers: Jacques Cousteau and Edmund Hillary.

"The cycle of life continues."

Bruno's pet phrase. You ignored it the first thirty times you came across it. Affirmations had never been your thing, because they were food for idiots, and because they were incompatible with the negativity lifestyle.

But it was the little cliché that could. You'd be walking through Grand Central, or clicking a pen, or leafing through box scores. Then, boom: "The cycle of life continues." Just kept popping out. Initially, it just seemed in keeping with your tendency to repeat rhythmic or alliterative (or megalomaniacal) phrasings: "Hail to the victors valiant," "I am the lizard king / I can do anything," "In Xanadu did Kubla Kahn / a stately pleasure-dome decree . . ." But the "cycle" bit was corrective. It was what came out in lieu of bile.

You weren't even sure what it meant. You weren't even sure Bruno knew. He used the expression as a catchall. Sometimes he meant "trust nature"; other times, "it's a mystery"; other times, god only knew.

But you had to admit. The man was onto something.

By the time you flew to Russia, it was all Bruno, all the time. You chased down anyone who'd so much as seen him sneeze. Cabbies. Women he'd picked up in clubs. Scores of mismatched characters spread across four continents. Virtually everyone, for openers, used the same words to describe him. Boyish. Restless. High-strung. Friendly but detached. Single-minded. Easily bored. Adrenaline junkie. Kept his distance. Limited interest in social interactions. Lived in his own head. Extremely private. Odd duck. Peter Pan. International man of mystery. Bruno's record of accessing Cold War hot spots off-limits to most Westerners had sparked rumors that he'd had friends on one side or the other (or both). "It was impossible to know everything about Bruno," said one of Bruno's former colleagues. "The mystery is what made him interesting."

You studied everything you possibly could about penguins, all seventeen breeds of them. You spent entire nights watching emperors on video. They'd shuffle to the edge of the sea, grandparents-in-Sarasota-style, then tumble straight forward, beak-first. Or they'd take a running start, but dive too early, belly flop onto the ice, and faceplant into the water.

But Bruno had been right: there was a reason why emperors were called emperors. Whereas most of the other species were more buffoonish, emperors evinced a dry, Noel Coward–ish aloofness. They did everything all the other penguins did. But they didn't pander.

And their chicks looked like tiny gray moppets.

And emperors mate for life.

Increasingly, the emperors in Bruno's photographs assumed distinctly human aspects. When Bruno photographed a rookery from above, it looked like a Magritte street scene; a male emperor, chest swelling, looked like Orson Welles; a mother emperor gazed anxiously at her chick, whose beak was frozen shut—and briefly you forgot that these were birds.

"He saw himself in their shoes," a friend said of Bruno. "In this world, with all these people around, he also felt remote. Like he didn't quite fit. A penguin doesn't fit anywhere other than *there*. Penguins can't survive anywhere else. And they don't seem to mind. And they didn't expect anything from him. He thought that people should be more like penguins."

Certain dynamics were obvious to a Lost Boy short on irony but long on sentimentality and metaphor. Bruno projected human characteristics onto nonhumans. Pulled a Rex Harrison. Anthropomorphized. He did this because his desire for human relationships conflicted with his distaste for human contact. Penguins were people minus all the demands, complaints, and awkward questions. He could come and go but always be welcomed home.

When the plane touched down in Russia, on a bleak fall day in Saint Petersburg, the place felt like home. It was in your DNA. Your blood ran thick (those long Michigan winters) and cold (that sunny Russian temperament). Admittedly, there was also the matter of bloodlust. You were a reporter. You were attempting to piece together the details of a horrific death. Without human tragedy, what would you do all day?

You checked into the Grand Hotel Europe, a gilded nineteenth-century colossus that stood as the best example of why the Romanovs had it coming. You sat at the hotel bar, wolfing a plate of smoked fish and caviar that cost more than most Russians made in a year.

Bruno's friends declined to join you there because only assholes wasted that much money stuffing their faces while everyone else got by on pierogies and borscht. The friends preferred McDonald's and vodka bars, though not necessarily in that order. One of the bars had drunken puppets on the walls; it was empty save for you, an ever-changing cast of Bruno's friends, and a few permanent customers, each of them drinking in stony solitude. This was Russia.

Bruno's friends, though occasionally given to slurred obscenities and long silences, were a sharp, highly skilled bunch; most worked as scientists, researchers, or support staff at Mirny, a forty-man research-and-supply base in East Antarctica, a place of unfathomable darkness (only three sunny weeks per year) and arctic-ness (three hundred blizzards). Winds could reach 180 miles an hour—powerful enough to send sled dogs flying. To empty a scalding-hot cup of tea into the air would be to see the tea shatter when it hit the ground.

The Mirny crew remembered Bruno as one of their own, almost despite themselves. During Bruno's first trip to Mirny—he made three altogether—the Russians didn't know what to make of the grinning, glad-handing Westerner, with his fancy cameras and individually wrapped Swiss chocolates. Bruno peppered the Russians with personal questions while revealing few details about himself. He carried a small tape recorder and turned it on without telling people. "I work for the KGB *and* the CIA," Bruno would say, milking it.

Over time, though, the crew succumbed to Bruno's boyish, almost evangelical enthusiasm for "polar pigeons." Day after day, he would bounce around the tight quarters, telling penguin stories, searching for cleaning products, nuzzling up to the few women on base, and listening to the Beach Boys' album *Pet Sounds,* repeating his favorite lines from his favorite track, "Sloop John B":

Let me go home
I want to go home.

He seemed impervious to the loneliness that periodically befell even the saltiest crew members; on rare occasions, the toll rendered men catatonic. "When I am in nature," he would say, "I am never alone. I have learned to listen to silence."

Sometimes he just sat and stared at the birds, which numbered in the thousands; sometimes he walked among them. Mostly, though, he photographed them. Endlessly. Day after day: *psing . . . psing . . . psing.*

Then everything began to change.

"There was a darkness about Bruno," said Ludmilla Pisarevskaya, a scientist he'd befriended during the final trip to Mirny, in 1997.

Their relationship was platonic but intense. (All of Bruno's relationships with women were, by definition, intense.) "He would shut down, disappear."

"Bruno was a great and complicated man," said Vladimir "Wowa" Popov, Bruno's closest friend in Mirny. "He was, how you say, *troubled*."

He was bipolar. Manic-depressive. Mental.

Hadn't occurred to you. You'd never known one of those people. Your knowledge of the subject pretty much began and ended with a limp movie starring Richard Gere called *Mr. Jones*, about a guy who was always either way too up (jumps onstage during an orchestral performance of "Ode to Joy") or far too down (prostrate in a psych ward).

Wowa's news flash clarified a few things. The all-night carousing and round-the-clock working binges. The relentless pursuit of adventure and danger. The *women*. Ten years earlier, Bruno had persuaded one of his girlfriends to join him on a five-month expedition to Antarctica. Then he persuaded her to marry him in an ice cave. On the spot. Surrounded by penguins. Then, after organizing a reception featuring 250 Argentinean soldiers, Bruno somehow arranged for the couple's wedding photo to appear on the cover of *Guinness World Records,* even though no records had been set.

Then the marriage was over.

And the cycle of life continued.

Your flight back to JFK was turbulent. Passengers stared. Earnest head tilts and Elite Gold luggage tags.

"Sir," said the stewardess, "are you okay?"

"Fine," you said.

You couldn't recall the last time you'd burst into tears. In a public place, no less. In *business class*. You weren't even sure why this was happening. Initially, you attributed the distress to a week's worth of vodka and pickled cabbage.

"You seem pretty upset," the stewardess said. "Turbulence upsets a lot of people."

She offered, in lieu of tissue, a napkin.

"I'm fine," you said.

"Sir, please—"

"Do *not* touch me."

She started to say something, then thought better of it and retreated.

The cause of your upset was twofold. To leave Russia, you felt, was to in some way leave Bruno. That Bruno was neither Russian nor alive—nor a person you'd ever met—was incidental. He was, in addition to a misunderstood genius, a disturbed one. Bipolar. Half of you felt sorry for him. The other felt sorry for you.

Back to the cruel world.

For the next month or so, you nudged and prodded Bruno's friends, relatives, and exes about his Troubles. Most acknowledged the problem, albeit warily. They were protective of Bruno, who guarded nothing so much as his own privacy. The best way to lose him was to press him. He hated personal questions and obligations. He rarely told anyone what he was doing, where he was going, or why. He kept the world at bay. Literally. Rare was the person who got anywhere near Bruno's apartment, a cluttered one-bedroom on West 110th Street. "It's a bad time," Bruno would say. "I can't explain."

One day, outside Lincoln Center, he found his latest project, a gorgeous ex-model named Kwami Handy. But he never once invited her over. "What do you have up there?" Handy asked. "A body?" After finally wearing him down, she discovered that Bruno's front door was covered in handwritten quotations and affirmations, among them ANGER IS THE WORST ENEMY and PRIDE FEEDS ON FEAR. The shelves were strewn with journals; the closets, locked. "Hermetic," Handy said. "His own little world."

He grew ever more elusive. "Don't take this personally," he'd tell Handy. "But I'm going underground for a week or so."

God only knew where he went. Sometimes he'd call an old friend in Switzerland, Ronald Bernheim. "I'm coming to Zurich," he would say. "Are you still up?" He would arrive after midnight, chat excitedly all night, then leave at dawn. "He had two extreme elements," Bernheim recalled. "Introverted and extroverted. There was hardly anything in between."

"Manic depression influenced and structured his life in many ways," said his ex-wife, Heather May, yet another ex-model. "He suffered tremendously. He tried to hide it. But that was an uphill battle."

Bruno was prescribed lithium, to even out the mood swings. But he hated the side effects (weight gain, lethargy, a feeling of blankness) and often went off the program. Cycling. Cycling.

Especially in Antarctica. In New York, he said, his moods swung wildly; in Antarctica, he was cured.

He was fifty-one. The vagaries of bachelorhood and age were upon him; New York was suffocating. "I am out of the normal," he wrote in his diary. "The decision is clear! It is either die or go to my beloved feathered friends."

Bruno dropped his middle name, Joseph, in favor of Penguin. "By my thinking," his brother Guido said, "it was all just a little bit too much penguins."

In his diary, Bruno wrote: "Antarctica will clear my mind." He laid plans for one final expedition. The goal was clear. "I must get that one last picture, of an emperor chick being born," he later said. "The perfect picture."

In April 1997, he traveled to Mirny aboard the *Akademik Federov*, a cherry-red, 460-foot Russian icebreaker; the journey, through violent seas, lasted seven long weeks. "This is a godforsaken white hell," Bruno wrote in his journal. He would lie on his bed for hours, listening to

Mahalia Jackson and staring up at two inexplicable footprints on the ceiling. He referenced, in his journal, "those negative thoughts."

"Day has become night and night has become day," he wrote. But three days later, when the ship's captain spotted Mirny, Bruno was born again.

"My home," he said.

The next day, Bruno bounded past glimmering icebergs until he detected a telltale fishy smell. Fifty yards ahead, he spotted a cluster of dark spots. "Like the center of a giant sunflower," he later wrote, recording the presence of five thousand emperors. "Yes! Yes! Yes! My heart is found!"

Most of the time, Bruno seemed the picture of health. But on days when Bruno was restricted to the base, due to bad weather—and there was plenty of that—he sulked in his room. Or scolded the crew about their drinking. Or bitched about being persecuted. The base chief refused to let Bruno go out without a partner. Bruno called the chief "the Leninist."

Other times Bruno just holed up in his room, subsisting on chocolate. "I think of the penguins," he wrote. "What might they do if stuck under the snow? Will they suffer?" He refused to let a German visitor photograph the penguins, for fear of spooking them. "You have to *earn their trust*," Bruno said, storming off.

By July 7, he looked wrung out, even by Russian-sailor standards. "Very bad," said one of the crew members, Leonid Popolitov. "Very unhealthy." Two days earlier, Bruno had watched in horror as a male emperor slipped on the ice, fumbled his egg, and ran away, flippers flapping.

But now, on the morning of the seventh, Bruno had only one thing on his mind. He had to get back to the emperors before the next blizzard swept through. Bruno hurriedly put on his work clothes, grabbed his satchel, and shambled outside, at 11:50 A.M., looking for all the world like Antarctica's own Ignatius J. Reilly.

His friend Wowa urged him to eat lunch first. He was a worrying sort, especially now that Bruno had persuaded the base chief to let him travel solo.

"Oh, no," Bruno replied.

The half-mile hike to the rookery took about forty minutes, each step a small negotiation requiring delicacy, focus, and dumb luck; at any point, a hidden crevasse could have snapped his ankle or swallowed him whole. He was panting and red-faced by the time he reached the penguins, offered his usual greeting, flopped onto his belly, and began working. He continued in peace until 1:45, when Wowa radioed with news: "We're having a storm," he said. "Come back."

"Oh, I can't," Bruno replied, cheerfully. "I'm finishing my work."

Wowa implored him.

Bruno went radio silent until 3:20. "Wowa," he said. "I can see nothing."

The sun was sinking; winds were at seventy miles per hour; visibility was down to fifty feet. Once darkness fell, the Russians sent up flares and headed out into the storm, tethered by "blizzard ropes." Radio contact became frantic, confusing. Bruno kept saying that he was near the base, that he was following the flares.

"I am looking," he said, in staccato bursts. "See light."

More flares.

"Yes," Bruno said. "See light."

Then, silence.

Bruno had been walking in the wrong direction. And the flares he'd seen had actually been their reflection, bouncing off the snow and ice—a glitter ball effect.

The next morning, the Russians finally found Bruno lying on a smooth sheet of ice, on the wrong side of a natural ice barrier. He was flat on his back, gloved hands over his face, which was covered by an inch-thick mask of ice.

So there was that.

Who dies chasing birds in a polar hell storm? A bipolar adventurer.

Emperors are not people.

Emperors do not mate for life.

Bruno maintained otherwise. He believed these things because he needed to believe them. And he needed to believe them because he needed to believe *something*. And he needed to believe something, because otherwise the sun would go black and the stars would fall from the sky.

Because that's how crazy manic fools think.

Bruno's friends and relatives had been right to downplay the matter of his Troubles. The latter were by turns notable and beside the point. You were pretty sure about that. Bruno was a little out there. A little . . . unconventional. But so was every other adventurer and explorer you'd ever heard of. Dian Fosse was a paranoid freak. Lewis and Clark were bat-shit.

Every time someone said "Yeah, well, the guy was obviously out of his fucking mind," you resisted the urge to Taser them—only you were allowed to criticize Bruno, because only you understood his dark magic. Instead, though, you told the doubters a story about Bruno's memorial service in Mirny, a few weeks after his death. As the crew stood shivering in the cold, thirty penguins toddled out of nowhere—until this moment, there hadn't been birds anywhere near the area. The penguins mixed in among the humans. Joined the congregation. In silence.

That nobody seemed to buy this story was distressing. You squirreled away in Brooklyn, plotting your escape from the cynics and heathens of this infernal city. Burning endless hours cursing the Toastmasters self-esteem meetings one floor below. *I am a strong, sexy man who happens to be a tad overweight.*

You jettisoned a woman you'd been dating because she was making all sorts of outlandish demands. She expected you to return calls, commit to dinner plans, invite her to Brooklyn—it never ended. One morning, after she'd had the nerve to question your commitment, you said, unbidden: "I can't do this anymore. I'm moving to California."

That the plan had just now come to you, on the spot, only made it feel more profound, in a Brunoesque sort of way. Adventure called. Bruno hadn't done shit until he was thirty-five. All in all, then, you were on pace.

But the clincher occurred weeks later, when you came across yet another newspaper headline. The *Los Angeles Times*, November 17, 1999:

ONETIME SUPERAGENT, DRUG ABUSER IS FOUND HANGED

CHAPTER THREE

Every reporter at some point comes to terms with his obsession for the dead. This revelation, though disquieting in certain respects, is a watershed; it marks the point where the reporter shakes off the folly of youth—all that dorm-room crap about Making A Difference and Championing Truth—and sees himself for who he truly is.

That all the best stories begin with a dead body was a given. This you learned at age thirteen, after stealing your brother's copy of *In Cold Blood;* its opening chapter, with its gory farmhouse on the high wheat plains of Kansas, revealed everything you needed to know about storytelling. But Capote's technique, though masterful, was notable only in relation to his subject matter. You would have been less enamored had the book been subtitled "A True Account of a Multiple Second-Degree Assault and Its Consequences."

Your career, from the start, had evinced the telltale stench of death. There had been dispatches from Starke, Florida, a prison town that's home to the state's only electric chair, known as "Old Sparky." And a profile of true-crime hack Joe McGinnis. And the tale of two brothers on Florida's death row, Ernest and Bobby Lee Downs, who had committed wholly separate offenses. Bobby Lee was a dimwit who shot his estranged wife in front of their children; Ernest, a sharper tack, was a rent-a-killer. He mailed you passages from Ecclesiastes, which he'd rendered in calligraphy. After reading your article, however, he wrote, "Thanks for nothing, asshole."

And Bruno Zehnder, photographer, fifty-two.

But death, in each of these cases, was as much carrot as stick; it framed and justified the exploration of larger areas of interest. American gothic. The sixties. Capital punishment. Wild adventure. Or at least that's what you told yourself.

But the newspaper headline marking the events of November 16, 1999, The Day The Agent Died, precipitated a great leap forward in your development as a ghoul. Or, at least, that's how you initially analyzed the situation. Inasmuch as you were inclined toward self-analysis. Which you were not. Because you were too busy conniving ways to highjack a prime story assignment before any of your charges got their greasy little paws on it. Fucking writers.

The subject matter, on the face of it, was tailor-made. The departed, Jay Moloney, had been a Hollywood wunderkind, rocketing from mailroom grunt to swaggering, starlet-nailing Armani Boy at Creative Artists Agency: the CIA of Hollywood, but with scarier agents. Jay had been first among equals, slashing his way into the good graces of Steven Spielberg, Martin Scorsese, David Letterman, Dustin Hoffman. And he'd done so thanks to the mentorship of Michael Ovitz, CAA's feared and omnipotent founder, godhead, and James Jesus Angleton figure.

From the *Los Angeles Times*:

Moloney was on the fast track to become one of the most powerful figures in Hollywood, a boy wonder who owned Picassos and Warhols and was earning $1 million a year by age 30. Tall, handsome and cocky, Moloney used his charm and boyish appeal to become the quintessential young deal maker in an era when agents became a powerful force in shaping popular culture. But he could never beat his cocaine habit.

Bingo!

Wonder Boy blew it all. Up his nose.

Another cautionary tale. Hollywood-style.

Suicide on Mulholland Drive.

Yes! Supertrifecta!

Glamour. Debauchery. Death.

VF, more than any other publication, elevated the crash-and-burn story to an art form; virtually every issue contained one or two epic tales of colossal demise. The disgraced media mogul drowned under mysterious circumstances. The rogue commodities trader on the run in Biarritz. To receive such coverage was to enter a pantheon. You weren't dead unless you died in *Vanity Fair.*

So your timing was top-notch. Bruno had made an impression on the editors, and the editors were people who could make *penguins* look cool—Hollywood's It-birds. Your article appeared in *VF's* first issue of the new millennium. You took that as a sign. This was even before you opened the issue, which featured four photographs of Cameron Diaz but nine of penguins. How many other writers could lay claim to that?

Mostly you profiled movie stars: people whose stories, like their brow lines, remained locked in suspended animation. Julia Roberts still howled about the scene when Richard Gere snapped the jewelry box; Will Smith still got goose bumps when recalling that first kiss with Jada. To write about celebrities (or about *any* living creatures, for that matter) was to write stories that, by definition, began and ended in act 2.

But Jay's story was a *story.* A three-act tragedy, with a classical narrative arc. A morality play. That much was clear, based on the waves of media coverage. The loudest *j'accuse* came via *New York* magazine's Hollywood reporter, Nikki Finke:

While authentic tears were shed after Moloney's suicide, the truth is that he achieved success not merely by embracing Hollywood but by reveling in its dark side. . . .

It's always hard to know whether bad people are drawn to Hollywood or good people go bad here. But one thing is certain: Unfettered access to Hollywood's renowned excess brought out the worst in Jay Moloney.

"Doug," you said. "Help me get this story."

"Jesus," he said.

"I know Hollywood. I knew this guy."

"Really? How?"

"Friend of a friend."

Elizabeth. The fashion-editrix. Show pony supreme.

"So I *essentially* knew him," you said.

"So *I* essentially knew him."

"Doug. Please."

"You're pushing it."

"It's what reporters do."

"Don't you have some editing to do?"

This prompted a changing of tack.

"Okay," you said. Softly. Expertly.

Doug, as an editor, was known to be flawless in every respect but one. He liked his writers. Liked helping them. Felt their pain.

"What's wrong?" he said.

As if he didn't know. As if he and Evgenia hadn't spent more than two years ministering to your anxieties about (a) work and (b) everything else.

Doug started to say something, but folded. Loosing a long sigh, he slouched toward the big corner office.

"Sir," the blond man said. "Are you here for the Moloney memorial service?"

A nod. A grunt.

"Sorry," he said. "No eating till after the service."

These people. You'd flown cross-country, at immense personal inconvenience, to get there. Draining, these cross-country flights. Blood sugar and whatnot. The memorial service was nowhere near the hotel; it was way over on the east side of town, at Paramount Pictures. Dead civilians were eulogized in churches, temples, mosques; dead agents, at movie studios, in a private theater with circular staircases and plush stadium-type seating.

But now, having arrived on time, you were assaulted by some twenty-year-old rent-a-waiter looking for someone to blame because he didn't get a callback for *Suddenly Susan*.

"Sir," he said. "The brownie."

You returned the brownie to the tray, but only out of respect for the dead, and only after punctuating the gesture with a grand flicking of crumbs, fingers at full extension. Once the waiter left, you commandeered three more brownies, while establishing a beachhead near the refreshments table, with its golden sierra of baked goods.

Waiter Boy steered you through the doors and into a theater stocked with mourners and their assistants. You took one of the few unoccupied seats; it was directly behind a man everyone else seemed to be giving wide berth. Only after you settled in, and hid the brownies beneath the man's seat, did you identify him as the great and powerful Ovitz. Crisp dark suit. Tight brown hair. Golfy tan. He was, like everyone in Hollywood, smaller than expected. Compact. He sat quietly, trying to look inconspicuous. Because that's what the devil always does.

Ovitz was the one guy in Hollywood who made CAA agents seem like decent fellows. He was now three years removed from the agency, having abandoned it, in typically cloak-and-dagger fashion, in order to assume the presidency of the one Hollywood racket even less sympathetic than CAA: the Walt Disney Company. CAA's brass felt betrayed, even though it was Ovitz, more than anyone, who had made them all both rich and respectable. Thanks to his Ovitz-ness—the Jasper Johns flags, the Sun Tzu *Art of War* crap—agents fashioned themselves as aesthetes rather than as the glorified car salesmen they actually were. But this was Hollywood. History didn't exist.

When one of the eulogizers made a veiled reference to Ovitz—"The O," he called him—Ovitz manufactured a smile. But the back of his neck blanched, and he reflexively slid his feet backward, underneath his seat. The heel of his black wing tip crunched one of the brownies. He reached down, removed the offending treat, and shot a glance at you. He looked like he wanted to say something.

Meantime, as the memorial continued, it occurred to you that Jay's memorial service was being held at a *movie studio;* that most of his eulogists were colleagues; and that these people spent a whole lot of time recalling Jay's penchant for gratuitous and self-congratulatory extravagance. *Remember when Jay rented the entire cruise ship in Turks and Caicos? And that suite at the Hotel du Cap! God only knows what he paid for that fireworks show in Maui!* It occurred to you that this was a memorial service for a tool.

Ovitz, at least, was the tool's tool. Self-made. Jay was manqué. He was a product of Hollywood, of *Malibu*. His father, an actor/agent/screenwriter, wrote the 1980 Peter Sellers flop, *The Fiendish Plot of Dr. Fu Manchu*, and represented Charo, Xavier Cugat, and Burt Ward, of *Batman* fame. Few kids, aside from Jay, had birthday parties starring the original Robin.

Naturally, Jay attended USC, the finishing school for Hollywood's jerk-offs of tomorrow. By then he'd refined his act, supplementing his boyish, eager-to-please excitability with equal parts glibness and schmooze. The "package"—Jay, like all agents, loved such words—landed him one of CAA's coveted summer internships. He eventually wrangled a job as Ovitz's assistant, thanks to a signature blend of craftiness, charm, and toadyism. He was a natural, as agents went.

Jay fetched the boss's dry cleaning, confirmed dinner reservations at Drai's, and arranged tee times at the Bel-Air County Club. "Get my golf clubs!" Bill Murray would demand. Jay knew what Ovitz wanted before even Ovitz did. And he soaked up the great man's teachings on life, work, and back-end grosses. Leverage well, Grasshopper.

Ovitz, a man who wouldn't relinquish a bar of soap without a fight, handed his charge a murderer's row of clients, which they represented in tandem. "Steven" and "Marty." "Dustin" and "Leo." He affected Ovitz's manner, from the way he spoke ("How can *I* help *you,* Steven?") to the way he dressed (dark-blue, two-button Armani). He began saying things like, "I'm gonna head up to Dublin, to see Bono." He was coddled—"Mike's boy." And he did the boss's dirty work, bullying reporters (calling one "a fucking pig") and spreading rumors about competitors (saying one rival agent had AIDS).

The rest of the story wrote itself:

Jay's annual income exceeded two million dollars. Suddenly he was an art patron, a collector of Picassos and Warhols. Blah, blah. He befriended strippers and romanced B-movie starlets—one from *Twin Peaks,* one from *Showgirls*—at the height of their celebrity half-lives. Blah, blah, blah. He drove a BMW 750, rented a beach house in Malibu, and lived high in the Hollywood Hills, in a gleaming modern colossus his friends nicknamed, in a nod to *Scarface,* "Tony Montana's summer house."

Cue the cocaine. Jay hoovered half the Bolivian flake in Los Angeles. The young buck, once so strapping and full of potential, began unraveling. A skipped meeting here; an unreturned call there. A master of the half-truth, he made half-believable excuses. Covered his tracks. Played with house money.

Soon enough, though, clients and colleagues smelled trouble. CAA demanded answers. But the warnings went unheeded. Jay snorted and snorted, lied and lied. At one point, in great detail, he told a doozy about having been carjacked, kidnapped, tied to a motel bedpost, and terrorized. The story seemed unlikely, given that he was still driving his BMW.

The rumors got out. Clients began freaking. Everyone felt for the poor guy. But jeez.

Jay came undone. He abdicated. Fortune dwindling. Reputation crumbling. Nose bleeding. Finally, in a parking lot on Sunset Boulevard, he found himself cornered by friends/colleagues. Ovitz pulled out a baseball bat and said, "If you don't go to rehab now, I'll break your legs."

Jay did the Hollywood Rehab Dance, starting at Promises, an unnaturally swank treatment center in Malibu. Following his month's worth of massages and tanning, he remained committed to rehab. Of his image. While describing his triumphant recovery, in *Premiere* magazine—his reconnection with Judaism, his Taoist influences—Jay posed for photographic portraits. He was shown sitting solemnly. Dressed in white. Hands in prayer position.

He went right back on the powder. Hitting the town with Chris Farley. Conning friends into loaning him money. He spent six months Working On Himself at a luxury resort in the British Virgin Islands. The resort, located on the private island of Guana, was owned by two of Jay's many rich, gullible friends; the cheapest rooms rented for 765 dollars a night. Jay returned to civilization with a killer tan and a new client, singer Ben Taylor, whom he'd met in Guana, and who happened to be the son of James Taylor and Carly Simon.

In April 1999, after acquiring a girlfriend named Ginger, Jay parlayed his connections into a five-hundred-thousand-dollars-a-year job at Paradise Music & Entertainment, a struggling management-and-production firm. The CEO of Paradise was Jesse Dylan, who happened to be the son of Bob. The firm was cofinanced by a company belonging to a money manager named Dana Giacchetto, whose client list happened to include Leonardo DiCaprio, Cameron Diaz, and Matt Damon. The stars also happened to be represented by a talent-management company called AMG, which happened to be owned by Michael Ovitz.

But Jay's packaging skills were waning. He lasted less than three months at Paradise. Which was probably for the best, because the company's stock price would soon plummet, because Giacchetto was about to be exposed as a fraudster. Jay wasn't involved in the crimes. Wasn't involved, period. A month into the job, he stopped showing up.

Then he died.

Quite a legacy, Jay. Hosannas.

Your verdict, pure and simple. You fled the memorial service a few minutes before it ended, in order to get first dibs on the coffee and treats before heading for the car. The last thing you needed was to wait in line with a bunch of sad-sack haircuts. Also, the thought of spending even one more millisecond in that memorial service was unbearable, given the degree to which the deceased represented everything that was wrong in the world. If you had to listen to one more story about Aspen, they'd have a second swinging corpse to deal with.

Also, the hotel had finger sandwiches and freshly baked Toll House cookies. This was your second go-around at the Beverly Hills Hotel, the famed pink palace on Sunset Boulevard. But the first stay had been during the hotel's nadir, a decade earlier, when the Polo Lounge smelled of Don Henley and *Spy* magazine could book a room for eighty bucks and a carton of Luckies. But now, postfacelift, the place sparkled. Top-shelf scotches in the minifridge. Bed that could fit a soccer team. And the cookies. Toll House, oatmeal—it was a guessing game. They just materialized, unbidden, on the wings of angels.

An email pinged:

From: Lizz
Dinner at 7. Ben and Daniel's.

The main attraction. The main reason why this story was so important.

You'd returned to Los Angeles regularly over the past two and a half years, supplementing the occasional work trip or holiday weekend with vacation days. Whenever people asked why, you'd cough up something about a friend's wedding, or a hiking trip, or whatever. In truth, Los Angeles was where you went when you crashed; it's where you went for therapy.

The therapists there worked round-the-clock, free of charge. They were a team of three: Lizz, Ben, and Daniel. They had formed four years earlier, in 1996—a year before you moved east.

Lizz and Ben had been friends since high school. They attended the prom together, under a cloud of conflicting expectations, Lizz being the rare classmate who had yet to connect a few dots pertaining to Ben's sexuality.

But by the time you all united, in Los Angeles, Lizz had worked things out. Ben and Daniel were married under the laws of the universe, if not the state of California. And they were, despite significant variances in temperament and interests, a package deal. They reminded you, in this way, of your parents. Seamless. You couldn't imagine one without the other. But Ben and Daniel even shared physical resemblances. Ben had broader shoulders and glasses; Daniel was wiry, boyish. But both had olive complexions, dark hair, and similar dimensions. They wore clothes and shoes interchangeably and evinced the kind of stylish antistyle that looks gay only on straight guys.

Ben was the front man, a reluctant charmer who could make a lamppost want to be his best friend forever. In conversation, he tended to tilt forward, as if pulled by wonder. "*Innnn*teresting," he would say, with Holmesian flourish. If the news was especially delicious, he would draw a sharp, deep breath. "That . . . is . . . *shocking*," he'd say. "Shocking. Shocking. Shocking." And when dispensing wisdom, as he often did, he tended to begin with the same five words. "*I need you to know,*" he would say, before explaining whatever it was you needed to consider/accept/understand/be/do/stop doing. Which was inevitably the right call. Because he was an old soul. And because he smelled lies the way dogs smell fear.

He was a transplanted New Yorker, raised on the Upper West Side, with all the other Marxists and Jews. By writ, he went on to Hampshire College, one of those namby-pamby schools where nobody gets graded and everybody calls the dean "Jeremy." Then he spent several years as an actor, then as a casting director, then a designer of bags, children's clothing, and other things you didn't understand.

Daniel, being from the Main Line suburbs of Philadelphia, had taken a more old-school route. He went to prep school and then to Yale, where he belonged to a British-style "social club" whose members held afternoon teas, leafed through Shakespearean quartos, and undermined democracies. Unlike most Yale graduates, however, Daniel broke free of his jar at CIA Headquarters. He wanted to direct movies, not coups. So he moved to Los Angeles, to get an MFA at the USC film school. That Hollywood was really just the CIA for cowards, and that USC was "the Farm" without guns, had not occurred to him. Yet.

Initially, Daniel was tougher to read. He rarely sought people out or showed his cards. Ben, when in the presence of idiots or assholes, didn't stand on ceremony. He'd say "I need you to know you're a ridiculous person," then walk away, having already deleted that person from his memory bank. Daniel would try diplomacy, then reason. As such, he was the one more inclined to eventually succumb to rage and profanity. So you had that in common.

But those who got to know Daniel soon found themselves in his warm embrace. He was a Hugger. He hugged professional acquaintances. Tightly. He lacked any sense of proportion or propriety; he was indiscriminate, unmanageable. At parties, he gave good-bye hugs to people he'd met an hour earlier—people you'd spent years not hugging. Which made you, in addition to uncomfortable, the asshole who wouldn't hug.

Initially, you dismissed the grappling and squeezing as some sort of nervous tic. Daniel had his moments of anxiety and fear. All in all, though, he was a model of stability and decorum, educated by Quakers, Yalies—people who masturbated with gloves on. Finally, under questioning by you regarding the hugging, he said, "Did it ever occur to you that it's just a nice thing to do?"

All four of you tended to externalize your internal monologues, the bulk of which tended to be eerily similar in both content (self-doubt) and style (hyperbole), i.e.:

Daniel: I can't tell you how stupid I was today.
Ben: You don't even know what stupid is.
Lizz: If I don't eat soon, I'll literally eat Daniel.
Ben: What if you actually did eat Daniel?
Lizz: What do you mean what *if*?
Ben: Fine. Eat Daniel.
Daniel: What? You don't love me?
Lizz: Couldn't love you more.
Daniel: More than Ben?
Lizz: More than Ben's mother.
Daniel: What if you were in love with Ben's mother?
Lizz: What do you mean what *if*?
Ben: I need you both to stop talking. In a loving way.

On this night after Moloney's memorial service, as per usual, you gathered at Ben and Daniel's house, a tiny, adobe-style place whose rough-hewn outer shell concealed a warm, gooey center. It was the most comfortable cave in human history, replete with overstuffed chairs, background music, and mood lighting.

That you and Lizz were now exes in no way destabilized the group dynamic. The breakup had seemed organic, civilized, and in the best interests of everyone. You and Lizz, as a couple, had been developmentally stunted. Your concerns about her increasing alcohol consumption fell on deaf ears. Her concerns about your utter inscrutability were wasted breath. So, thanks to the gentle guidance of Ben and Daniel, you'd found a happy medium. As siblings.

They watched you like hawks. Even after you moved cross-country. Even after Lizz replaced you with a new and improved boyfriend. When you started sinking, they knew it immediately. And they didn't suffer fools.

"How are you feeling?" Ben asked.

"Hard to say," you said. "Good days, bad days."

"Fine. Now I'd like the truth, please."

"That is the truth."

"No, it's not."

"How do you know?"

"Because I know you better than you know yourself."

Months earlier, from three thousand miles away, Ben had arranged for you to see a psychiatrist one of his cousins had recommended. Your experience with shrinks, up until this point, had been limited to a single therapy session in 1978, when you were a thirteen-year-old plagued by nightmares about escaped mental patients. You had, as usual, been watching too many horror movies. Enter Shrink One, a cuddly mensch whom your parents had known socially. "Go home," One said. "Watch each movie two more times, in daylight. Really look at them— that's the trick. By the third viewing, you'll be cured." Modern therapy: your one-stop shopping solution.

Shrink Two looked the part of an Upper West Side psychiatrist. Bow tie. Beard. Glasses. The insomnia and depression, he said, stemmed from "social anxiety disorder." He prescribed an antidepressant (Prozac) and a tranquilizer (Ativan). The pharmacy needed to order the Prozac. But the Ativan worked so well, so fast, you declared yourself cured, nixing both the antidepressant and the shrink.

Whenever troubles arose, you knew where to go. Whatever the problem, they handled it. With a smile.

You missed them. You needed them.

"Just move back," Daniel said.

"I wish," you said.

The next day, at the hotel, boredom sparked a cursory review of the news clippings contained in a manila folder marked "Dead Agent." One article, in *The New York Times,* offered the usual post-mortems until the sixth paragraph:

The coroner's office also said Mr. Moloney had a history of depression.

You contacted the coroners office.

"So he battled depression?"

"He did."

"So was that the root cause? Depression?"

He paused.

"Not exactly," he said.

"So what then?"

"You're familiar with manic depression?"

Suddenly everything smelled like burnt hair.

You spent the afternoon chasing down two books you'd halfheartedly skimmed while writing about Bruno. Both were authored by Kay Redfield Jamison, a clinical psychologist expert in the field of manic depression (in part because she herself had it). In her most famous book, *An Unquiet Mind,* Jamison noted the degree to which bipolars can become addicted to mania—"the force that through the green fuse drives the flower," she wrote, quoting Dylan Thomas.

Enter the party drugs. By many estimates, roughly half of all bipolars at some point abuse drugs or alcohol. This neutralizes the effects of mood-stabilizing drugs and prevent doctors from knowing whether a patient is manic or just shitfaced. And the combination of mania addiction and cocaine addiction is the ultimate marriage from hell: Two codependent beasts assume each other's worst qualities, then mutate into one symbiotic monster, which ultimately devours itself.

You leafed through your interview notes. It was the same story, over and over:

"He was a tornado," said his former assistant, Jessica Tuchinsky.

"In excess," said his ex-girlfriend Lisa Wong. "Everything in his life was becoming in excess—buying, playing, working in excess."

"He moved in the lightest and darkest ways," his friend Tom Lassally said.

During a romantic sailing trip in Anguilla, Wong watched the lightness drain out of him. "He would go off on his own at the end of the boat," she recalled. "And he'd just sit there, alone. He said he just felt lonely." Jay's friends called the phenomenon "vapor lock." "He'd just sit out on a rock for hours, perfectly still, and just be sad."

Occasionally, Jay tried to explain. One day, out of the blue, he asked Lassally to meet him at the Los Angeles Farmers Market. "Why?" Lassally asked.

"I can't tell you," Jay replied.

When they met, Jay looked like shit.

"I've done some cocaine over the last few days," he said.

Lassally recoiled. Jay didn't even drink.

"You're only as sick as your secrets," Jay said, backtracking. "No big deal."

"If it isn't a problem," Lassally said, "then why are you sitting here?"

"No big deal," Jay repeated.

That Jay's drug problem began shortly after Ovitz's abrupt departure from CAA was noted. "There was always that safety net," said one of his CAA friends. "When Mike left, it traumatized him. I don't think it's a coincidence that his crash happened at the same time. We talked about it, and Jay was aware of it."

Life on his own proved daunting. Sometimes he asked his partners for tips on basic agenting techniques and protocols. "He didn't trust his skills," said one colleague. "He seemed terrified. He always thought he was going to get found out."

Publicly, at least, Jay talked the talk. "A lot of people who don't understand addiction want to blame my using on what was going on with Ovitz and CAA at the time," he told *Premiere* magazine. "My sincere belief is that it had nothing to do with it. I had a predisposition toward it." Still, he acknowledged the impact environment can have on an addict, suggesting that work pressures had perhaps "compounded" his problems.

He was a hell of salesman.

One gram every other weekend had become three per day. He couldn't get through a day without cocaine and had a dealer at his beck and call. He almost always snorted in seclusion, locked in a bathroom or bedroom, too ashamed to let anyone see him and half convinced they'd never notice. After Wong's thirty-first birthday party, she discovered powder all over her bathroom floor. He began canceling on her with lame excuses; other times, he just didn't show up. One day, arriving at his house, she found blood was everywhere.

"What's going on?" she asked.

"Don't worry," he said.

The relationship tanked. His mind moved too fast. Except when it moved too slow. He'd stay up all night, sorting photographs or alphabetizing the thousands of CDs he bought at a Tower Records. Or the boxes of stuff—scuba gear, clothing—he'd bought that day. He'd sleep through the day, then wake up in a fugue. One day he walked to the garage, closed the door, climbed into his BMW, turned on the ignition, and waited. Then he changed his mind. He paid his coke dealer to stay away. Then, an hour later, he asked him to return. With a pile of cocaine.

"I have a hole in my heart," Jay often said. He had a congenital heart defect that required surgery. Everyone saw this as Jay's ticket to sobriety, since he couldn't show up at the hospital with a heart full of coke. His friends watched him night and day, solicited the best addiction specialists. He brought that out in people. They wanted to mother him.

The surgery was a success. Jay was not. It was then that his national rehab tour began, eventually stopping in Oregon, near his mother's home. He checked into the famed Hazelden rehab center, where he remained for several months, and where he persuaded a CAA client to stay with the agency. He was determined to, in his words, "rock this place." This was typical of Jay. "His enthusiasm to get better was off the charts," said one of his CAA friends. "Just as his depression was off the charts."

Then, boom. Jay persuaded a friend that a murderous drug dealer would kill him if he didn't settle a six-thousand-dollar drug debt. The friend hand delivered the money to Jay, who scored the minute he left Hazelden.

Jay returned to Hollywood, determined to rehabilitate his image, if not himself. CAA kept the media jackals at bay by stating that Jay had—in that time-honored excuse by all great Hollywood hopheads—become hooked on postoperative painkillers. Which was also true.

He missed more work meetings. He summoned the strippers, who found him out cold. He somehow ended up totaling his car in Alhambra, an industrial wasteland in the San Gabriel Valley. Though uninjured, he was dazed. Medics transported him to the psych ward at Cedars-Sinai hospital, on the cusp of Beverly Hills. It was there that he was diagnosed as bipolar.

Lithium smoothed him out a bit. Until he stopped taking it. He went Bruno. "Fucking side effects," he'd say. It made him feel flat, empty. "They just kill something inside me."

CAA allowed Jay to "step down" in the spring of 1996. He informed most of his clients directly, among them Scorsese. "I just can't continue," Jay told him.

Jay's identity crisis, his lack of *credentials,* accelerated his odyssey of fluctuation. "Good days and bad days," he'd say.

He tried everything. Prozac. Zoloft. Wellbutrin. He would stick with the program for a few weeks: exercising, returning calls, apologizing. "He'd be ashamed," recalled his friend Barry Josephson, an executive at Columbia Pictures. "He'd say 'I'm sorry I didn't make it.'" He would pore over spiritual texts, self-help manuals, the Bible. "For a while," Wong said, "it was God this, God that." He considered collecting his photographs into a book titled *I'll Burn That Bridge When I Get to It.*

Cycling.

He would disappear for days. Go underground. Typically, friends found him at home, passed out or squirreled away in darkness. Sometimes he covered his windows—twenty feet tall, best city views in town—with garbage bags, T-shirts, underwear. "He didn't want to see it," said his friend Dewey Nicks, a photographer. "He talked about how he just wanted to keep it out."

Round and round.

Salvation was out there somewhere, anywhere. Jay put in six successful months at the Menninger Clinic in Topeka, Kansas. When he finally left, six months later, he bombed across rural highways, picking up speeding tickets in Minnesota and Wyoming. Back in Hollywood, he snorted rails with Chris Farley, whose drug-related end was only seven months away. A visit to New York proved especially unconstructive. While arguing with cops, Jay tried cutting his throat with a shard of glass. So off he went to Four Winds Hospital, a private psychiatric facility in Katonah, New York.

"He'd always get excited about the *next* place," one of his friends recalled. "When that wouldn't work, it was always the *next* one. He was always moving, searching."

Next stop, Guana. Six months of exercise, sunshine, and work. He cleaned pools, folded laundry. His friends let him stay for free, as long as he passed regular drug tests. A travel writer, having stumbled upon

Jay, described him as an "affable" and "hilarious" character, whose chief responsibility was to feed Cheepah, a giant rock iguana who lived on the island. Jay spoke to Cheepah as if to an old friend. He asked the iguana how his day was going, and whether he'd missed him.

It was the best he'd felt in four years, maybe more. His body, once flaccid and pale, had become lean, beveled, tanned; his green eyes sparkled anew. He'd passed every test and was as he looked. Clean. His confidence was returning. To celebrate, he got a tattoo: a Taoist symbol. "The pressure was off," his mother recalled. "He felt that he had his problems under control. He said he felt a peace there that he hadn't felt in so long."

"I think I'm ready," Jay told friends. "I think I'm ready to go back."

When it came time to reenter civilization, in May 1998, he stayed with friends in New York. For five months, they provided the support system he dearly needed, and watched him closely. His money and valuables were placed in a trust, from which he received a modest allowance. He'd given his friends no choice, having previously blown six thousand dollars on an antique edition of the AA *Big Book* (signed by Bill W. himself) only to sell it for two thousand dollars he used to finance a binge.

One minute, Jay was working out like a fiend, leading Narcotics Anonymous meetings—"Just fucking do it!" he'd tell other addicts; the next, he'd be a puddle. "You must be disappointed in me," he'd tell friends. At a benefit event, he dissolved into tears. "I've got everything, and just look at me," he said. "I'm *pathetic*."

That's when he met Ginger, a neophyte actress who'd had a bit part in the teenster movie *Cruel Intentions*. He made his move while she was working out at his gym. With her mother. "I'm taking your daughter on a date," he announced. On their first date, however, Jay barely mentioned his professional bona fides. "I haven't worked in three or four years," he said. "I've been in and out of rehab, and I've been sober for eight months."

"Okay," Ginger said.

Emboldened, he moved into his own apartment, on the Upper West. He spent his first night there with Ginger. Which was also his last night. Jay had scored drugs on the Lower East Side, gone to pieces, and bolted back to Guana. "He felt he was such a burden," Ginger recalled.

Finally, after righting himself in Guana, he visited Ginger in Los Angeles, slipped again, then set his sights on Kansas. There he put in six solid months at the Menninger Clinic, except for the time he received a two-day furlough, headed straight for an ATM, scored drugs, found a hotel room, climbed into the tub, and slashed his throat and wrists. Hotel staff found him near death. Jay's first words, upon being revived: "I'm sorry."

Soon enough, though, Jay was attributing his scars to an "accident" and keeping up appearances. That's when he commenced his short-lived "comeback" with the Paradise company. He had always assumed that he would get back in the game and return triumphantly to CAA. Stay straight for a year, the partners told him. "That's the saddest part," one later said. "There was no evidence that he could."

He tried two more rehabs in 1999, including California's Impact treatment center, a kind of Last Stop Before Prison. He had the system down cold. "When he talked to a doctor, he'd speak as if he were a physician," a friend recalled. "He knew every drug, side effect, and combination. He played along. A doctor would say, 'He's okay and on the road to recovery!' We'd just look at each other and say, 'Yeah, right.'"

By now home was a rented house atop the Hollywood Hills. The L-shaped house, while modern and comfortable, was a far cry from his old place. Ginger spent every day and most nights there. First thing every morning, Jay bounded out of bed, in search of coffee, coffee, coffee. Then, while scribbling in his journal or listening to Buddhist meditation tapes—he burnt through cigarette after cigarette. He'd start crashing.

"I just need to go take a nap," he'd say, mortified that he was sleeping so much. "Is that okay?"

Minutes later, though, he might well pop out of the bedroom, shouting, "Let's go to Virgin Records!"

More than once, usually before or after attending an AA meeting, Jay relapsed. He would return home saying he'd had "too much coffee"—a lie even Jay couldn't sell anymore. He was too mortified to face his friends. He ducked calls and retreated to the bedroom. He'd cry for hours.

Then he'd rally Ginger for a trip to Universal Studios, in search of roller coasters.

On November 13, a Saturday, Jay and Ginger watched a Holyfield fight on TV, before turning in.

"You're gonna have a birthday tomorrow," she said.

He just groaned and rolled over.

The next day, Jay joined his friends for brunch at Casa del Mar, a beachfront hotel in Santa Monica. He and Ginger spent the evening back in the hills, watching *The X-Files*.

"Happy birthday," she said, before heading home.

He groaned and shut the door.

The next morning, after he missed an AA meeting, the Jay Alert System blinked red. One friend alerted another until Jay's last remaining client, Ben Taylor, forced open the door to Jay's bathroom. The water was running. Jay, having fashioned his belt into a noose, dangled from the shower nozzle.

He had just turned thirty-five.

You were speeding along the westbound lane of Mulholland Drive, at about 10:00 P.M., when the dead guy summoned you. The road was otherwise empty; this was usually the case, especially at night. The skinny two-lane blacktop was poorly lit and at times wended sharply;

it was largely a road to nowhere, except for stoners, sightseers, and the small sampling of residents—celebrities, celebrity-dentists—lucky and stupid enough to live high atop the canyons.

Mulholland at night had always been your favorite spot in Los Angeles. You made the drive whenever possible, for the same reason the stoners and sightseers did. It was like driving through a desert above Times Square. You saw the city, in its twinkling entirety. But the city couldn't see you.

It was a Thursday night, at the tail end of your work trip. Most of the interviews were in the bag. You'd spent the evening eating pasta and pie at Ben's and Daniel's house. Lizz was there, cheerful as ever. Dinner proved that nothing had changed among you, except for (a) the amount of alcohol consumed and (b) the fact that you couldn't go visit the cats at your old house. Evidently, Lizz had met the man of her dreams. He was staying at her place for the night. So your open-door policy had to be revised.

So Mulholland it was. The peace and quiet would do you good. The week had been a productive but taxing one. You had taken to crying in the shower. You had begun to view Jay Moloney as a fellow inhabitant of The Island Of Misfit Boys.

You rolled down the windows and took in the particular smell of the high canyon: that signature blend of wildflowers, scrub, and decaying eucalyptus.

That's when it happened. You were rounding a gentle bend, fiddling with the radio, when you felt a powerful urge to brake. This was unscheduled. And yet.

The rental car rattled to a stop, in that rental-car way. Then you pulled into a small, patio-like driveway on the north side of street, before turning off the car and stepping out. Behind the driveway, only ten feet from the road, was a modest bungalow-style house, painted off-white. The house was dark; the blinds were drawn, though not entirely. Through one window, you deciphered the lines of a foyer and some sort of living area.

That this was Jay's house was obvious, even though you hadn't set out to find it and didn't know the address. Whatever doubts you harbored—and you didn't harbor many—died the instant you saw, on the floor, a busted door handle.

You retrieved a crumpled receipt lying near the driveway. It was from Virgin Records. He'd bought a Santana album called *Lotus*.

Your first impulse was to laugh. *Lotus* being a personal favorite.

Your second was to make sure no one saw you laugh.

Your third was to move back to Los Angeles by April 19—your thirty-fifth birthday.

CHAPTER FOUR

Every morning, starting in the spring of 2000, you awakened to the sweet smell of decay. The smell—with its clashing notes of mold, smoke, menthol, and perfume—suggested an arsoned whorehouse in British Columbia. But it was intoxicating nonetheless, because it was the smell of home.

Laurel Canyon wasn't the swankiest section of the Hollywood Hills; it was a colossal thicket of overgrown scrub, wildflowers, and eucalyptus trees, all locked in warring states of expansion and rot. The place had only one commercial enterprise, the Canyon Country Store, which mostly stocked beer, cereal, and Doritos. The fauna—snakes, coyotes, Jackson Browne—defied eradication. The place looked much as it had when the founding fathers—Morrison, Moon, and Zappa; Crosby, Stills, Nash, and Young; Mama and Papa—established a community of peers hip to double albums and unprotected sex with strangers.

And now here you were, having persuaded Graydon to make you a contributing editor. Same pay, half the work. Just jeans, sunshine, and a laptop. The writer's life. Here's to new beginnings and a sun-filled bedroom in a secluded hillside house in Laurel Canyon. The "master suite" had a large bathroom with a Jacuzzi tub; a spare bedroom, across the hall, became an office. Between the two rooms was a turret-style skylight straight out of *The Song Remains the Same*—there were medieval themes at play. The skylight illuminated a spiral staircase leading to the main floor, which housed the living room and the kitchen, which had a certain rusticity. The house was the sort of place where David Crosby's sound technician would have lived comfortably and died mysteriously.

But the best part? The neighbors. Lizz lived in the canyon, in your old house. Ben and Daniel were still around the corner.

And Jay, of course. You passed his place all the time. It was the one with the realty sign.

You were doing all the right things. Seeing a new shrink. Getting a trainer. Mixing with the humans. Usually there was a girl in the picture, if only a potential one, or part-time one, or a not-quite-dead-yet one—or, in a pinch, one who was none of the above but might one day be. You were bullish about the latter, because relationships that don't exist never fail, because it's impossible to disappoint (or to be disappointed by) a conceptual girlfriend.

There had been, for example, the baby-hungry actress who really just wanted to date your sperm; the actress who exited middate, crying "I'll never find love!"; the clothing designer who liked you, then abruptly announced her engagement to a guy she'd met the same night you'd met her; the lit professor who was doomed even before she asked "Can I keep some clothes here?"; and the restaurant owner who was kind of perfect in every way and therefore couldn't be trusted.

You thrived. The therapy sessions had paid off. All four of them. You *identified* the error of your ways and *acknowledged* the problem. You *accepted* that things had to change, and that *only you* could change them, and that *real change* comes only through *real commitment*. It was about being *proactive*.

An entire year: gangbusters.

Then: a few issues.

They began in the summer of 2001, when you visited a physician at UCLA Medical Center, complaining of hellfire in your throat and chest. The culprit, he said, was "hiatal hernia." The muscle that should have separated your stomach from your esophagus was flawed, allowing acids to burble northward. It was just something you were born with and in no way life threatening. But corrective surgery was advisable for asthmatics and posed virtually no serious risks. Also it had a fantastic name: "laparoscopic Nissen fundoplication."

"Minimally invasive," they said. Just one inch-long incision, hidden at the base of the navel, plus four little punctures through which surgeons extended tubes and cameras. You would be on a liquid diet for a month. But that was the worst of it. You would be out of the hospital in a couple days, a little sore but otherwise fine.

Except that's not how it went. For four days, in the hospital, you puked and howled. For days thereafter, at home, you bled, oozed, and lay sweating like Nixon. Couldn't sleep. Couldn't eat. Your esophagus remained constricted in anger. A pinhole. Even Jell-O was an ordeal; anything thicker—those infernal protein shakes—may as well have been Play-Doh. You spent five days on a fold-out in Ben and Daniel's TV room and didn't become fully ambulatory for five more. Stitches popping and bleeding. All bedsheets tie-dyed.

Bad time to hole up in your bedroom, without eating or sleeping.

Bad time for a guy who can't look in the mirror to get his face cut open.

That's why you now found yourself on your back, on the floor of your office, in a state of What The Fuck. It explained many things: the wayward bandage and the throbbing cheek.

My face. The fucker cut my face.

Earlier that morning, having neither consulted nor notified any of your friends, you had returned to UCLA, to undergo your second surgical procedure in as many weeks. This procedure had nothing to do with the earlier one and was in no way necessary at this time.

But you had your reasons. The ladies wouldn't be banging down your door anytime soon anyway. Might as well do it when you already look like shit. And, really, it was a surgery in name only. Outpatient. The removal of a tiny basal cell skin cancer on your face, between your nose and your right eyelid. Nonmelanoma. Garden-variety.

The doctor did the deed in less than five minutes, using a pinky-size scalpel. A few stitches. Done.

Everything was great until the doctor tried to make you look into the hand mirror. "Take a look," he said brightly.

"No need," you said. "I'm fine."

Really.

"Go on. It's much better than you think."

"I trust you."

"Really, once you see it, you'll see it's no big deal."

There was a brief struggle over the mirror. Then the doctor backed off and exited, leaving everything to his nurse, a Filipino with perfectly symmetrical breasts.

"Normally, I'd show you how to clean the incision," she said, shifting to a slight baby-doll voice. "But I know some patients get squeamish."

"Oh, I'm fine with it," you said, ashamed.

"The doctor said you don't wanna look—"

"Mirror, please."

You took the micro approach, holding the mirror just two inches from your face, so you could see the hot zone only. It was a swollen half-inch line intersected by a handful of black stitches. But it looked just as the doctor had said it would, maybe even better.

Here two things happened:

1. The nurse reported the presence of a second basal cell, on your forehead.
2. You glimpsed the rest of your face.

Your *face*. Complexion the color of canned tuna; a cubist mess of misaligned features. The wound tugged at your lower eyelid, exposing gooey red unpleasantness and making the eyeball look far larger than the other.

You said something like "Agggh" or "Igggg," before dropping the mirror, which clattered at the nurse's feet. She did her best to keep you in the chair, the room, the office, the building. Her voice resounded: "You need to make an appointment for your next procedure!"

The freak-out began in earnest in the car, in an eastbound lane of Wilshire Boulevard, en route from Westwood to Laurel Canyon. Pulse was audible and quickening. There was a tightening in your chest, then in your throat—classic harbingers of an asthma attack. You fished an old Albuterol inhaler from the glove compartment and took two deep drags.

The fail-safe failed. So you pulled over, opened the door, and dry heaved. The action tore loose your surgical bandage and ripped a stitch on your belly. Stanching the blood, and determined not to bleed out in front of Trader Vic's, you grabbed a bottle of water, splashed your wounds and hands, and gulped the remaining water.

Onward you drove, bowed but unbroken, and aided by open windows and a blasting air-conditioner. At home, the heat was a little surprising. The house, being the enemy of sunlight, virtually never got hot—that was its main appeal, aside from its general inhospitability to outsiders. But this was late August, after all. Baking sun. No breeze. Haze over the canyons, locking in the heat.

Too much hot, dead air can make anyone bonkers, even cats. There were two of them, siblings: Buck, a gray boy, and Scrub, a calico-white girl. They were bug-eyed and prickly in the heat, the way the coyotes get when the canyon grows dry, leaving them no choice but to venture out into the streets and parking lots in search of sustenance. The cats circled you, hewing close to the living room walls, as if assessing the world's biggest mouse.

"Hey there," you said, rubbing together your thumb and forefinger: the universal cat greeting sound. But they were unmoved. And, frankly, a little rude. Their food and water bowls, in the kitchen, were flush. You had given these cats everything, often at your own expense. The refrigerator was empty but for condiments and two apples; the water cooler was down to its last gurgling ounces, which you splashed on your face, having neglected the doctor's orders to keep the gauze dry. The bandages slid down your cheek and splatted onto the floor. As you knelt to retrieve it, a whitish blur rocked toward the soggy lump, pounced on it, then spirited it away.

You watched Scrub, the calico, tear the thing to pieces.

"Okay," you said. "Come on."

They seemed to find this amusing and paused to enjoy the moment. When you made the mistake of stepping toward them, however, it was Formula One. Buck ran hard on the heels of Scrub, nipping at her tail and generally lighting a fire under her ass. They thundered out of the dining area and past the fireplace. They took the hard corners—around one side of the sofa, then the next—before hitting the other straightaway, which stretched from the front door to the side of the dining area. Where you now stood.

"Guys," you said. "Come on—"

They looped faster and faster, gaining brio. By lap three or so, they merged into an eight-legged machine of speed, sound, and impending danger: clipping chair legs, scattering fire pokers. You chased and lunged. They adjusted. Effortlessly. In stride. *Obstacle,* to the rampaging cat, is just another word for *opportunity.*

Yet still you persisted, having reasoned (not incorrectly) that the last thing you needed now was a home front out of control, but also having reasoned (incorrectly) that stability would best be served by chasing cats.

"Hey! Enough! Stop!"

Finally, after a couple more laps, you slumped to the floor, sucking wind and near tears. Also bleeding a little, facially. This served as a reminder that you were now, in addition to emotionally unsteady and increasingly dehydrated, a cyclopic freak doomed to a life of ridicule and quarantine. Meltdown was at hand. Your Michigan T-shirt felt wrong, too *close,* so you took it off and buried your face in it. Blood. Sweat. Et cetera.

That's when you heard them, on your left flank. Soft paws on hardwood flooring. Galloping.

Instinct took over. Only way to explain it—how you tossed the T-shirt, at just the right time and angle, to catch Scrub flush in the face, startling her to the degree that she slammed on the brakes—too suddenly for her brother, who rear-ended her at full force, propelling both of them across the floor, in a yowling ball of paws, tails, and fur.

"Oh!" you said. "Sorry—!"

But already they were airborne, leveling off at an altitude of five feet, front legs at full extension—the spooked cat knows no bounds. The two of them careered off a bookshelf (second from the top, nonfiction, hardcover) and slammed onto the dining room table, which was bare save for a crystal-blue glass vase.

"No!"

A whipsaw. Wayward paws.

"STOP—!"

The vase went flying, over the length of the table—sideways, like a bowling pin—and slammed into the top of a tall wooden chair; it occurred to you, shortly before you passed out on the floor, that the resulting explosion—sapphires everywhere, uncut and twinkly—was something like elegant.

Peering up at two figures.

"We're here," Lizz said. "It's us."

"You can hear us?" Daniel asked.

"Uhhh," you replied.

"It's okay. It's okay."

They eased you up into a sitting position, supporting your back and head with overstuffed brown sofa pillows. Previously, it seemed, you had been lying on the floor, with the back of your head slumped against the base of the sofa.

"What do you need?" Daniel asked.

"I'm okay."

"Do you know what happened?"

"Uhhhh."

"We're gonna call the shrink."

"*No,*" you said, snapping to. "I'm okay."

Nothing stirs the senses like the fear of therapy.

"I'm fine," you said. "Just a little—"

You were alert enough to spot Lizz discreetly move across the office, to the desk, and return the telephone's handset to the receiver.

"You left me a voicemail," Lizz said. "When I called back, you didn't answer. So I called Daniel."

"Drink," he said, offering water.

You drank. And drank. This bought precious time in which to determine what the hell they were talking about.

"You said you felt panicky," Lizz reported. "You'd gotten home from the doctor, and the cats were out of control. You were upset about your face."

You throbbed, quietly.

"What's going on with you?"

You started to reply.

"And don't lie, please," Lizz said, scanning for signs of deception. "I'll know."

There was a lasting silence.

"I'm okay," you said. "I probably just need some breakfast."

A look passed between them.

"It's three o'clock," Daniel said.

You awakened to a flash of white-yellow light, as from a motorcycle passing in the opposite lane at dusk in Scotland. The light came and went so fast, and so unthreateningly, you would have missed it altogether, had you not been locked in a mental hospital.

Nobody sleeps well in a psych ward. This always comes as a surprise to civilians and rookies, who tend to envision Night Of The Bagged Elephants. In truth, the deep drooling comes only to those who, absent whopping doses of tranqs or sleepers—your new-school Ativans, Klonapins, and Xanaxes or your old-school thumpers (Seconal, Librium)—would be crawling on the ceiling or pacing like jungle cats. And "fast asleep" is not to be confused with "daisy sleep." Mummies don't pop out of bed, restored and ready to embrace the day. Houseplants do not dream.

Don't knock it, though. There's something to be said for nothing. Nobody seems to understand this, except monks and mental patients. The latter have their epiphany in the wee hours, when the ward falls quiet save for the occasional rattling of med carts and squeaking of thick-soled shoes on linoleum. Drowsiness begets sleep, and dreams enter the picture, and Barbiturate Brain takes full effect. No boring dreams in a psych ward, only boring dreamers.

Anyway. The light awakened you.

Actually, that's not quite accurate. Initially, you dismissed the light out of hand, deeming it unworthy of further action. To open your eyes would be to lend credibility, to legitimize. That's what they want, the terrorists. A seat at the table. The trick was to stay the course. Blinders.

But the little beam struck again, courtesy of the night orderly, a laconic sort, black, midthirties. His main function was to make sure nobody committed suicide—though how anyone could do so, in these surroundings, remained a mystery. Everything was bolted in place, from the glorified cots to the midget-schoolboy desks beside them. No fixtures, ledges, or knobs suitable for hanging. No sharp edges for slicing. No loose metals, bolts, or nails to swallow or insert. No breakable wood or plastic fit for impalement. The shatterproof windows were externally barred and bolted; the walls, constructed of an unyielding material, NASA grade.

It was almost as if the place was calling you out. Challenging you to outfox it. You dismissed the lowbrow options: head banging, bedsheet swallowing. Too noisy. Terrible odds. A fit and focused mental could, by employing classic sprinter's technique—by exploding out of the blocks, head forward—impact the opposite wall with sufficiently destructive force. More likely, though, he'd wake up singing nursery rhymes in a rubber room.

The Big Gulp? The standard-bearer. But also the riskiest. (The long cons always are.) Tough to hoard a boatload of Schedule 1 narcotics (forty pills, minimum) in a place with routine tox screens and swallow checks. Plus, because narcotics rarely achieve full effect in less than thirty minutes—bed check!—you'll likely be apprehended in no-man's-land, where incontinent meets comatose.

So those were out.

At least once per hour, the orderly peeked into the room and shone his flashlight at you. He did so in the gentlest way possible, considering. His first couple visits came as a surprise, causing you to duck and cover. "Just checking," he whispered. "Anything you need?"

"I'm fine," you said.

You began clocking his visits. The anticipation made sleep impossible. The process went faster if he could glimpse both your face and hands, so you lay on your stomach, arms high around the pillow. Better to feign sleep during each visit, to spare everyone these awkward exchanges.

The minutes immediately following each bed check were dicey. It was always then, during the big in-between, that the mind drifted. You pictured your parents in their bathrobes, shuffling around the kitchen, busying themselves with make-work tasks—the sweeping of crumbs, the rolling of dough—while your brothers offered assurances that Everything Is Under Control And Purely Precautionary. There would be nods of agreement and gallows humor. Your brother David makes cryptic allusions to "that weekend with Drew Barrymore." The other brother, Peter, is just relieved the cops didn't find any heads in my freezer. The parents laugh, then go back to concocting reasons why they were to blame for a son gone mad in Hollywood.

"Everything okay?" the orderly asked.

"Fine," you said.

You were of two minds about the larger situation, and strove to keep things in perspective. You weren't chained to a radiator; this wasn't a *Frances* situation. A day earlier, you had met with Shrink Three, whom you'd been seeing since the move from New York. Three had leaned forward, scanned your eyes, and said, "You're so tired, aren't you?"

A nod.

"Maybe you need a safe place to rest. Just for a few days—till you feel strong and safe. But only if you think that's a good idea."

"Voluntary?" you said.

"Absolutely. Nobody's *committing* you. Nobody will make you stay. Just for evaluation. And a safe place to rest."

On the other hand: *mental hospital*.

Items prohibited while in the hospital: Firearms, cameras, tape recorders, knives/daggers, lighters/matches, any type of weapon, alcohol, illegal drugs, over-the-counter drugs/ medications, prescriptions drugs/medications, coat hangers.

Items to be locked up by nursing staff and checked out by patients: Aerosol spray cans, cigarettes, glass items, scarves, sharp items such as scissors, tweezers, nail clippers, nail files, razors, mirrors, sewing kits, knitting needles.

Hitherto, your exposure to psychiatric hospitals had been limited to a scene early in *Halloween*. Donald Pleasence, as the jaded psychiatrist Dr. Sam Loomis, drives a chain-smoking nurse through the gates of Smith's Grove Sanitarium. It's a dark, rainy night. They see, in the distance, zomboid patients wandering loose on the grounds. This makes things doubly ominous, since one of Dr. Loomis's patients is Michael Myers. Fifteen years earlier, as a doe-eyed child in a jester costume, Michael had hacked his topless sister to death with a kitchen knife. Now Adult Michael hurtles onto the roof, smashes open the windows, commandeers the Buick, and speeds toward his hometown, Haddonfield, to finish what he started.

When you first saw *Halloween*—your brother David was happy to take a thirteen-year-old to the most disturbing movie to date—the flying-maniac bit got the biggest jump out of the audience. That's because they were stupid and drunk. Cheap scares left nothing to the imagination. The hand that emerges from the grave, in *Carrie*, was, like most Stephen King inventions, doofy-scary. It lacked credibility. Ditto zombies, werewolves, demonic possessions.

But that one image in *Halloween*, of those ghostly maniacs in hospital gowns, was a horror trifecta. For one thing, it portended—the unseen being scarier than the seen. (See also *Jaws, Rear Window*.) For another, it portended the possible: Maniacs exist; maniacs escape. And, not least, it exploited that freakiest primal fear of all: insanity. That's why the movie kept you awake in the dark for months: because *it could happen to you*.

That's also why your first day at the UCLA Neuropsychiatric Hospital, ward A-South, proved edifying. The place had a sunny communal area, replete with freshman-dorm-style furnishings and stacks of

Entertainment Weekly. On one end were the kitchen, the dining tables, and a few small rooms used for therapy and classes. The other end housed the bedrooms, separated by gender. The place suggested a garden-variety rehab clinic, or a Local Community Center For The Very Sad. This one just happened to have a reinforced-steel door at the entrance—think Brink's, think bank vault—and armed guards stationed there.

The twenty-odd patients wore their own clothes and circulated as they pleased. They were polite, if not always chatty. Many were adjusting to new antidepressants or mood stabilizers, or to new dosages or combinations, few of which go down gently. When the side effects come—an inevitability, in the beginning—they do so by way of fatigue, dizziness, nausea, insomnia, somnolence, headaches, diarrhea, constipation, loss of appetite, aching joints, nightmares, sweating, itching, or various other possibilities, among them *increased depression and/ or anxiety.*

So there's that. Depression or anxiety or both had brought most patients here to begin with, so everyone could be forgiven a few quirks. The first patient you met, a whippet-thin woman, fortyish, had just awakened from a catnap on the sofa. She smiled warmly, introduced herself, and went back to sleep. Twenty minutes later, she did the whole thing again. Then she paused. "Already did that, didn't we?" she asked, and shrugged. "It's the Ativan. It's fantastic."

Shrink Three awaited in a meeting room near the Brink's door. She, like your previous therapists, looked like she could have been one of your *alter cocker* relatives. She talked with her hands, wore necklaces beaded with African stones, and hated George Bush.

You felt safer the instant Three reached across the table and squeezed your forearm, then acted in accordance with standard shrink protocol: smiling bittersweetly, lips pursed, head tilted and nodding.

"So?" she said.

"So," you said.

"How do you feel?"

"Okay. Tired. Weird."

"It's a little scary, I know." Another squeeze. "Do you feel like they're taking good care of you?"

Shrug. Nod.

"It's voluntary, though, right?"

"Completely your choice. Just a safe place to rest. How did you sleep last night?"

"Weird."

"The Ativan didn't help?"

Shrug. She scribbled, then asked, "Do you feel safer here?"

The -er was concerning.

"Safer," you said.

She handed you a folder containing the whats, whys, and hows pertaining to your current adventure:

> **Mental Status Examination on Admission:** The patient was well-groomed and had no behavioral abnormalities. His attitude was cooperative, and he was pleasant on approach. His speech had normal rate, rhythm, and tone. His thought process was linear and coherent. His affect was mildly constricted and sad. His thought process did not contain homicidal ideation.

A glance up at her. She shrugged.

> **History of Present Illness:** The patient has been experiencing worsening depressive symptoms and passive suicidal ideation for the past two weeks. His symptoms worsened since he underwent a Nissen fundoplication. The patient reports feeling depressed mood, insomnia with early morning awakenings, and also has been ruminating on issues with his life. He also feels anxiety and experiences racing heartbeat and diaphoresis [sweating] and feels more irritable . . .

Arguably, you had picked a bad time to go off your Wellbutrin. This you had done two weeks earlier, without consulting your doctors, because what did they know anyway? They weren't the ones stuck like a pig and withering away. They weren't the pathetic invalid attractive to no one and ticketed for a life of loneliness and pornography. You had gone to them, torn asunder. You put your fate in their hands, at 250 dollars an hour. And what did you get for it?

Wellbutrin. The "antidepressant" for those who wish to feel worse, faster. Wanna maximize that insomnia? Try Wellbutrin. Nightmares not graphic enough? Wellbutrin's for you. It made Jell-O intolerable. It made you kick bedsheets and cry. It made you say, repeatedly, "Fucking Wellbutrin."

Patient told his doctor on the day of his admission that he did not feel safe in his home and was having vague thoughts of death, but he denied an actual suicide plan—

"Whoa," you said. "I'm *not* suicidal—"

"Ideation," she said. "Not directly intending or planning to kill yourself, but ruminating about death or dying, in a general way. Sound about right?"

Felt like a trick question. Granted, you frequently expressed a hope that somebody would hit you over the head with a hammer. But who didn't sometimes? Granted, once or twice you conjured images of being hit over the head with a hammer. And, sure, if you had a little extra time, a death-scene scenario wasn't out of the question. Stroke? Climbing accident? Ventilators? Police tape? Any play in the *Times*? Or just a couple paragraphs in *The Oakland Press*?

But still. Shrinks ask the million-dollar question—"Are you feeling suicidal?"—as a matter of course; it's their "You have the right to remain silent." Always your response was clear and consistent.

"I'm not suicidal," you said. "Really."

"I believe you," she said. "But we have to be careful, because ideation can lead to worse."

She offered another document:

Reason for Admission: Depression with passive suicidal ideation, vague plan (i.e., when he broke a vase, thought to self "this would be an easy way out").

"Do you remember that?" she asked.

A period of time elapsed. Things shook loose, in bits:

The cats, spooked, crouched low, fur standing on end, eyes wide . . . The squirrel, watching through the window . . . The jeweled quality of the shards . . . The sparkly, pale-blue fairyland circle they formed at your feet . . . The biggest shard, triangular, a shark's tooth . . . Sound, absent . . . Air, stagnant . . .

"Hot," you said. "It was hot."

"Do you remember how you felt?"

"I don't know."

"You said you thought 'this would be an easy—' "

"I see that."

"So that's correct."

"Maybe for a split second, but—"

"But why?"

"I was just freaked-out—"

There was a pause.

"Relief," you said. "I felt relieved."

She nodded.

"I was just freaked-out," you said. "It wasn't serious."

"You also said you didn't feel safe at home."

"Look at me," you said, pointing to your various and sundry physical wounds. "I'm a mess. I couldn't take care of myself. Physically."

"You know what I'm asking," she said.

"I'm not suicidal."

"So it was more of a general feeling? You were just generally very what? Scared?"

A shrug.

"Scared of what?" she said.

"Just something bad," you said. "Generally."

"Because you're very depressed. And tired. And weak." She leaned close. "It'll be better soon."

"Can't wait."

"You know that, right?"

She took a good long look.

"Absolutely," you said.

News of your surrender was restricted to close friends and family, in keeping with your overall policy of emotional nondisclosure. The family remained a going concern. Worry: a family tradition since 1600, when the men with foreskins first began chasing and raping your forebears. The parents worried if you didn't finish lunch. So you thought twice about letting them see you in the crazy barn, particularly since you looked in some ways more fucked-up than the screwballs over in B-South. You were the only bleeder, the only one who appeared to have charged a moving vehicle.

The friends and brothers posited that perhaps your parents were stronger than you thought—that they had managed to survive, among other things, the Great Depression, Nazis, and the loss of loved ones who had died awful and untimely deaths. The gallery also posited that your nondisclosure policy had in some way contributed to your fucked-up-ness by leaving you alone and alienated and thus giving you even more time to spin worst-case scenarios of the self-fulfilling variety, i.e., worrying about worrying.

You understood, even then, how important it is for the mental patient to project an air of thoughtful calm, lest he confirm the suspicion harbored, on some level, by every civilian who dares visit—that you'll soon be one of those poor, howling slobs forever demanding copies of the Constitution or phone calls to the White House. As such, a spirit of compromise was at hand. The parents would be kept in the loop, but also at a distance, until your parole, after which you would fly home to Michigan, to recuperate at their house.

Meantime, because Lizz was out of town on business, the grunt work fell to Ben and Daniel. They ran interference with doctors, kept your family posted, ran your errands. Fortunately, they didn't have much else to do, aside from their full-time jobs and their round-the-clock responsibilities for the care and welfare of a scared young birth mother who didn't know a soul in Los Angeles; she'd traveled from Wisconsin farm country, alone, to surrender a newborn to a gay couple. She was due any day.

Daniel played it breezy when visiting, as if visiting his orthodontist. He pretended not to notice the Cryer on a nearby sofa or the Dozer by the TV. "Don't worry about anything at home," he said. "Everything's fine."

"Did you talk to my parents?" you asked.

"Your dad. He was great."

"Was he upset?"

"Maybe a little. But fine—"

Looks passed.

"He was just a little quiet," Daniel said. "He just called and said 'Thank you for taking care of my son.'"

That night was unquiet.

By morning, you wanted out. The whole thing had been a mistake, an overreaction. You just needed a little peace and quiet. Not captivity. This was hurting more than helping. There were risks, consequences. The longer you stayed, the greater the likelihood that friends would steal peeks at your wrists and keep their children at a distance and squeeze your hand and say "You look *really good*." Those friends tell other friends, who tell others, and suddenly women are averting their eyes and Graydon's marching into Doug's office, saying, "The secretaries are terrified." Done. Blacklisted.

"Soon," Dr. Three said. "The eagerness is a good sign. Means you're feeling stronger."

You charged Daniel with a perilous task: muling contraband past security. Daniel, being both merciful and susceptible to emotional manipulation, reluctantly hid bags of miniature candy bars (Twix, Hershey's) inside a blanket you had requested. The guards searched visitors for many things, but gooey caramel deliciousness was not among them.

You hid the treasures in a dresser drawer, cushioning them with a blue University of Michigan sweatshirt (whose drawstring had been confiscated). Each little chocolaty gem was unwrapped and consumed slowly, a process learned the hard way. Your upper esophagus, which remained constricted, claimed the first Twix in a python strike; the bar remained lodged there for three minutes, until squeezed into syrup, as you thumped and coughed and cried.

So now you bit the bars into smaller pieces, then pressed each piece between your tongue and the roof of your mouth until melted. The enterprise was a perilous one, because orderlies and nurses regularly appeared out of nowhere, unbidden, looking for outlaws like you.

"Are you *chewing*?" came the voice.

"Whuh?" you replied.

She hovered in the doorway, in all her majesty: pushing fifty, hair dyed jet black and rising toward beehive territory. "Nurse Black" was no less able or dedicated than the ward's other staffers, whom you very much liked and appreciated. She was aggressively so, and therefore problematic.

"Crumbs on your face," she said.

"Whuh?"

She beelined toward the dresser, claiming the contraband with alarming skill. This did little to improve a relationship that had been shaky since Day One. You were among the few patients who had declined to attend art-therapy class; it just wasn't in you to paint sunsets on coffee mugs, or whatever the hell they did in there.

"For your own safety," Nurse Black said, tucking the candy under her arm. "No more squirreling."

"I'm not."

"Mr. Squirrely Squirrel. You wait for everyone to leave the dining area before you eat."

Also before approaching the common areas, the bathroom, and the pay phone. The latter was the trickiest. Calls had to be made from the ward's one pay phone, which was constantly in use, even when nobody was there; incoming calls were answered by any patient who happened by. "Hello," he would say. "Looking for who? Okay, I'll find him."

Tranquilized mental patients proved less than reliable messengers. They would forget whom they were seeking, or why; even when they did find the right person, the latter was equally likely to falter. As such, the phone's receiver could often be found hanging low to the ground, swinging gently, and emitting the faintest voice: "Hello? Anybody there?"

Mostly you avoided the food-service area, the one space where A-South met B-South. Certain B-Teamers were a bit out there: shuffling schizos and muttering delusionals, the occasional psychotic in need of restraints. They weren't raving or menacing, but you gave them wide berth anyway, as did most of the A-Team. Apples, oranges. Leave the poor things be.

Except for Larry. Everyone had an opinion about Larry. Most figured him for a bipolar gone off the deep end. Everyone used air quotes when saying his name, because everyone knew he wasn't a "Larry." He had the misfortune of being, in addition to a delusional wreck, an

A-list actor. You couldn't look at the guy. You felt humiliated on his behalf. Nobody wants to be famous in a psych ward.

"You're being Mr. Squirrel again," she said.

She just stood there.

"Yes?" you said.

"You know," she said.

"I'd rather not."

"Everyone likes clay."

"It's not required."

"A silly children's exercise—that's what you're thinking, isn't it?"

Yes. Also: Go fuck yourself.

She returned a day or two later, to escalate the conflict. "No clay," you said finally. "I'll do animals."

"Animal therapy" amounted to a few volunteers bringing in a few dogs to be pet. Seemed workable. Dogs wouldn't ask nosy questions or "share their stories" of self-mutilation and incest. So you headed down the corridor and into the common area. Joining a handful of other patients, you spent a half hour rolling around on the floor with two ragged, wheezy dogs. It was the highlight.

The humans weren't half bad, either. This being Los Angeles, there was talk of the summer movie slate, and why the hell Spielberg had made *Jurassic Park II*. One of the older patients, a Hollywood sort, asked to see a movie script he'd seen you editing with a pen. This was *Emperor Zehnder,* the script you and Daniel had written about Bruno Penguin Zehnder. He returned the script an hour later, saying only, "It's all box office."

A young sadster from down the hall studied your Michigan sweat-shirt. "Fuck Ohio State," he said.

The sweatshirt was now his.

"You finally got some sleep," said the reed-thin lady. "You don't look like a ghost anymore. What's the secret?"

"Drugs," you said.

They put you back on the Wellbutrin, whose side effects were cushioned by a tranquilizer (Ativan) and a second antidepressant (Remeron) with mildly sedating properties. The sum effect was even better than sleep, although that part was fantastic, too. The new regimen—the "cocktail," as they say—didn't knock you out, the way sleeping pills would; it didn't stone you, the way a bong hit would. It brought only one effect: peace of mind.

No more teeth grinding. No sweaty palms. The pastel walls seemed a little sunnier; the pleather chair, softer. You spread out in the crowded TV area, arm slung over the back of the sofa, legs splayed across it. Just one of the gang, debating the finer points of *Who Wants to Be a Millionaire?*

Strewn across your lap were six individual-serving puddings. You blazed through them, licking clean the lids with a newfound appetite. Remeron: the antidepressant of choice for anorexics, chemo patients, and you. Two pounds gained in thirty-six hours; a body fueled by butterscotch; a soul in repose.

That night, before lights-out, something drew you to the bedroom at the end of the corridor. The room was darker and tighter than the rest. A triple. The first guy said little more than "hi" or "excuse me"; the second avoided eye contact. The third never seemed to leave his cot. He had scruffy brown hair and whiskers and resembled a long-haul trucker. He slept and slept.

He caught you staring. "It's cool," he said, propping himself up and waving you inside. "You're the reporter guy, right?" he said. He asked you to name the story you had most enjoyed writing.

"It was about a photographer who died in Antarctica," you said. "Chasing penguins."

"Was he fucked-up?"

"Well, he froze to death—"

"In the head, I mean."

"A little, maybe."

He mulled. "So," he said, "are we 'off the record'?"

That got a laugh.

"Fuckin' hate it here," he said. "And I fuckin' hate the meds."

He briefly detailed his slow, steady spiral into depression, then suicidal tendencies, then virtual catatonia. He had gone off his meds, ditched his doctors. "Sometimes I don't know what's worse," he said. "Feelin' that way, or these shitty drugs. They work for you?"

"I think so. You?"

"I guess. I'm talking, so . . ."

How long you been here?"

"Not long enough," he said, sinking toward supine. "Feel better, man."

He rolled onto his side, facing the wall.

"Penguins," he said.

In the morning, you called your valets, Ben and Daniel. "Ready to go!" you said.

"The doctors agree?" Ben said.

"They say I'm much better."

"You feel that way, too?"

"Yeah—"

"And not just because you wanna get out of there."

"I do. Really."

"That's *fantastic*. We'll be there in an hour."

"Thanks. They need you to meet me at—"

"Wait, sorry, call you back."

Several minutes passed. A pay phone vigil. You flipped through your paperwork:

No sign of delusion or manic depression . . . He has a mood-congruent affect . . . Has strong motivation and insight . . . He receives ongoing therapy and has strong support from family and friends—

"I'm so sorry," Ben said, having called back. He sounded completely different. Scattered. "We can't get you."

"Whuh?"

"The birth mother just called. She's in labor. I'm so sorry."

"Ohmygod."

Had to be a sign from God. Rebirth, baptism, et cetera.

"Are you okay?" Ben asked.

"Are *you* okay?"

"You're not mad?"

"I'm so excited I'm gonna wet my pants. Go!"

"We took care of things. Paula is picking you up."

"Who?"

"Paula."

"No!"

Click.

The challenge now was to remain calm, to keep things in perspective. Battle, war, forest, trees. The situation was not an ideal one. Granted. Paula was certainly a friend, and a promising one, having recently received Lizz's stamp of approval. Paula was a warm, playful little thing with giant brown eyes. She evinced a nervy, self-flagellating sense of humor, plus most of the other requisite characteristics. Generalized anxiety. A tendency to verbally acknowledge her anxieties, in real time. An ability to simultaneously deflect the conversation away from herself.

But still. She was a new friend and therefore viewed with fear and suspicion. Whereas the rest of the group had spent years together, collectively honing skills, Paula had arrived fully formed, speaking your shared language of addled hyperbole: "I need you to know I'm the worst person in the world" . . . "I've never loved anything more than this Popsicle." She was, after all, an *actress*.

You wouldn't be comfortable letting many of your oldest friends, *made* friends, see you at a moment of weakness. The vetting process could take decades, and Paula was twelfth on the waiting list, at best.

She pulled up in a silver Porsche. Suspicions: confirmed.

"Please don't feel awkward," she said.

"I feel awkward," you said.

"You're embarrassed by the car, aren't you?"

"No."

"*I'm* embarrassed by the car."

"I'm embarrassed for both of us."

She loosed an explosive two-note laugh: "Ha-HA!" She did this whenever especially tense or overstimulated. The Porsche, she said, had been a silly impulse purchase, after she finally divorced her deadbeat husband. That she loved the Porsche didn't mean she was entirely comfortable saying so. She apologized all the way to Laurel Canyon.

She lived there, too. This was a good sign, to be sure, but possibly a deceiving one, a trick. She lived in higher style than the rest of the group, in a very grown-up house on Wonderland Avenue. Wonderland was one of the swankiest streets in the canyon, despite a good measure of infamy; the 1981 Wonderland murders—four bludgeoned, by "associates" of Johnny "Wadd" Holmes—trail only the Manson attacks in the pantheon of Freaky Hollywood Bloodbaths.

Paula's home resembled a Normandy farmhouse, replete with weathered shingles and flowers everywhere. The backyard was a tiered garden filled with daisies and bougainvillea; the front porch was awash in red roses. She parked you there, in the fresh canyon air. She served you moo-shoo pork. When the pork lodged in your gullet, she fetched water and cleaned you up, pretending not to notice your scars.

It was appreciated. It was degrading.

Sensing this, Paula said something she'd mentioned earlier, briefly. This time, though, she didn't pass it off. This wasn't her first rodeo, she said. As a teenager, she had been hospitalized for ten days. For depression. For anxiety. "I got better," she said. "It gets better."

There was a silence.

"Now *I* feel awkward again," she said. "I've never felt more awkward."

That drew a laugh.

"It was probably different back when I went in," she said. "I mean, everyone had to use this one pay phone. Somebody would answer a call, then wander off—"

"But they'd forget why," you said, quickly.

"And they'd leave the receiver off the hook—"

"You'd hear 'Hello?'—"

" 'Anybody there?'—"

"As the receiver swung back and forth."

"Ha-HA!"

You moved through your favorite place on earth. Everything was clean and white; the only sound a slight crackling underfoot with each step you took. The terrain was flat, more icy than snowy; it twinkled a bit. Your pace was slow but steady; your breathing, quick but smooth. You never tired, even in this cold. The white had a warmth to it.

Also the emperors helped. Emperor penguins radiate warmth— that's just a given. Additionally, they keep things lively. The faster they walked—toddling along, flanking you—the faster you walked. They're world-class walkers. Resourceful. Eggs or bust.

Nothing else seemed to *happen* here. The procession just went on and on, into the white.

Until.

"Wake up."

A faraway voice. From beyond the glaciers.

"Wake up. Pick up."

"I know you're there. Pick up!"

Dream deferred.

"Pick up! Pickup-pickup-pickup!"

Levels of consciousness. Movements. A lunge.

"Fine. Call me as soon as you wake up."

Click.

Hand hits button. Crackling sounds.

"It's Lizz. Call me."

"It's Mom. Call me when you get this."

"It's Ben. Pick up. I know you're there."

"It's Lizz. I know you're there."

Six messages, 8:00 A.M.

"Pick up!"

"Hulluh?"

"You're awake," Lizz said.

"Uhhh."

"Why didn't you pick up?"

"Uhhh."

"Are you okay?"

"Uh-huh."

"I need you to do something for me, okay?"

"Uh-huh."

"I need you to stay on the phone with me and turn on the TV. Can you do that?"

"Uh-huh."

"Okay, go."

The issue was locomotion. The new drug cocktail produced solid sleep and magnificent dreams for eight to ten hours. Terms were non-negotiable.

Three minutes. To press "on."

"What do you see?" Lizz said.

A giant building, vaguely familiar. Smoke. Fire.

"Do you see it?"

Something smashing into a giant building, vaguely familiar. Building collapses. Scene repeats.

"Hijackers flew planes into the World Trade Center, the Pentagon, and someplace in Pennsylvania," Lizz said. "But *not Los Angeles*. Okay?"

And repeats.

"How are you now?" she said.

"Fuck," you said.

"Tell me what you're thinking."

"I'm thinking *Fuck*."

She apologized for not being there. She was en route to the Toronto Airport—she'd been covering the annual film festival there—and now had to turn back and find a place to stay. But already she had found time to communicate with Ben, Daniel, and Paula, who stood ready and able to look after you.

After hanging up, you watched TV for a minute or so, head slightly tilted, dog-style. Burning chaos. Flying accountants. Powerful stuff. The mental fog thinned, giving way to bona fide human emotions. There was sorrow. There was anger. Together they produced burning clarity:

My flight home better not be canceled.

The raisin brain has a way of simplifying life; it eliminates needless distractions (empathy); it separates gold (your needs) from dross (everyone else's). The world is viewed through a pinhole aimed at a mirror.

Terror hits home. Hogging all the channels, even ESPN. All these network haircuts biting their lips and jockeying to out-solemn each other, to have their President Kennedy Is Dead moments. Already Fox News had declared martial law and shuttered all the airports, perhaps forever. Nobody was going anywhere, except to their TVs—the ultimate ratings bonanza!

Casualty of war. That's what you were. Held captive. Stripped of your freedoms. Tortured by a series of rolling panic attacks, each more insidious than its predecessor, because nothing triggers panic attacks more efficiently than the question "Why do I keep having panic attacks?"

You were halfway to A-South, and bombing down La Cienega, when the receptionist answered your call. No walk-ins, she said. No vacancy, she said. "It's been a challenging day for everyone."

You drove home and hunkered down. The siege lasted about three days—until LAX reopened, and you booked the first available flight to Detroit. A red-eye, departing at 11:00 P.M.

The passenger to your right was a mousy Chinese woman. Thankfully, she spoke no English and limited herself to two brief interactions. The first came immediately, when her smile expressed approval of your flannel pajama top, specifically its adorning penguin motif.

The second came ninety minutes later, when you awakened from deep Ativan stupor to find the lady sheepishly tugging your pajama sleeve. She was sorry to disturb. She needed something, please. She searched for the right word.

"Tawa," she said.

"Whuh?" you said.

"TAWWA!" she said.

"Ma'am, I can't—"

"This is your captain speaking," came the voice from above. *"Prepare to make an emergency landing."*

The smoke appeared in a couple tiny wisps that hung at eye level, moving from fore to aft. More evident was the smell, an acridity you associated with pizza bagels cooked too long in dorm-room toaster ovens. The flight crew shuffled about, assuring everyone that, although the source of the smoke had yet to be located, it was in no way connected to terrorism.

"TAWWA!" the lady said.

The crew also noted that, although pilots typically proceed to the nearest operational airport, in this case they would be landing immediately, at an abandoned community airfield in the Utah desert. No, a flight attendant said, the airfield was not built to receive large aircraft.

The news did not go over well with the passengers, who remained controlled but . . . involved. As everyone assumed the position—read those emergency-briefing cards!—the airstrip came into view: a single lane, surrounded by sand. You focused on the Chinese lady's hand. She held tight to your sleeve, squeezing penguins.

The landing was firm but level; the "deplaning," orderly. You were hustled to a small, dark hangar—the only sign of civilization; everything else, in all directions, was desert and darkness. It was after midnight.

Once inside, the crew told everyone to get comfortable, because a replacement plane wouldn't be arriving for ten hours or so. No food (except for a small box of donuts, which were too thick for your insides). No blankets or pillows.

One Ativan.

The emergency pill. The little white messiah you housed at all times. You gulped it dry, lint and all, then slumped down in an empty corner of the hangar. Hugging yourself for warmth, squeezing penguins, you shut your eyes.

CHAPTER FIVE

Love.

Felt good just to say it. The lilt. The rolling of the tongue.

Love, love, love.

The possibilities. Loves rules. Love comes to town.

Felt even better to feel it—toward family, friends, cats, trees, the whole package. Love returned slowly at first (expressions of warmth or gratitude), then faster (physical contact; concern for others), then as a bat out of heaven.

There was a girl. Her name was Mimi.

Two years had passed since 9/11, after which you had done as great nations do. You rallied. Rebuilt. Came together. Your wounds, within and without, had healed. Bigger, better, faster stronger: You were exercising, doing things right, mixing with the humans. You had a good shrink, a consistent "program." You bought a small but sweet Cape Cod–style house five miles east of Laurel Canyon, in Los Feliz. The house, which had "two-and-a-half" bedrooms, was an easy choice. Also the only one. Ben had come across it while house shopping for his family. "You're buying a house," he said. "Just show up at 3:00 P.M." By 3:15, it was yours.

Best of all, Richard Gere had entered your life. He would play Bruno in the movie. Hollywood, city of dreams. Work was gangbusters, even when it wasn't. You reported an article about a faded action star gone thug. There was gunplay, of a sort; one night, outside your darkened house, somebody stuck a gun in your face, said "bang," sped off.

It was bad Elmore Leonard—if the Armed Assailant had wanted to hurt you, he would have. But the magazine provided a round-the-clock bodyguard. This was awkward until you saw its effect on the woman you dated pre-Mimi. Until then, she'd been a little out of your league. Now she couldn't get enough. You were a man of intrigue, muscle. A dangerous man.

She left when the guards did. Didn't matter. Water off a duck. She was sort of a slag anyway. Never would have passed the Ben and Daniel test. Only one woman had passed of late, and rightly so. Caitlin had a glow. Caitlin was warm and gracious, a true keeper. Caitlin *took in stray dogs*.

Caitlin lasted a month, having had the misfortune to meet you in the immediate wake of 9/11. When you still weren't ready. When love still hated you.

Can't hurry it. Mysterious ways.

Mimi was a lovely little thing, a hundred pounds soaking wet, with pale blue eyes, translucent skin, and a delicate, birdlike quality; her voice was scratchy soft. She spoke in a revving sort of way and was stronger and pluckier than she looked—a zippy little Mighty Mouse forever skittering here and there, in her girlish, tiptoed way: down the street, in between the rooms of her apartment. She skittered even in heels, which she wore pretty much all the time, along with the outfit issued to all New York fashionettes, black skirt, black halter top. She looked like a Mimi.

She lived in New York and was very much of it. Raised on the Upper East Side. Educated at the requisite private schools and colleges. And she, too, was a journalist; she edited a magazine aimed at the sort of women who can spot a Marc Jacobs knock-off from five blocks. She read *The New York Times* from inside out, starting with the Sunday

Styles section. Every night she met someone out for drinks, then someone else for dinner elsewhere. Her refrigerator was pristine.

You started as acquaintances, occasionally thrown together while she was in Los Angeles. She visited regularly, as fashion/media types do. But business wasn't the main attraction. She had friends in Los Angeles, one of whom she had recently begun dating. This was Brian. He was of your New Friends—the happy result of your current mission to earth. Brian was endearing, an inveterate mingler. He lived to engineer parties, dinners, and the romantic entanglements of others. He remained unconcerned that he'd introduced you to two women who now held you in contempt.

It was through Brian that you got to know Mimi, during three or four dinners over the same number of months. Although you and Mimi enjoyed each other's company—same nervous energy, same "quirky" social skills—you plateaued at idle conversation about bad movies. At one group dinner, somebody let slip that, back when Brian and Mimi were platonic, he had envisioned a spark between Mimi and *you*. Then everyone laughed.

Four months passed before you and she had anything resembling a private conversation. You had been charged with making a dinner reservation and had emailed the details to Brian and Mimi. Neither replied. A follow-up email, sent the next day—the dinner was that night—also went unheeded. This baffled, given the communal cyberaddiction. You had no choice but to do the unthinkable, to make a phone call. No answer at Brian's. No number for Mimi. No dinner for you.

Dinnertime. An email arrives.

Mimi: "What's your phone #?"

Number entered. Phone rings.

"It's Mimi," she said. The phone made her sound even tinier.

"So I guess dinner's off."

"Well, we broke up."

Two issues. You hadn't seen this coming. And you didn't know each other well enough to be talking about it.

"Oh," you said. "I'm sorry."

"Yeah, well," she said.

"Guess dinner's *really* off."

"I guess. I know we're not friends."

"We're friends."

"We are?"

"Well, it's not all up to me."

"Friends!"

The friendship began.

You joined Mimi at Orso, an Italian restaurant that had long been one of Hollywood's most low-key high-end gathering spots; it was her haunt in Los Angeles, only nominally due to its New York pedigree—the original is near Broadway, in the Theater District. She loved, in addition to the soup and wine, its back patio, an airy, candlelit oasis adorned only by a natural canopy of eucalyptus-tree branches. She was fiercely loyal to soft, soothing old-school spots and disdained any-place crowded, loud, or look-at-me. It was a good thing, too, because whenever she was trapped inside noisy rooms, her scratchy little voice became inaudible.

Also, she smoked like a sailor.

You arrived five minutes early, per standard protocol, only to find Mimi already at a corner table. This was thrilling, New Yorkers being even worse than Angelenos in the punctuality department. *Couldn't find a single taxi. Wilshire was a parking lot.* But there she was. Wait-ing. A woman who hardly ever drove a car, and who needed a map to find Wilshire Boulevard.

She was enjoying a smoke as a waiter set down a mini-decanter of the house white. Laying eyes, she ran toward you like a silly schoolgirl. Pitter-patter.

The subject of Brian was not on the table long, Mimi being skittish by nature and more so given the situation. She frequently pulled back her hair and tightened her ponytail. She spoke faster than usual, in staccato bursts.

"Sorry," she said. "I'm a kook."

She said this periodically, punctuating the last bit with a quick shrug and soft titter; once or twice, she wrapped her knuckles against her forehead.

"You have no idea," you said.

The goal was to assuage her anxieties while also staking your claim as the bigger, better head case. For a while, she proved a spirited challenger, enumerating her various and sundry issues (insomnia), stylistic fetishes (black halters, white walls), compulsions (email, skittering), and habits (jogging, smoking). Every day, after running at least seven miles, she beelined to a bodega, to buy cigarettes. One pack per day. Exactly.

"Kook," she said, with a lower-case *k*.

She tucked her chin toward her neck and peered up at you, flashing blue eyes somewhere between puckish and help-me. This was when everything began to change.

"What?" she said. "Everything okay?"

"Huh?" you replied.

The scotch helped only by degree.

"It's nothing," you said.

"What?"

"Long story."

She waited quietly. In an avian way.

And out spilled the whole tawdry saga: the gory stitches and flying cats, the puzzle factory and the penguin pajamas. The unrated version. The director's cut.

Then, silence.

"Sorry," you said. "I'm really sorr—"

"No," she said. "Thank you."

"Huh?"

In a flash, she rose, skittered over, gave you a quick squeeze, and returned to her seat.

"Just thank you," she said.

The friendship was over.

The romance began in earnest a month later, during Mimi's next trip to Los Angeles. Due to some flimsy sense of propriety, you hadn't spoken in the interim, communicating only via the occasional email; the missives were more friendly than flirty. They allowed for plausible deniability, i.e.:

> You: When are you coming back?
> Mimi: soon, two weeks
> You: Too long.
> Mimi: hope sooner
> You: Well, just do your best.
> Mimi: hokay!!

Professional status notwithstanding, Mimi never used capital letters in emails; alternately under- and overpunctuated; and occasionally succumbed to the dreaded emoticon: smiley faces, frowns, winks. In any other circumstance, these would be deemed major infractions—Daniel's twisted relationship with commas could send you into a tailspin. But Mimi got a flier, in part because she sent a thousand emails per minute—what's a modern career gal to do?—but mostly because she smelled like dandelions.

The kiss was a modest one—a peck, really—and took place at the end of a second dinner at Orso, in the parking lot. This required Mimi to stand ramrod straight, knees together, lips extended northward.

The Brian situation loomed, fostering much hand-wringing in the coming days. The breakup had been amicable. So Mimi felt strongly that she should break the news to him, and that he would prefer it this way. You ceded to her wishes, despite a nagging certainty that the responsibility fell to the friend, not the ex. But you demurred, for two reasons:

1. The lady gets what the lady wants.
2. Conflict deferred.

She did it. He didn't like it. Your absence was noted.

You emailed Brian a letter: explaining, prostrating, requesting an audience.

He replied. Short and sweet.

"I don't want to kill you," he wrote.

Probably he did. Certainly he should have. Had the situation been reversed, already you would have been at Lowe's, buying bleach and a shovel. Actually, you *had* been in his position once, when a grad-school buddy took up with a recent ex of yours. The ex made The Call.

The friend received, via FedEx, a dead fish.

You were so young back then—just a bunch of wild, crazy kids in the go-go eighties. New York, New Day. Bygones. You attended their wedding, for crissake. Perspective—Brian needed some. He and Mimi were a blip. A *dead* blip. The guy just needed to See Things As They Really Were. To grow a pair. To stop being so fucking *selfish:* me, me. Seriously, with friends like him . . .

Love made life's little complications fade away.

Love was tunnel vision, a crystallization of focus and concentration, in Imax 4-D. You were motivated, goal oriented.

Mimi flew back to New York; you would follow two weeks later. Period. Flights full that day? No problem. Hotels, too? Whatever. Half the price if you go the following weekend instead? Fuck that. Go. Now.

At work, both Doug and Daniel noted upticks in quality, quantity, and profanity; it had long been Daniel's position that your mental health was best gauged by the degree of blasphemy and insults you spewed. The more polite you were, the more he would ask "Everything okay?"

Gym, every other day. In between, you hiked the canyons—Runyon, Bronson—without breaking a sweat, headphones blaring, head bobbing, iPod replaying the same song. "I Feel Alright," by Steve Earle, lasted an entire week.

Posthike. Gatorade in one hand, newspaper in the other.

Skimming, skimming: Vivendi, Valenti, Terrorism, Taubman.

Treadwell.

ALASKA: BEAR KILLS EXPERT

A self-taught bear expert was one of two people fatally mauled by bears in Katmai National Park and Preserve. The bodies of the expert, Timothy Treadwell, and Amie Huguenard, both of Malibu, Calif., were found on Monday at their campsite. . . . Troopers said they found a tape at the scene that contained the sound of the attack, in which Miss Huguenard told Mr. Treadwell to play dead, then to fight back.

Alaska. It called to you.

Naturally.

Open heart, open ears, world's your oyster.

The *Times* called. Doug called.

Onward, to Alaska.

Kodiak Island, Alaska. Sits at the heart of a 177-mile-long archipelago off the state's southwestern coast. Looks like the love child of Ireland and Hawaii. Feels like a dream.

The island's hub is the town of Kodiak, a windswept, lovably humble seaside community (population: six thousand) of fishermen, hunters, and the people who sell them stuff. Locals—as opposed to The Fucking Tourists, with their Cabela's boots and Patagonia-ness—embrace certain archetypes. They wear galoshes to formal occasions. They shoot reindeer and skin moose and hang heads on mantles. They smell of cigarettes and brine.

The hallmark of Alaskan oysters is sweetness.

Among the town's most well-known locals was Willy Fulton, forty-two, a ruddy ex-cowboy with a thick gray moustache, Marlboro Man brio, and a taste for seventies-era conceptual rock. Willy was the most seasoned bush pilot in town, with six thousand flights under his belt. His fearlessness was legendary. He was one of the few pilots who willingly assayed one of the island's most dangerous areas, Kaflia Bay, a mountainous jungle land accessible only by bush plane. That's where the two campers had met their ends.

Timothy Treadwell.

Amie Huguenard.

Bears.

Ew.

Basically the extent of your knowledge, at this point. Things moved fast, postheadline. Alaska wanted you there yesterday and went the extra mile to make things happen, to wit: the moment doubt entered the picture. This was two days into the story, after you'd promised Doug and Graydon an epic tale of beauty and death—"The Penguin Man meets *Jaws*." You were at the gym with a friend, jogging and whining. Not a single source had called you back. The nerve of Those Fucking Eskimos—

"Tim *Treadwell*?"

A woman on the next treadmill. An actress. Giggly.

"*So* weird," she said. "My sister lives in Kodiak. She dates this guy. His name's Willy."

The mother lode. The guy hadn't returned anyone's call. Now he was your regent and guide. And he didn't give a shit about certain namby-pamby regulations set forth by the desk jockeys in Anchorage nor certain logistic snafus he'd encountered during his last trip to Kaflia.

"Nothing to worry about," he said.

Willy's plane was a classic four-seater, a 1958 de Havilland Beaver, painted orange and yellow. The wee plane resembled, to those on the ground, a flying jack-o'-lantern—hence its nickname, "the Pumpkin." The plane evoked, to those inside it, a flying lawn mower. The wind-force made it bump and career, sometimes sickeningly. This, combined with the roaring engine, mocked the ears. Conversation required headsets. "Smooth so far," Willy said, as the island disappeared from view. "Wait till we get some weather."

The cloudy skies were clearing, allowing increasingly unfettered views of the water below and beyond. This was the Shelikof Strait, a 150-mile-long stretch of emerald gloriousness running along the island's southeastern coast. Kaflia Bay was 75 miles down the coast from Kodiak, in a kind of cul-de-sac inaccessible from the north. Willy would first have to swing well eastward, over the straight, before knifing due west toward Kaflia Bay. This would increase the flying time, to about an hour. Thank god. In heaven, nobody asks, "When do we land?" The only bad thing about screaming over emerald waters and through electric-blue sky, in an orange pumpkin, was the knowledge that it wouldn't last forever.

Sunlight hit the water just so, turning the atmosphere orange, then orange-purple, then into a Pink Floyd show. Possibly that last part was goosed a little by Willy, after he popped *Animals* into the stereo and cranked it.

Not another plane in sight, even as the plane approached land, and even though the land was part of Katmai National Park, a tourist mecca. This particular stretch, which included Katmai Bay, was temporarily closed to outsiders, by order of the National Park Service. Willy mentioned this, in passing, while bombing low toward the bay.

"Pussies," he said.

He made a water landing—softly, on floaters—and idled toward land, some twenty yards away. Clouds convened as Kaflia promptly established why virtually none of the park's fifty thousand annual visitors dared trod here. The "beach" was a brownish swamp thick with boulders and alder trees, notable for their spiky, skeletal branches; the land sloped sharply upward, into a series of mounds and hills. No sight lines. No sounds. Kaflia, though never anything less than inhospitable, hit its stride in the dead murk of November.

Willy climbed out, splashing into the shallows. He pulled the Pumpkin toward shore, by rope, and let you believe he needed assistance tying the plane to the "dock"—a series of planks he had jury-rigged previously.

Then he grabbed his shotgun.

"Twelve-gauge," he said. "Ever shot one?"

"Sure," you said.

A look.

"No."

"Stay this close," Willy said, indicating a ten-yard circle. "No exceptions."

Over the rocks and through the alders. Ascending a rugged series of humpback hills. Negotiating alders, loose footing, and a series of criss-crossing dirt trails and tunnels leading everywhere and nowhere. This was "the Maze," a cocktail of menace, isolation, and claustrophobia. Even now, when all but abandoned, the Maze put the fear of god into all comers, including a heavily armed ex-cowboy. In a way, Willy said, the silence made things spookier. He much preferred the seen to the unseen, despite everything he'd seen here, during his previous visit.

That was a month earlier, when the Maze was the most dangerous spot in Alaska, a no-man's-land ruled by the biggest, baddest predators on god's green. The Alaskan grizzly bear (a.k.a. brown bear, a.k.a. Kodiak bear) is to the woodlands as the great white shark is to the seas: the top of the food chain, the *capo di tutti*. The largest stand upward of eleven feet tall and weigh as much as 1,500 pounds: the size of three Bengal tigers, five mountain gorillas, or eight writers. Grizzlies behead moose with a single swat and occasionally cannibalize. Not by accident came the Latin name: *Ursus arctos horribilis*.

Nor "the Maze": a misnomer suggesting dark chaos when in fact the site stood as a triumph of urban planning, having been constructed by and for the community it served, while prioritizing functionality, pedestrianism, and growth. Each summer, scores of grizzlies, if not hundreds, decamped in an area no bigger than a couple of football fields; in secluded idyll, they fattened up on sockeye salmon—and also had sex, dealt with cubs, and fought for dominance—until October arrived, rendering the rivers barren and the elderberries scarce, and nudging everyone up into the hills for The Big Sleep.

The grizzlies of the Maze were old-school. Hardcore. Most were not habituated to humans; those who were didn't much care to be, having abided the park's unwritten interspecies law: "Bears shall tolerate, in all designated areas, the aiming of Sony Handycams and the pointing of greasy fingers and shall periodically humor onlookers with the occasional belly scratch, fish toss, or cannonball plunge. In exchange, humans shall stay the fuck out of the Maze."

Null and void. The contract had been officially terminated, with cause, on October 5. That was the day a thousand-pound grizzly, a.k.a. The Big Red Machine, came upon a tent smack in the middle of the Maze, courtesy of two blond New Age freaks from Malibu. They'd been hanging around all summer, walking on all fours, making silly bear sounds, and Being One With Bears. As if they were fooling anyone.

All summer he'd ignored them. He'd been clear and unequivocal.

Kept his distance. Growled when need be. But they couldn't take a hint. Wouldn't get the fuck out of the way. And now it was cold and rainy, and he was too old and tired for this shit. He expressed his displeasure by ripping them to pieces and tearing off their heads.

So that was something to think about.

But still. Hibernation season was now in full effect. Or should have been. By the looks of things—random paw prints, bear scat—a few stragglers had passed through in the last week or so, looking for one last bedtime snack.

"They just hide in the alders, circling, waiting," Willy said. "You won't even know he's there till he's *there*." He said this after pivoting to his right, drawn by a sound audible only to him. He pointed his rifle toward a brushy knoll twenty feet away, less aiming than intuiting. The brush shook slightly, then fell still, then did both again. Willy scanned widely.

"Instinct," he said. "Gotta trust it."

With your life. Flight instinct was your special gift and came complete with a lifetime guarantee—*flight instinct* being synonymous with *survival instinct,* and the latter being the one developmental imperative you lovingly nurtured. Stimuli + fear + flight = survival = propagation of the species. To defy the equation would be to defy the rule of law, natural and otherwise. *Inherit the Wind,* 1960. Court finds for the defendant, Spencer Tracy.

And yet. Now, in Alaska, instinct screamed "Stay!" The fear only made it shout louder. The fear was *fantastic,* because it was True Fear (i.e., that which is prompted by a legitimate threat to life and limb, such as a bear mauling), as opposed to The Fear (i.e., that which is manufactured, for no good reason, by a sick, sad imagination). To experience the former was to feel your lungs grow—asthma, be gone— fueling capillaries and neurotransmitters long abandoned; it was to enter the secret world of Breathers.

There was no bear.

This made you sad.

"Because you're an idiot," Willy said.

You walked in silence.

"Think Tim was an idiot?" you asked.

"Great guy. Loved the guy. But he could be an idiot."

"How?"

He started to explain, then thought better of it. Moving slowly, he scanned the perimeter and hewed close to rivers, which served as natural barriers—bears are doltish swimmers. Willy knew how to bag a bear (carry a big gun) and how to keep one from bagging him (don't miss). He managed to do both during his previous trip to the Maze, when he arrived just in time to see The Big Red Machine finishing off The Blond Tourists.

Willy had flown alone, intending only to shuttle them back to the island. He ended up facing down none other than the biggest, meanest, hungriest bear in the Maze—its alpha, its Big Red Killing Machine—during what was surely its greatest hunter-gatherer moment ever. A second bear had also joined the fun. The only thing more violent than a grizzly with its prey is a grizzly who feels threatened. The Machine chased Willy all the way back into the plane.

By then Tim was scattered all over the place, but Amie's whereabouts remained unknown. So Willy gave chase. Opened fire. Tried to distract the bear with flashlights. Three hours elapsed before rangers joined the hunt, at dusk, in the rain. The trail went cold. Until, out of nowhere, The Machine spirited out of the alders, silent and fast, coming within five yards of them. He took twenty-one bullets before going down.

"That's why I advise against sleeping here," Willy said.

"You said that to Tim?"

He just stared.

Detecting something underfoot, you peeled from the dirt a

pale-blue woman's sock, frozen stiff, half shredded. Also a fingernail, cracked, dirty.

Willy examined them both, nodded, and continued on. He stopped at the sight of two stacks of bones lying side by side, one a bit larger than the other; most of the bones measured between two and three feet in length; none lay in accordance with their god-given order—they were literally just piled together, like kindling. Each had been whitened by the sun and picked clean. No heads in sight.

"You look a little gray," Willy said.

"I'm fine," you said.

He grabbed one of the thicker bones. "Leg," he said, waving it. "Got a little cartilage left. Take it. Souvenir."

Your tenfold experience, chronologically:

1. Gagging.
2. Regret.
3. Contempt for this land of savages.
4. Pity for two dead Malibu morons.
5. Flight instinct.
6. Relief.
7. Shame.
8. Gagging.
9. Flight instinct.
10. Contempt.

By now Willy had established that human remains were inappropriate souvenirs (see item 6); that the bone now clutched tightly in your fist was quite obviously too large to be human (7); that it and all the others were born of The Big Red Machine and his wingbear, also KIA (8); and that the remains were few because the grizzlies had been eaten, immediately postmortem, by their fellow grizzlies (9).

Thoughts turned to Tim Treadwell (10).

Silence fell. Returning to the Pumpkin, in silence, you sat fiddling with two spent shell casings retrieved from the crime scene. They smelled like burnt hair. By takeoff, however, the odor had ceded to that of rotting tissue, thanks to the souvenir bone in your possession. "Gonna smell like death in here the whole time," Willy said.

Willy commenced a sickening low-fly tour of the area. He buzzed tree lines and grassy plains. He whisked in and around the lower mountain peaks, as if negotiating pylons.

"So what are you gonna write?" he said.

"Still digesting," you said.

He laughed. The plane leveled off, at low altitude.

"Gotta love Tim," he said.

"Yeah?"

"*Hell yeah*. Just a big kid—a little out there, sure. But, damn, he *went for it*."

"And died."

"Yeah, well."

Again he started to explain, then reconsidered. Again he cranked the Floyd. He banked the plane sharply, flying just higher than the tallest peaks. The sinking sun served as a kind of burnt-orange spotlight. You widened and rolled your eyes, to make sure they weren't just reacting to the smell of death, before refocusing on the mountain.

The two grizzlies stood side by side, on a semiflat little ledge three-quarters of the way up the mountain. They were adult males, thousand-pounders, more golden than brown. They were fatter and logier than you'd imagined they would be, especially in their bellies and asses, which carried the few hundred extra pounds they'd need for hibernation, in one of the mountain's hidden caves or warrens.

At first the bears hardly acknowledged the Pumpkin, giving it a cursory over-the-shoulder glance, the way they do at geese. Willy kept circling back around to them, at a distance of about forty yards. They looked either bemused or amused, depending. Finally the larger bear nudged the other, as gently as a grizzly can, and some sort of oral communication passed between them.

During your next and final flyover, at precisely the same time, the bears teetered back onto their hind legs and stood upright—eight feet tall, old-man bellies hanging low—while simultaneously raising their arms overheard. Coats shimmering in the twilight, the great golden bears waved their giant paws at you, and roared.

The universe loves a gambler.

Nobody seemed to understand this. Nobody except you, Mimi, and the good people at American Airlines.

And Tim Treadwell.

Together you and Mimi would defy The Loveless Majority. Godspeed all those cynical losers who had long since given up on love, having spent decades regretting their own desperate, lazy choices, and who now lived only to destroy the brave few who dared seek a relationship born of something other than convenience, boredom, or fear. They said: "Long-distance romances never work." They meant: "My marriage is a cancer."

Transcontinental love, transcendent love. The rewards were infinite. There was a point system. Membership Rewards points begot gold status, then platinum, then super-mega-turbo-titanium. Love *accrued*. Occasionally JetBlue, acknowledging your commitment to excellence, flew you cross-country. Gratis. The universe upgraded you. To *elite* status. To broad leather seats and melty soft Toll House cookies. *Welcome, young lovers, to the Admirals Club.*

Mimi preferred The Friendly Skies; you tended toward JetBlue, though sometimes you switched things up, just for the hell of it, because that's the kind of crazy love-struck kids you were. No limits, no boundaries. Either way, win-win.

You preferred flying to Mimi, as opposed to vice versa. That was mostly by design. Travel got you out of the house and into the big happy world. (Get out, get in—*very Taoist,* probably.) The benefits of same were manifest, from Alaska to Tribeca. New York was shinier, cleaner, a cool embrace. Possibly you'd underestimated the place. Possibly you needed to rethink things.

Mimi lived downtown, in Greenwich Village, a neighborhood devoid of skyscrapers and full of green spaces, topflight restaurants, and preserved eighteenth-century brownstones with slanted floors, private terraces, and cruel mortgages. It was the neighborhood of the moment, and Mimi had gotten in early, buying a sunny corner apartment in a doorman building on lower Fifth Avenue. The apartment had a large, loft-y feel. This was partly because it had bay windows and expansive views of the Village and partly because of scale: It housed a tiny person with tiny belongings.

By day, for hours at a stretch, Mimi could be found tucked at her little wooden farm table. She sat on a wiry little chair. She typed lightly and fast, her slender fingers skittering over the keys of a mini-laptop, writing abbreviated emails in tiny fonts. She sat by an open window, even in wintertime, her scratchy little voice hushed by breezes and city sounds. A kitten on a windowsill in a dollhouse.

This left 99.999 percent of the apartment to you. Workspace was essential while you worked on the Treadwell article, in addition to a screenplay you and Daniel had been hired to write. Your journalistic role model, Mel Gibson, was "attached" to produce, direct, and star in the "project," about an outlaw biker gang. There were expectations. Deadlines. Pressures.

Mimi appreciated, as all writers do, the importance of shutting up and going away. She never offered the dreaded "Hey, whatcha thinkin' over there?" She let you hide in far corners, acknowledging only your laptop; you were free to shuffle randomly, unshaven, wearing last night's T-shirt and jeans, in an autistic-like fugue. *Was Tim* disemboweled *or* eviscerated? *Who should the biker blow in this scene? Or is it* whom? Such behaviors were welcomed. Honored.

"Two kooks together," she said.

Things moved fast: tribunals assembling, litmus flying. First came Mimi's best friend, Samantha, a ten-foot-tall Brit who had mulched Mimi's last two boyfriends. *Approved*. Then came Mimi's mother and sister. *Sign and date, please*. Then Mimi went before your parents, Miles and Evelyn, while they were visiting New York for the weekend.

"Lovely," Mom said.

"Charmer," Dad said.

"And Jewish," Mom said.

Next came your other parents, Ben and Daniel. They posed the biggest threat of all, given the high standards to which they held your prospective girlfriends, and the middling marks most of them had received. Ben, after meeting one of the candidates, said only three words—"I just can't"—before walking away.

They met Mimi in a new Japanese restaurant of the sort Los Angeles too often produced; it was aggressive, mediocre, and noisy. Mimi's voice faded; the yellowtail perspired; the check came to eight hundred thousand dollars, plus tip. Ben and Daniel were as they always were at such times, by turns charming and noncommittal. Mimi excused herself to smoke. A passage of time was noted.

"Nicely done," Ben said.

Oh, the places you went. Mimi, even more than you, was a forward mover. The itch to keep moving, to *progress,* was embedded in Mimi's limbic brain. She had been to every major international city twice. Since Christmas.

She had it down. She, like you, could pack for a six-week trip to another dimension in thirty minutes, on a moment's notice. But, in addition to certain more advanced skills—she could squeeze thirty sets of heels into a carry-on—Mimi belonged to a shadow organization tasked with cracking the most inaccessible hotels and restaurants, anywhere, any time. She denied this. They always do.

"I wanna go," she would say. Here she would vibrate, nearly pogoing. "Let's go."

"Me, too," you would say. "But I've got all this work and—"

"You can work there."

"Hmmm."

London. San Francisco. Colorado. Arizona. Washington. Boston. Paris. London again.

"How's the hotel?" That was her favorite question, whenever you called from out of town. If it was a nice place, she probably already knew the answer, but liked hearing it anyway. If you were off the grid—if you were calling from, say, a Best Western in Alaska—her interest skewed toward the anthropologic.

"Is it stinky?" she asked.

Two words never associated with Mimi: *motel* and *rustic*.

"No," you said. "It's fine."

"Is there really a big mean bear in the lobby?"

Stuffed. Adult. Male.

"Eww," she said. "And please don't get eaten."

"It's beautiful here," you said. "We should come back sometime."

She just laughed and laughed.

The next time you saw her was at friend's wedding, in London. You had dinner with two of Mimi's other friends, a handsome British couple that owned things, in a new-old restaurant with blood-red walls and a menu free of mutton. Mimi sat across from you, sipping broth. She looked up, birdlike, spoon at chin height.

And that was it.

Now many things happened internally, in a split second. A review of all work commitments and scheduling issues. An urge to pour scotch over your head. An audit of bank savings, retirement accounts, likely future earnings. An image of your cats on a window ledge. A chronological review of all hotels visited in the past year, including lobbies and public areas. A flash-forward to five years hence (no change). Another financial review. A loss of appetite. A debate as to whom should presently be consulted, and whether that should be done from afar or in person. An estimate of which consultant would say what, and who was most likely to laugh, cry, or berate (none, none, and none, respectively). An urge to spray champagne everywhere, as if in the Detroit Pistons locker room, circa 2004. A flash-forward to ten years hence (ibid). Another image of the cats, skittering along a sidewalk. A feeling of flushness. A sense of pervasive whiteness. An awareness of the white tablecloth before you. An urge to clear it of all plates, silverware, and finery, with one swift swing, before climbing atop the table, looking straight into those pale-blue bird eyes, and shouting "IF YOU DON'T MARRY ME, I'LL DIE!!!"

"BEST FEELING EVER!"

First thing you wrote in your reporter's notebook, in the immediate wake of The Great Alaskan Bear Encounter, weeks earlier. Actually, that's not quite accurate. The notebook was already filled with random jottings, written in your barely legible schoolboy scrawl: "bonerotpuke," "pnkflyd airline," "bluedeathsock"). But the aforementioned one was fully rendered and punctuated. And whereas the others appeared on various pages, the first appeared on the cover, in fat blue lettering, as if written by an eighth-grade cheerleader.

The Great Alaskan Bear Encounter produced a rush unlike any other, a full sensory explosion: ringing ears, hair standing sentinel. There was a sense of internal movement, of organs weightless and untethered: floating, shifting. There was light and more light, a Crayola 48. And there was, audibly, a kind of low sniggering, Deputy Dawg–style—*hee-hee-hee*—that tempted but ultimately defied hyperventilation. The surge, in toto, harkened to the old days of childhood—of choked awakenings and frantic midnight runs to the ER and needles jammed into biceps and the sweet, saving glory of epinephrine.

But this rapture came without cost. Organically. This one endured—through *The Dark Side of the Moon* and deep into hibernation season. It followed you back to the Lower 48. It awakened you in Mimi's apartment, in the middle of the night, in the middle of a dream. It dragged you out of bed, turned on your PowerBook, and wrote:

"He was in love."

And there it was.

Since the moment the dead man had entered your life—since the day he'd died, really—everyone had asked the same question, above all: "What the hell was that guy thinking?"

"Well," you'd say. "It's complicated."

"He wanted to live with bears? *Grizzly bears?*"

"Yes."

"He slept with them?"

"Well, *among.*"

"Is this something others bear experts do?"

"Not really."

"So he was nuts, right?"

"Well, that's a strong word—"

"Well, what normal person does that?"

Usually, at this point, you pretended to see someone across the room. Answers proved elusive; doubts, lingering.

Tim, though long on experience, wasn't a scientist and had no formal training; prior to the killings, most official bear experts regarded him as a lovable naïf with a gift for melodrama and self-romanticism; some deemed him a dangerous crackpot who ignored the key tenet of the interspecies relationship: respectful distance. By selling people on a "relationship" he *desired,* rather than the one that actually existed—"these bears just *tolerate* us," one warned—he was inviting savage reality.

Tim wouldn't even use standard protection—bear spray, electric fencing—for fear of discomfiting the grizzlies. He ignored pleas by a renowned expert named Barrie Gilbert, who regretted not having had a fence back in 1977, when a grizzly tore off half his face.

Tim endlessly clashed with the park service, due mostly to his one-man antipoaching crusade. Poaching officially fell under the purview of rangers, who were trained for such dangerous work, and who, in any case, felt strongly that Tim was talking out of his ass, by turns imagining (because he was nuts) and conjuring (because he was a narcissist) a heroic stand against dark legions that existed only in his mind—poaching, they said, was quite rare, due to strong policing efforts.

Also: the bear thing. Katmai's superintendant, Deb Liggett, implored Tim to reconsider, saying "My staff will never forgive you if they have to kill a bear because of you."

"God forbid, if a bear takes me, let him go," Tim would say, whenever the issue arose. "If I don't come back"—and here he would shrug, calmly—"this is what I *love* doing."

That word again. (Emphasis *his*.) Just kept jumping out of the notes and tapes. To ignore it would have been to defy The Nature Of Things. As They Really Were.

The ocean refuses no river.

"Even those who had long predicted Treadwell's death granted him this," you wrote. "He was a believer, who walked the walk. And he was in love."

Chills.

So simple. So obvious. Yet so elusive to so many.

You had to be there. With us.

Tim and you. Yin and Yang. That much was obvious. Twos were everywhere. Golden pairs.

Tim, like you, had been raised in a peaceable suburb, Ronkonkoma, Long Island, amid loving family and friends. He felt more awkward than he looked. He was tightly wound, friendly from a distance. Though reasonably smart, he valued cleverness over intellect, shortcuts over rigor. He was inconsistent, either all-in or all-out. Concentration was an issue, boredom ever present, amusement the goal. He lived in his head, and wished to be anywhere but here.

Just when Tim seemed to come into his own, he started coming undone. In college, at Bradley University, he was a record-breaking diver. Two years later, in Los Angeles, he was sleeping with a loaded M16. He was twice arrested (assault, illegally discharging a weapon) and twice nearly died. The first brush involved a speedball of coke and heroin; the second, an LSD-fueled nosedive off a third-floor balcony. (His technique remained precise; the beach rendered a perfect imprint of his face, including his sunglasses.) He described both mishaps as accidents, but allowed that the line between "accidental" and "suicidal" can be a fuzzy one.

When Tim was a boy, grizzly bears calmed him. "I became a grizzly," he recalled. "In my chest beat the heart of a wild animal." Ever since, he had dreamt of bears. Or of being one. Often he was a bear with wings that transported him above and away from the cruel world and deposited him in a cool, clean wilderness of mountains, snow, and silence.

Bears saved him. Bears showed the way.

"I need to be somewhere really remote," Tim told a friend. "Far away from people."

He struck out for Alaska, solo, despite shortfalls in experience, resources, and nuance. In Kodiak, the locals deemed him "goofy" and "Hollywood," owing to his shaggy Prince Valiant haircut and his standard all-black outfit: coat, jeans, sunglasses, baseball cap worn backward. They also described him as "sweet," "naïve," and "excitable" and as "a big kid living in his own fantasy."

During Tim's first trek into the wild, fifteen years earlier, a grizzly surged out of the bush, raging. Man and bear locked eyes. "The encounter was like looking in a mirror," Tim later said. "I gazed into the face of a kindred soul, a being that was potentially lethal but in reality was just as frightened as I was."

The grizzly demurred. Whereas philistines would have seen a grizzly being grizzly—bears commonly "bluff charge" before fleeing—Tim saw the glory. His appetite for drugs disappeared; a lifetime's worth of fear and alienation melted away. The answer was clear:

Be the bear.

Tim's mantra. He said it all the time, in one way or another, from this point forward. Sometimes, when anxiety crept or courage proved elusive, he dropped to all fours, quietly chanting "I am grizzly . . . I am grizzly."

Turn off your mind.

Trust your heart.

Give yourself over.

For fifteen years, Tim's faith saw his faith rewarded. Although every group seemed to have one threatening or aggressive scofflaw—the "25th Grizzly," in his words—the big browns never laid a paw on him. They just observed from a distance, in much the same way the fanny-packers observed them. Tim welcomed them, and reached out. Literally. At times, when the cameras were off and the time seemed right—and despite all conventional wisdom about bear relations—Tim crossed the Rubicon. He *touched the grizzlies.*

And the killer bears were fine with it. And the universe smiled. Tim scored a book deal (*Among Grizzlies*) and a profile in *People* magazine. He starred in specials for Paramount Television (*Wild Things*) and Animal Planet (*The Grizzly Man Diaries*). He became catnip to the ladies. "It's my bear work they're attracted to," he told a friend. "I never got laid like this until I started talking to bears."

David Letterman couldn't resist the guy's shaggy charm, twice inviting him on the show. Tim's fund-raising organization, Grizzly People, attracted corporate sponsors (Patagonia, Konica Minolta) and celebrity benefactors who shared his passion for wildlife preservation and lustrous hair: Leonardo DiCaprio, Gisele Bündchen. *A couple.*

Tim took meetings at CAA. Just down the hall from Jay.

Tim headed to a frozen nowhere, to be found. Just like Bruno.

Tim, like Bruno, was in love.

It was almost creepy. Each had found love (or vice versa) after resolving to be a lone wolf, wild and free. But Tim! He and Amie had begun as friendly acquaintances: he the oversize kid, friendly but aloof; she, a self-effacing little wisp, five-feet-nothing, one hundred pounds soaking wet, but far stronger than she looked; she regularly ran for miles, tirelessly. "She's my girlfriend," Tim told a friend. "She's wonderful."

Amie embraced, rather than tolerated, Tim's . . . whatever it was. *Singularity.* She saw through his eyes. "Like heaven," she told a friend, after returning from Alaska. "You haven't lived till you've bathed in a river with bears."

By all accounts, Tim was healthy of body and mind. His bedroom walls were free of handwritten grievances; his L.A. drug spirals, ancient history. He was not the latest addition to Team Bipolar, R.I.P. High-strung? Sure. Audacious dreamer? Yep. Prone to the occasional overstep? Absolutely. These were prerequisites. Wildlifers live in and for the *wild.* Dian Fossey would have made a lousy nanny. But she made one hell of a Sigourney Weaver.

So. Notwithstanding your occasional disparities in judgment and execution, and setting aside certain differences in decorum and styling—the Eighties James Spader Look was unacceptable in the eighties—and despite the fact that you represented everything Tim stood against, and that he would have bored you to the point of savagery, you were practically the same person.

Plus: *bears*.

Who couldn't relate? Kings of the forests *and* the box office. Stars at pretty much every zoo everywhere. Pandas and polars, being few in numbers and many in publicists, were the "event bears." They were divas; they were flakes. The surest values were the killer teddies. Grizzlies: bigger, better, faster, stronger. The American bears.

Tim, for all his excesses, was onto something real—in a way Bruno had not been. Bruno knew the penguins, but they didn't know him back. But there was a reason why the experts always spoke in terms of "man's relationship with bears." Because one really existed. The evidence was everywhere, and mounting. A hundred years earlier, who would have believed chimps were capable of speaking sign language? Or that elephants could tell a real Picasso from a fake?

Tim did as all wildlifers must. He tested boundaries. Stepped out of the comfort zone. Without a crackpot like Tim, a slob like you would never have seen Alaska. Or been greeted by a delegation of bears. Or been inspired to shop for wedding rings.

Or maybe it was just the Adderall.

dderall.

A central nervous system stimulant prescription medicine. It is used for the treatment of attention-deficit hyperactivity disorder (ADHD). Adderall XR may help increase attention.

More than six hundred million dollars' worth of pills sold in 2004, courtesy of the good folks at Shire Pharmaceuticals. The world's most widely prescribed "psychostimulant."

Everyone remembers their first time. Where they were. What they were doing. The *power*.

First lover.

First childbirth.

First Adderall.

For you it was Dublin, Ireland. Kildare Street. 11:50 A.M.

Sunny but cold. That peaty smell.

Moving through the workday bustle. Legs heavy, breathing labored—the weight of miscalculation. Regret having not flown in a day earlier, to cushion the jet lag. An entire night spent staring at barmy Irish sitcom reruns.

Fell asleep: 10:00 A.M.

Wake-up call: 10:30 A.M.

Second wake-up call: 11:00 A.M.

Adderall: 11:30 A.M.

Life: 11:50 A.M.

That first heartbeat, that one booming baritone *thump,* was itself worth dying for; already it's given you a full and enriching life as Dublin's favorite son. All eyes met yours, and twinkled with acknowledgment. The women wanted you, and the men wanted to be you. The park ahead, Saint Stephen's Green, became Saint Stephen's Greener. A distinct popping of reds, from scarves and signs, was noted. The city was old but fresh, a diorama liberated from its shell.

It was established that all the women had emerald eyes and smooth ivory skin, and that it was high time you obliged a grateful nation, in a Jameson-soaked blur of chanted limericks and dangerous group sex: *"There once was a gal from Kilkenny! You could have her arse for a penny!"*

Meantime, though, duty beckoned.

After the Bruno story appeared, suddenly you had all the writing assignments you wanted, the lion's share of them being high in sex appeal, low in degree of difficulty, and abundant in perquisites, resources, and frequent-flier points. Rare was the celebrity-profile writer who could match your singular blend of shallowness and inanity. And escapism.

You'd just show up at the appointed hour, at The Celebrity's hotel or home in Malibu/Beverly Hills/Miami/London/Dublin. You'd spend an hour feigning interest about their latest piece-of-shit romantic comedy; their blatherings about Method and their first acting coach; and their gibberish about using their twenty-million-dollar paychecks as a means to finance documentaries about flipper babies killed by land mines. You'd spend the second hour asking about his latest divorce/arrest/ bankruptcy, and nod thoughtfully while they ducked the questions, complained about the media, and said "Well, I've got an early call to-morrow." Then they'd direct all further questions to their publicist, Marci.

Then you'd return to the hotel, take a swim, order a shank of some such drizzled in a light aioli something, then spend the rest of the night swaddled in handwoven bedsheets and eight-thousand-year-old scotch.

Then, returning to New York, you'd cherry-pick The Celebrity's least canned-sounding quotations, along with those of his Celebrity Friends ("he stays so *grounded*") and Celebrity Colleagues ("at the end of the day, he's all about The Work"), before culling anything that seemed even remotely provocative or controversial. Weepy confessions were virtually unheard of, unless The Celebrity was pushing a book about same. Ideally, then, you'd mine something derogatory or embar-rassing about a Celebrity Colleague—you were golden the instant George Clooney mentioned punching a director. Otherwise, you'd settle for any hints of on-set discord, marital woes, spending habits, preferred vacation spots, or real estate purchases. Or sex. Of any kind.

Then you'd spend five thousand words trying to make the subject seem fun and lively, while simultaneously signaling to the reader your smirking contempt for the whole process.

You entered the Shelbourne Hotel, a classic red-brick beauty, and bee-lined into its Horseshoe Bar, an ornately detailed space occupied by exactly one customer, who looked as if he'd been drinking there since the hotel first opened, in 1824. His eyes were rheumy; his T-shirt rum-pled; his complexion, the color of death. He hadn't slept since god only knew, and sat slumped at a corner table, consuming a breakfast of cigarettes and beer.

This was Colin Farrell, obscure actor-boy and human train wreck—potentially the least promising interview subject you'd encountered since Madonna, who at least had had a real career, and who had been courteous enough to arrive sober and bathed. "My fuckin' head is throbbing," Farrell said, in a sloppy Irish brogue. "I think I'm gonna puke."

He headed to the bathroom, returning several minutes later. "Happy to answer anything you want," he said, sliding a pint across the table. "But I say let's just get pissed."

Colin Farrell, the gift that kept on giving. He insulted the leaders of Ireland's sacrosanct Catholic Church, calling them "motherfuckers" and "dirty hypocrites." He waxed about substance-abuse and wanking and hookers. He named starlets he hoped to bang.

The joyride continued for four blessed hours, at a rate of 1.6 pints per. Normally the consumption of that much alcohol would have doomed you to a bathroom stall, fetally curled. But not this time. This time you held firmly in the sweet spot, buzzed but never drunk. You *sharpened*, absorbing not only his words and actions, but also those of others. Nothing escaped you, and everything inspired. The ornate ceiling, the lilting voices—maybe you should read more Seamus Heaney.

The Adderall Boilermaker:

99 ounces of Guinness Extra Stout

15 mg Adderall

Stir gently.

Exiting the hotel, you felt so clear, so present, you almost missed the sweet warmth rolling down your legs.

This was two months before Mimi and Tim.

A single-entity amphetamine product, Adderal combines the neutral sulfate salts of dextroamphetamine and amphetamine with the dextro isomer of amphetamine saccharate and d, l-amphetamine aspartate monohydrate.

See also: speed.

Amphetamines are thought to block the reuptake of norepinephrine and dopamine into the presynaptic neuron and increase the release of these monoamines into the extraneuronal space.

See also: epinephrine shot, minus needle.

Adderall should be used as part of a total treatment program for ADHD that may include counseling or other therapies.

See also: Shrink Five.

Until she entered the picture, after all, your reentry into the world had been wobbly, rudimentary. You had gotten off to a decent start in the post-9/11 era. Out went Three and Four—clean slate and all that— and in came Five, who would save you time, money, and aggravation. Five, a psychopharmacologist, provided both therapy and prescriptions, and an altogether better parking situation. She worked out of a tidy white house on a quiet upper-middle-class street in the Valley. The suburb evoked those of your childhood. Apples to oranges.

Five was younger and less shrinky than her predecessors, in both appearance and approach. She was a transplanted Southerner with a gentle twang and a fondness for neutral colors; she mixed gal-next-door warmth with a formal reserve, suggesting a childhood of South-ern Baptist bake sales. When floating an issue—and that's always how she did it, as if wondering aloud whether she'd put too many nuts in the brownies—she adjusted for degree of difficulty. Low: "Just won-derin' why Daniel might be annoyed at you." High: "Ever notice how often people misuse the term *self-deception*?"

Five was easy. You didn't even need to seek her out, let alone vet her, having once again ceded the legwork to Ben, Daniel, and Lizz, in addition to the newest member of your full-time and all-purpose ex-ploratory committee: Paula. They had soured on Three and Four, but especially Three.

"Idiot," Ben said. "Fell for all your bullshit and lies."

"Pushover," Daniel said. "Didn't call you on your shit."

"Burnt out," Lizz said. "Checked out."

"Devil," Paula said.

Their hostility toward Three far exceeded yours, if only because they needed *someone* to blame for the disaster, but were disinclined to point fingers at a poor flailing friend, even despite his noted proficiency for dissembling, dishonesty, and noncooperation (*bullshit* was *their* word) and never mind that even the world's top jockey finishes out of the money atop a horse that won't run. They shot the jockey.

You selected a new doctor the same way you had selected a new house. By proxy. Happenstance. It was a nice house.

There is a method to everything.

There is no *i* in *team*.

Team is another word for *trust*.

Five transitioned you from larva to chrysalis, thanks in part to her light touch. How liberating therapy was in the absence of difficult questions and unchallenged nonreplies. No more embarrassing subject matter; no more awkward exposition. There was an economy to the process, especially in the early going, pre-Adderall:

Five: I'm thinkin' you look a little down.

You: I guess so.

Five: Any specific cause, ya thinkin'?

You: No. Maybe. I dunno.

Five: Hmm. Worse than last week?

You: Eh. Maybe. I dunno.

Five: Well, that's no good.

You: Nope.

Five: Thoughts of harming yourself?

You: Nope.

Five: Thoughts of death?

You: Not directly. Just the usual.

Five: The hammer? Hitting you?

You: Passively.

Five: The Remeron? Feel any changes?

You: No. I dunno. I sleep a lot.

Five: How many hours a night?

You: Nine, ten.

Five: And during the day?

You: No. Just . . . dull.

Five: Still hard to focus, write?

You: Still hard.

That's when she handed you a prescription for the moon and stars. "Like turning on a light switch," Five said, days later.

The following have been reported with the use of stimulant medicines:

Mental (Psychiatric) problems:
- *new or worse behavior or thought problems*
- *new or worse bipolar illness*
- *new or worse aggressive behavior or hostility*

Five noted that virtually all prescription medications pose some degree of risk, however nominal. Those taking psychostimulants may experience, among other things, vomiting, racing heart, high blood pressure, headaches, diarrhea, constipation, sweating, dehydration, insomnia, panic attacks, or swelling of hands, feet, or ankles; a tiny fraction of users (i.e., those with major or undiagnosed diseases or abnormalities, or just really bad luck) may risk seizure, stroke, kidney damage, anaphylaxis, tachycardia, heart disease, or sudden death.

Always the fine print. Always so vital, when taking any medication, to carefully review all labels and literature; indications and contraindications; guidelines for dosage and potential for abuse; common side effects and rare side effects; and general warnings and precautions, including (but not limited to) Potential Adverse Events; and to immediately discuss all questions or concerns with a doctor or health care professional.

And yet.

The love you'd been feeling, in so many ways, was indeed *love*. The genuine article. In no way drug-induced. There's no such thing as an XR Love Pill, at least until spring 2013. Had Adderall been Robitussin, still you would have chased Mimi around her sofa (albeit sluggishly) and seen glory in two great bears. A psychostimulant is literal; it grabs hold of your dusty snow-globe brain—and everything presently contained therein, from hardware (neurons, blood vessels) to software (emotions, psychology)—and gives it a good shake.

Adderall, while not a hallucinogenic, produced its own magical effect. Only subtler and more utilitarian. Adderall produced, in lieu of fantastical Dream Dances, a euphoria of the here and now—shapeshifting for the busy modern professional.

Adderall Love was a major motion picture about itself, taking creative license only when in the service of economy, continuity, and marketing:

Mimi & Me
A True Story of Epic Romance
Inspired by a True Story

Nobody wanted to see two train wrecks irritate and infuriate each other, almost from the get-go. In fact, the two of you had nearly been disqualified while still in the starting blocks, while blundering the Brian Situation. Mimi had agreed to let you know precisely when she'd be breaking the uncomfortable news to her ex, and to then report back, posthaste, so you could promptly make an informed follow-up call to him.

The matter came into sharp relief at a housewarming party thrown by one of her many anonymously rich acquaintances, in a canyon above Beverly Hills—the first time you and she had together mixed with other people (albeit after arriving separately). Ten people surrounded you, on a narrow backyard patio. The smokers.

"Did it," she whispered.

"Did what?" you said.

"Brian. The talk."

"Huh? Seriously?"

She puffed and exhaled, in her well-bred way: lips shunted leftward, forcing the smoke back and beyond.

"This afternoon," she said.

"This after—?!"

Prying eyes. You clawed a hand through your hair.

"Did we not discuss this?" you said.

"He called. Couldn't lie to him."

"Couldn't tell me till *now*? In the middle of ten strangers?"

The tone rattled her.

"Sorry," she said. "I got freaked out."

"It went badly?" you asked.

"Not goodly. He was pissed."

"At both of us, right?"

"Yes and no."

"He was more pissed at me?"

"A little more, I guess."

"What did he say?"

"Tell you later."

"Later? Are you joking?"

"Don't get upset at me."

"Why would I do *that*?"

She shushed. Exhaled left.

"I need air," you said, escaping her light grasp and bolting into the backyard/forest. Just need a minute to regroup.

But from a certain pacing-point, near your car, you noticed Mimi greeting an old friend. Laughing. Smoking.

By the time she stubbed out the cigarette, you were white-knuckling it toward Ben and Daniel's house.

"Sold me out," you said. "Right?"

"Wasn't good," Daniel said. "But talk it through with her."

"She made herself the good guy. Left me twisting until twenty minutes ago."

"You're right to be upset," Ben said. "But it *was* a messy situation."

"When I met Ben," Daniel said, "he refused to go out with me at all unless I was completely single. He wanted to set the right tone. He said, 'It's important how things start.'"

Despite the temptation to scratch their eyes out, you resolved to make things right. Mimi had other ideas. She ducked your calls for two days, having been wounded and alienated by your unilateral exit from the party: She would be left high and dry by no man, regardless of whether she'd previously left him twisting. A man, let alone a prospective boyfriend, simply didn't do such things. Not to her.

A tone, once set, cannot be unset. Mimi eventually ceded to compromise—the hangings were deemed offsetting penalties. The messiness endured, in sneaky fits and starts. There was, in the beginning, the occasional spat. She didn't get why, when she was in Los Angeles for only four nights, you seemed content to see her on only two of them. You couldn't help wondering why she always got to choose all the wheres, whens, and how-longs. She tended to let slip, after a night apart, that a guy had asked for her number. You tended, after she said this, to take the bait.

Spat was, for the first few months, just another word for *passion*. And passion was that which you most needed. *The logy bear emerges at last, and beholds the first salmon run of spring.* But "spat" had a practical application as well, being the conflict-resolution mechanism of choice for the conflict-averse, affording you both the opportunity to raise grievances and the freedom to avoid dealing with them. So much in common, you two. So much to not share.

"You vow to do *x*," you'd say. "Instead you do *y*."

"You're warm one day," she'd say. "Cold the next."

Then cocktails.

Usually this unfolded in the evening, in between drinks one and three, because (1) daytime communications hewed to the secret language of writers, with its Neanderthal mumblings ("coffee headache," "need shower") and e-grunts ("no thnx," "when eat"); (2) nothing makes writers reenter the atmosphere, and vent their misery, more effectively than a stiff drink; (3) the antidote to misery is a second and third drink; and (4) you were otherwise busy with your prescription narcotics.

8:00 A.M.: Awaken in a haze.
8:30 A.M.: Adderall taken.
9:00 A.M.: Adderall giveth.
2:30 P.M.: Adderall taketh away.

Abrupt cessation following prolonged high dosage administration results in extreme fatigue and mental depression; changes are also noted on the sleep EEG.

The most painful thing about Adderall Crash wasn't the crash in and of itself, hideous though that was: a half hour of portentous wooz—vision blurring, head filling with cement—ceding to a blackness blacker than night. The most painful thing was the creeping awareness that the longer you stuck to the program, the less it would work—that, week by week, Adderall Crash would arrive sooner and sooner.

Tolerance. The bugaboo of many or most Adderall fans, notwithstanding the manufacturer's best efforts to duck the subject:

The effectiveness of Adderall XR for long-term use has not been systematically evaluated in controlled trials.

Your devolution resembled that of virtually every other Addster you'd met. And you met dozens of them. Where once a basic ten-milligram dose kept you battle-ready all day, now the fight faded in four hours. Then three. Then . . .

Gradually, in half-pill increments, Five upped the dosage; usually this facilitated some forward progress, or at least fortification, but at no small cost. Surges proved ever more modest and short-lived; attrition, the opposite. The brutal escalation—enough "surge" bullshit, spade a spade—played poorly at home. Slam-dunk into quagmire. No endgame; diminishing returns. More Adderall only led to more Adderall.

Which only led to more sleep problems. And therefore more Ativan; more morning haze; *more* Ativan. Which only led to more devastation and bloodshed, i.e., teeth ground down and cuticles gnawed to the quick. Which only further destabilized and undermined that which you had originally intended to save.

Overstimulation, restlessness, dizziness, insomnia, euphoria, dysphoria, depression.

Dysphoria. Opposite of euphoria.

A state of unease. Distress. Anxiety.

Something to chew on, aside from nails. Or cuticles.

Amphetamines have been reported to exacerbate motor and phonic tics.

Four o'clock was the cruelest hour. By then you were a heap, sinking toward a slumber that would never be fully consummated. Adderall's long good-bye brought to mind every party your family ever attended. "Can we go now?" you'd say, at staggered intervals.

"Fine," Mom would say, at last. "Grab the coats."

One step ahead of her. But Mom spent more time saying her good-byes at the end of parties (nearing but never quite reaching the door, coat in hand but not yet on; reaching but never quite crossing the doorstep, coat on but not yet zipped) than she did attending the parties.

The long good-bye. The slow bleed.

Broke you down. Turned you.

Mimi, before heading out to run errands, stopped and assumed her standard good-bye-kiss posture: shoulders square, lips extended. The look you shot her.

A.k.a. *Ursus arctos horribilis.*

Every afternoon. Clockwork.

Daniel felt it. When partnered with a ticking clock, squeeze as much out of him as possible, as early in the day as possible. Then back the hell off.

Your family felt it. Communications—challenging in the best of circumstances—were largely restricted to the death period. Calls were verboten during your fast-closing window for productivity. Since Detroit was three hours ahead of Los Angeles, evening calls were no-go. Unavoidably, then, "conversations" with the family were brief, purely informational. *I'm fine . . . They're fine . . . The April Issue . . . She's fine . . . I ordered sea bass . . . She doesn't eat sea bass . . . Pan seared . . . ESPN2 . . . Movies take years to get made . . . Just tired . . .*

"Sure you're okay?" Dad would ask.

"Yep," you would say. "Just tired."

There would be a pause, followed by his standard sign of distress. "Hmmm," he would say.

"Talk to you soon," you would say.

The murk endured until dinnertime.

Conflicts tasted best when slow cooked, at low heat—when allowed to marinate in their juices, inside tightly sealed crockery. When at last they were ready for consumption—say, when Mimi had for the umpteenth time forgotten/ignored your request to please take *any* of the eight thousand flights available daily, *except* the one that arrived at the witching hour for traffic, at 6:00 P.M., and that did so not at LAX (which itself required the endurance of Shackleton) but at an airport in *Long Beach,* which was three times farther down Hell's Freeway, and which required you to spend nearly as many hours in traffic, round-trip, as she had on a transcontinental flight—the flavor just popped.

"Greetings," you said.

"What?" she said. "What did I do wrong this time?"

This was near the outdoor baggage claim, where you'd finally located her, after killing twenty minutes idling in vain at the curb, where you had agreed to meet, and where the police did not welcome idling at rush hour. A security fence separated the two areas. But you tracked Mimi down in the way you often did—as the Ojibwa had done for centuries—by reading clouds. Your voice, from afar, interrupted her twice-hourly Dream Quest: gaze far-off and dreamy, ears tuned to a private symphony, lips aiming smoke signals toward the sky.

Suitcase at her feet. Carousel empty.

"The curb," you said.

"Yep," she said. "Was on my way."

"Well, not exactly."

She dragged her suitcase. Hamster with a Buick.

Small talk until the on-ramp. It was 6:00 P.M. on the 405 highway. But she wanted to go straight to dinner—table booked for 7:15—despite the fact that no army on earth could get there that fast, and notwithstanding all your previous failed attempts to defy the time-space continuum in the name of arugula salad, balsamic on the side.

"Won't happen," you said.

"I'm starving," she said.

"You took the two-thirty flight."

"I had things to do at noon."

"Like what?"

A silence.

"Like go to the gym," you said.

By now, though, you ran a distant second to her BlackBerry. She typed more words in a minute than you had all afternoon. Because you'd spent most of it on the 405.

"You fly here," you said, "to talk to them there."

"I've got work stuff to take care of," she said.

"Do it later. We're here now."

"In a minute."

"Put that away."

The clatter of tiny fingers and keys.

"Can I smoke?" she asked, still typing.

"Not now."

"I'll open the window."

A few months earlier, her smoking suggested Grace Kelly in *Rear Window*; now, Raymond Burr. You hadn't suffered car smoking since the early seventies: On frigid winter days, when Mom couldn't crack the window more than an inch, her Pontiac became a biohazard. But because the smoking seemed to trigger your asthma—this was back when doctors lit up in hospitals—Mom quit smoking. Unlike a certain other young lady possessed of a foul habit that poisons innocent by-standers and really goes the extra mile with asthmatics.

"*Pleeeeease,*" Mimi said.

The tone. The plaintive gaze.

The sound of one head imploding.

Adderall doesn't make love more passionate. It makes passion more passionate.

"Jesus!" you said, squeezing the wheel. "You live in your little Mimi World, doing only what Mimi wants—"

"Can we be nice—?"

"Then you bitch about how 'distant' and 'aloof' I am! Guess what?! I can't commit to a spoiled little girl!"

"I wanna go home—"

"And what do spoiled little girls do when they get called on their shit?! They turn it around, crying, 'Why are you always mad?!' Then they run away!"

Adderall doesn't make love endure. It makes lovers endure.

You fought and fought. Always in your special way. Volume level never exceeding 6 or 7—that ten-second junior tantrum in the car (a 7.5, tops) should have incited some natural direct aggression; instead, it exposed both combatants as what they really were. Paper bears. All bluff, no bite. Retreating into the alders. Measuring vulnerabilities. The bear you can't see—that's the man-eater.

You fought about the fights, or nonfights. You had nonfights about nonfights.

You outworked her. Outwitted her. Surprised her.

She ate you alive.

Mimi knew a straight jungle fight would be her last. To expose herself would be to expose her every deficit, in terms of strength, skill, experience, wherewithal, and, not least, psychological edge. She'd seen just enough of you to know you'd rip her to pieces, and knew the only way she could win this fight was to not fight it.

Many challengers were stronger; none were nimbler, quicker, zippier. Mobility and elusiveness: her natural gifts. Can't kill what you can't catch. Endurance—another gift—sealed her greatness. Not for nothing, all that skittering and running and jogging. She ran when you called her on one of her half lies. Or broken promises. Or childish snits. She ran to kill.

Mimi, when cornered, responded in one of two ways. Most times, she simply made herself smaller. This made you hesitate. *All she really needs is a little warm milk and kibble.*

In tougher cases, she played dead. As if the wrath had finally proven too much. *I'm just so tired of apologizing.* This prompted you to retreat, for fear of being the bloodthirsty 25th Grizzly, cannibalizing a warm corpse.

Only under the most extreme circumstances, after having exhausted all other options, did she go on the attack. Once, a day after you fetched her at the airport, came word that you had to head east for some family business. Mimi, sensing your anxiety, offered to accompany you—a gesture appreciated but declined. Awkward time to introduce the girl-friend. "Back in two days," you said. "Just need you to be here then."

"Don't worry," she said. "I'll be here."

Or not. She'd flown home, after manufacturing some half-baked excuse about work meetings. In fact, she couldn't bear waiting around in Los Angeles. Made her antsy. Or something.

Cornered, do-or-die, Mimi did as she always did in dire situations. "When I was in San Francisco," she said, during a late-night call, "you weren't there for me!"

"Whuh?" you'd said. "Last February?"

"You weren't there for me."

Because you'd broken up a week prior. Because she'd done then exactly as she was doing now.

"We both know you fucked up," you said. "We both know you're trying to flip the subject."

"I can't take it," she said. "You're always angry."

"And she strikes again!"

"See? Angry!"

"See? That's why I'm angry! You do something that would piss off *anyone!* Then you say, 'The real problem is, you're just an angry person!'"

"Can't talk about this anymore."

"The next thing you say."

"Don't be mean."

That she was full of shit didn't make her entirely wrong. Adderall was merely the devil's helper. Mimi's bad habit, short attention span, and immaturity were complimented by your deep-rooted impatience, aloofness, and immaturity. Ditto the passive-aggressive silences and strained conversations about nothing. The more Mimi exploited your vulnerabilities, the angrier you got. Pin the blame on the donkey.

"She runs to duck accountability," Five said. "Also to make you feel bad, chase her, and say 'Didn't mean to hurt you. I love you.' Basically, it's third grade."

"Enough," you said. "Chase is over."

Chase continued. Drawing you out. Wearing you down.

"The thrill of the chase?" Five said.

"Doesn't feel thrilling," you said.

"Then why do it?"

"I . . . It's complicated."

"Is it?"

"Yes. No. I dunno."

"Maybe it's easier to chase something you know won't work out than to deal with something that might."

"So they say."

"Do you think Mimi's your one and only?"

Long silence. The inspection of shoelaces.

Skipped the next two appointments.

"It's hard when you love somebody," Daniel said. "But it's harder to stay in a bad relationship."

"Daniel's being diplomatic," Ben said. "You're both a little bit crazy. I'm sorry, because I know you love her. But that's just too much crazy. So—and I say this in the most loving way —*enough already*."

Lizz and Paula trod lightly during reality-TV night at Lizz's apartment (*The Bachelor: Rome,* featuring an obscure Italian prince, Lorenzo Borghesi, who owned a line of skin-care products for pets). "Love the photo of Mimi on your desk," Lizz said. "She's so cute."

"She drives me crazy," you said.

"I want her clothes," Paula said.

"I've got nothing at all against Mimi," Lizz said.

"I do—"

"But there's no way you can change her. Literally *none*."

"I know," you said.

"And, unless she changes on her own, you'll never be happy in this relationship."

"I know."

Three times you stopped the madness. Three times you scurried back for more, the last instance occurring after you'd finally persuaded Mimi that perhaps the conflicts might best be adjudicated by a dispassionate third party. A professional of her choosing. "Plenty to go around," said the Beverly Hills Shrink. "But, Mimi, most of the low-hanging fruit seems to be on your tree."

Surprisingly anticlimactic.

"Okay," Mimi said.

One minute you've got it all figured out; the next, you're a stack of bones in a godforsaken wilderness. Bleached by the sun. Picked clean.

PART TWO

CHAPTER SEVEN

You are an amnesiac. A person with impaired memory. In a major way. As in "Where are my pants?" and "What the hell am I doing in Yorba Linda?" As in today is June 15, 2008, and yesterday was January 15, 2007.

As in "Where'd my fucking life go?" and "I did *what? When?*"

You are a reporter. A gatherer and disseminator of facts. A drive-thru historian.

The Amnesiac Reporter.

First reaction? Script idea. High-concept. Suits eat that shit up.

Second reaction? Feels too TV. Too "Jennifer Love Hewitt *is* The Amnesiac Reporter."

Third reaction? Open the Tops Report's Notebook (4 x 8). Grab the Olympus tape recorder.

Report, Amnesiac.

In a way, you felt, this was journalism as it was meant to be.

Who? What? Where? When? Why? All that j-school crap. Second nature.

And so you turn on my tape recorder and defer to the reliable sources who got you through The Summer of Electricity. No puff piece, this one. After twenty years as a profiler, you finally see what it's like to be the profilee.

This is a reporter's brain on electroshock.

You identified as your home office the eight-by-ten sweatbox in which you now sat, flanked by twin desks crammed with computer equipment and sundries. The framed photograph of your parents (beaming, anniversary) was a no-brainer. You identified the Detroit Tiger bobblehead (gift from your brother David), the autographed 1959 Al Kaline baseball card (from David and Peter), and the bottle of 1991 Steven Seagal cabernet sauvignon (from the boss). You connected various finger paintings to the appropriate children. And you grasped the derivation and import of two yellowed newspaper clippings ("Bruno Zehnder, Photographer, 52, Is Dead"; "Alaska: Bear Expert Killed") and two photographs (penguins, bears).

You remained cognizant of the many tips and instructions you'd received from the whoziwhatzits at Cedars-Sinai:

"Some patients adapt easily."

"Amnesia fades gradually."

"Others do not adapt easily."

You adapted. Because you *remembered* to do so. Because you remembered to remember. Taped to your computer, on a separate stickypad, was a reminder about reminders:

"Make to-do lists."

"Carry a notepad."

"Keep a journal."

"Carry phone numbers."

"Study photographs."

Photograph one: the tree full of goats. At first, you think, "Why in holy hell do I have a photograph of six goats standing high atop a tree?" Then, on the back of the photo, you notice the word *Moroc.* Which evokes a trip to Morocco. Which evokes Rachel, the girlfriend with whom you took the trip. Caramel skin and hair. Surfer's looks and carriage. The only person you'd ever known, aside from your dad, who had zero vanity. Could quote Rumi while rolling a joint in the dark but couldn't find mittens lying in plain sight. Obsessed with tiny plastic pellets that litter the seas, having been discarded during the manufacture or transport of plastic household products.

"Nurdle," she called you.

Morocco. The dream destination ever since Dad gave you *The Sheltering Sky,* Paul Bowles's bizarro love story set in and around the North African desert, circa 1940s: the place and time of his first journey outside Detroit, as a twenty-year-old army grunt en route to the Italian front.

Morocco. Where goats climb trees. Where you found love. Where . . .

Blank.

Ah, well. Probably her fault.

Photograph two: (1) Dad reading *The New York Times* in the living room. Half acknowledging the camera, in his half-sheepish way, with that signature gap between his two top front teeth. His affront to vanity. Lean and lanky as ever, in his worn shorts and sneakers. The plainest clothing possible, in keeping with his contempt for designer labels and logos (and for those who wear them). Only a few signs of wear and tear. Arms a bit more wiry than usual. Skin tone, normally a deep olive, a shade paler. But still. The calves of teenage decathlete— the dividends of a life spent in perpetual motion. The youngest eighty-nine-year-old on earth.

You scribbled a note: "Call home tonite."

At the center of your desk, between the bobblehead and the cabernet Seagal, sat a stainless steel jar. The jar held all your best stolen pens—the A-list pens, liberated from the biggest desks in Hollywood. You remembered, even now, that a studio's financial strength could best be gauged via its choice of writing implements; the executive with a Bic Round Stic is the executive who will never buy your script.

Amid all the Staedtler Liquid Points and Sanford Uni-ball

Micros—personal favorites, along with Uni-ball Signos—loomed a pink plastic spoon. Tallest of the group. Dead center. Direct line of vision. Hugging the spoon's neck was a grinning plastic frog, an inch tall. The frog wore an orange and red cap, blue sneakers, and a yellow T-shirt with red lettering: "Dig 'Em." He had oversize, lidless eyes. They glowed yellow.

Amnesia, you decided, was underrated.

Memory, after all, was just a euphemism for *needless complication,* for *wide load;* it defied nature and evolution. Stymied personal growth. To regain it was to die faster.

But what could you do? The art of amnesia maintenance required props, teamwork. Couldn't drop an anvil on your own head. Couldn't drive into a light pole. Not since the friends and the girlfriend commandeered the car keys. Now that The Procedure was over and done with, and you were under house arrest for crimes unknown, the Days Of Ignorant Bliss were but a memory.

You sat there on this warm day, in the sweatbox, going nowhere. Except in your mind, which was going backward, making up for lost time—quite a bit of it, according to the blue sticky note you'd taped to your computer screen: "Procedure Day One—3/07/08." Three months ago, give or take. The interim remained a big fat blank, for the most part, but in a favorite-sweatshirt kind of way—the opposite of *regret* being *forget*. Actually, come to think of it, a long stretch preceding the interim wasn't exactly popping, either. Upwards of a year.

Ignorance was a blessing. Memory was a bitch.

The longer you sat there, staring blankly at the frog, the clammier you felt. The feeling had been there all afternoon, in a subtle sort of way; it felt barometric, as if the house had been gliding through different time zones, at different altitudes. Every now and again, you'd stop what you were doing and steal a peek around—the way nervous airline passengers do. Something *was* changing, somehow. But since nobody else seemed to mind, and since the earth continued spinning on its axis, there was little reason to dwell. The physical sensations—the queasy stomach, the cold sweat—were hardly unique. You were no stranger to the clam.

Better to keep busy. Finish what you started.

Lollipop Girl: Lucy.

A plastic frog, to a top-tier amnesiac, is a plastic frog.

A plastic frog, to you, was Dig 'Em.

And Dig 'Em was Lucy's frog.

And Lucy was Caitlin's daughter.

And Caitlin was your girlfriend.

Wasn't she?

Wait. Think. Rewind.

Caitlin. Caitlin.

Of course. You first met her in November 2001, shortly after the 9/11 disaster—the scar beneath your eye was still visible. Caitlin was the woman who took in limping stray dogs. Ben had masterminded the date, after meeting her through a mutual friend of theirs.

"I need you to know I found the girl," he told you.

"Oh, god," you said.

"I promise you'll like her. Couldn't be easier to get along with. Couldn't be more sane. Owns a restaurant—"

"But—"

"And, yes, very pretty."

"But—"

"And you know I know what I'm talking about. I sort of want her myself."

"Be my guest," Daniel said.

"Thanks," you said to Ben. "I'll think about it."

"Do not change the subject," Ben said.

"It's just . . . I'm weird. Even I don't know who I'd like."

"I know you better than you know yourself."

This became evident during your opening phone call to Caitlin, which for days you had dreaded and delayed. To call a friend, or a potential interview subject, demanded all the fortitude you could summon; to call a woman, blind, was to watch yourself die. *Gee, I hope my name rings a bell. No, actually, I'm Daniel's other friend.* With Caitlin, however, the pain ceased immediately. There was an easy grace to her manner, befitting her Midwestern roots (neighborly) and her Southern Californian lifestyle (breezy). She smelled like vacation.

"Oh, hey!" she said. "How are ya?"

Rather than let you fumble about, in an effort to appear restaurant literate, she suggested the place and time, made sure you didn't mind picking her up, and closed by saying "I really hope you like my dogs." To arrive at her house, in West Hollywood, was to be swamped by her yowling pack of rejects, among them a three-legged terrier and a pit bull scarred with old cigarette burns. Caitlin loved the strays.

Her appearance matched both her manner and Ben's sales pitch. She was tall and slender, in her Levi's and solid navy sweater. Her beach-blond hair flowed nearly to her waist, in waves, and required no maintenance. Her general air of vitality, punctuated by a big white smile, suggested a lifetime spent playing beach volleyball in Norway.

She looked you square in the eyes and shook hands with a bona fide *shake*, in the damn-glad-to-meet-ya way of yore. This reflected both who she was and what she did. After college back East, she had returned to Los Angeles, to make her bones in the culinary business. She trained at a four-star restaurant of the California nouvelle variety, rising from hostess to sommelier before opening her own place, in 2001. The early reviews were good; business, brisk.

But the date wouldn't be there. "God, no," she said. "I'm nowhere near that confident." Instead she took you to the first restaurant, taking care of everything. She was codependent in the good way. "Tell me if you mind *any* of this," she said. "I just want you to enjoy yourself."

"Will do," you said.

She evinced, at all times, a deadpan mirth. An unruffled self-awareness. "Lettuce in my teeth," she said, flatly. "I know there's lettuce between my teeth."

She checked. There was.

"Now I'm gonna take out the lettuce from my teeth," she said. "Then we're gonna pretend it never happened."

It was the first time, post-9/11, that you felt comfortable in the presence of a person outside the core four. A California girl with Midwestern values. Worldly but homey. Forthright but calm.

"Michigan, huh?" she said. "Like college football?"

"Do *you*?" you said.

"My family's from Columbus, Ohio."

The air deadened.

"I was deciding whether to let you kiss me good night," she said. "But now that's out the window."

You thanked Ben first thing in the morning, somewhat grudgingly.

"Must be lonely being so much smarter than everyone else," you said.

"Little bit," he said.

"This is amazing," Daniel said. "I'm so happy."

"Me, too," Ben said. "Now don't fuck it up."

There was laughter. Plans were made.

Then you fucked it up.

Then she moved East. For five years.

Then she moved back, in April.

With a three-year-old girl, Lucy.

And Lucy's toy frog, Dig 'Em.

And you loved them both.

And now they were gone.

Because you fucked it up.

. Again.

Somehow.

They say the worst moment in an amnesiac's life is the moment he remembers what he lost. But that's bullshit. The worst moment is when he *can't* remember what he lost.

At this point, only two options remain. The first required you to blow your brains out. The second, which you preferred, and which suited your skill set, required you to do what you were paid to do. Find your subject. Be a servant of his energy. Make his life your life.

All you knew for certain, in the meantime, was that something had gone terribly wrong, and that you had no one to blame but yourself.

CHAPTER EIGHT

Y ou!

*Looking like I might not get to see you to say good-bye.
That sucks, 'cause you are one of my favorite patients (which
I suppose is not saying much, since we are @ a mental hospital, ha-ha). No, but seriously, you are awesome. Best of
luck with staying well, your writing, being the cool uncle
guy, and just generally kicking it in L.A. Try to stay away
from Jamie Foxx. If you're ever in town, give me a holler.*

All my best, you.

Liza

One full page, handwritten. Girly swooshes, in bright orange magic
marker.

Also included, at bottom, in blue ink: the writer's phone number
and email address.

No surname. No date. No letterhead. No envelope.

No clue.

The letter just presented itself, atop a stack of unopened mail.
Couldn't be a long-forgotten missive from the 9/11 romper-room adven-
ture. The vignettes referenced the years 2004 and 2006. When Jamie
Foxx was nobody.

At the computer, you searched your email program for a "Liza." None. Then you Googled her email address.

The address belonged to a student at a small college in New England. But the school's website listed only the woman's surname and field of study. Literature.

Google took it from there, matching the woman's full name to a handful of articles published a few years earlier, in a newspaper in suburban Chicago. Liza, at the time, had been high school royalty, serving as both valedictorian and head cheerleader. The accompanying photos revealed a dimpled beauty with ivory skin, high cheekbones, and lush blond hair.

And a total stranger. This was discomfiting, adding specters of shame and fear to an already tenuous position, memorywise: the existential no-man's-land inhabited by the semiamnesiac, who remembers just enough to know he's a guy who can't remember many or most things. (*I forget, therefore I am*—riddle me this, Frenchman.) The natural desire, at this point, was to fill in the blanks, based on a series of assumptions, based on the scant information at hand. Letters from a dewy ex-cheerleader would have sparked some promising scenarios—a creative-writing workshop gone Bacchus, a lost weekend at Burning Man—were it not for the part about being @ a mental hospital.

The latter two words, when entered into your email search program (both individually and as a pair), produced way too many hits; other key words and phrases ("mental cheerleader," "mental valedictorian") tanked. "Jamie Foxx" produced a single email, in which an acquaintance of yours had referenced *Booty Call*—

Jamie Foxx.

Inklings. Flickers of . . . something. A stoop. At night. Outside. Chill. Blustery.

Booty Call. Ray.

Jarhead.

Laptop. Night.

Stoop. Talking.

Eyes. Face. Young.

Her.

Wait—

Fragments of fragments. A brown wooden desk. A TV. A skinny man in a yellow sweater. The smell of soggy leaves.

Leaves. Stoop. Night.

Your PowerBook housed seven downloaded movies, among them two documentaries (*Grizzly Man* and *March of the Penguins*) and five features (*Sexy Beast, The Insider, Blood Simple, The Thin Red Line, Jarhead*). The latter had last been viewed on November 15, at 8:04 P.M. Six months ago. Halfway through the lost year.

Of the twenty-four emails you had received on the night in question, only Caitlin's offered a compelling subject-line:

LUCY JUST WENT PEE IN THE POTTY!!!!!!!!!!!!!!!!

The email itself contained no text—some landmarks speak for themselves—but arrived concurrent with another one. You had first emailed her a photograph of a potted orchid. The orchid, along with an antique mirror and a Coke bottle, sat atop a lacquered, mahogany-colored dresser. The mirror reflected, in part, a bedroom painted off-white, a wall adorned with some sort of framed artwork (a pencil drawing, perhaps), and a made bed with white linens and a headboard that matched the dresser.

Bed. Mahogany.

Bed, mahogany. Blanket, blue.

This somber tableau, as represented in the iPhoto, brought to mind nothing beyond your general distaste for bed-and-breakfasts.

Next came a series of emails with your old friend Mark, a political reporter in Washington.

On November 15, 2007, at 1:07 P.M., Mark wrote:

I'd love to come visit you. How regimented are things there? I could fly up in the morning and get you the hell out of that place for a while. We could just watch the Michigan–Ohio State game somewhere—I'm guessing The Pavilion doesn't have Direct TV.

Google, first hit:

The Pavilion offers distinct, highly structured inpatient and partial hospitalization programs for the treatment of alcohol, drug, and psychiatric problems.

THE PAVILION
809 W. CHURCH STREET
CHAMPAIGN, IL 61820

Email archives: "Pavilion rehab."
Nothing.
"Pavilion OD."
Ibid.
"Pavilion drugs."
Nothing.
Scrambling around the office, looking for hard evidence. Rummaging the green storage shelves overhead; rifling the gunmetal-gray cabinet below. A sea of dog-eared news clippings ("Bear Advocate Killed By Bear"), research materials ("Map To Where Bruno's Body Was Found"), and movie scripts scattered amid the largely pristine booty

acquired during The Adderall Gold Rush: three laptop cases, two pairs of Bose headphones (one unopened), Harman Kardon minispeakers, two Apple keyboards, three brands of mice, plus various and sundry mouse pads, iPods, iPod cases, adapters, cameras, and Macwhatnots— all tangled in a vast series of power cords, extension cords, headphone cords, and stiff black tentacles of unknown origin.

Somewhere amid this filing system lay your personal papers, crinkled and scattered: letters, deeds, and receipts; documents financial, legal, medical. A summary of your stomach surgery beneath the warranty for your refrigerator; a May 2004 bank statement within the pages of one of your old *VF* covers ("Who Wouldn't Want to be GEORGE CLOONEY"). Then, atop a stack of papers sandwiched by the manuals for your blender and microwave, a swooshy signature: "Liza."

> *Thanks for your consideration, advice, company, etc. It*
> *would be amazing if you could read this. I added a few*
> *things here at McLean.*
> —*Liza*

Memories of memories. That's what it boiled down to, pretty much. That was the best-case scenario. The past year was mostly gone. The further back you went, Before Procedure, memory improved commensurately. Variable clouds. Limited visibility.

And so it began.

According to multiple sources, you arrived at LAX on the morning of November 12, 2007, and boarded a JetBlue flight bound for Boston Logan. You were dropped off by Ben, who had spent the car ride gently praising and prodding. "I need you to know I'm proud of you," he said. "And I need you to take full advantage of this."

A nod.

You were retrieved in Boston by a stranger with a quiet smile and a makeshift placard bearing your surname. He gestured at the black duffel hanging from your shoulder, then commandeered it. "What I'm here for," he said. "Los Angeles—bet that's one long, tiring trip."

A nod.

The drive to your hotel took twenty-five minutes, most of which were spent negotiating a mile of westbound traffic just beyond the airport, in East Boston. After forcing a few random questions about Kennedys, in order to preclude awkward silences, you fell silent. Boston Harbor was a soothing distraction, a sparkly blue green, until the sun fell from the sky, all city sounds dropped out, and you entered the long, dark tunnel.

The tunnel was concerning in a multitude of ways; it occurred to you that, had nature wanted us to force our way through seas and mountains, she wouldn't have put seas or mountains there; that this explained why everyone hates tunnels; and that this fear was to be nurtured, because it was a natural fear. Of nature. Beware: woman scorned. Don't touch penguins. Don't feed bears. Don't tunnel.

"Sorry?" the driver said.

"The heat," you said. "Could you turn it down?"

"The heat's not on. Want air-condition—"

"What's this tunnel?"

"Called the—"

"How long is it?"

"In length?"

"In *minutes*."

He gestured toward a pinpoint glimmer ahead.

"Still warm?" he asked.

"Fine," you said.

You spent the night at a hotel in Cambridge. There, seated on the bed, you scrolled the list of movies stored in your laptop. You'd watched all of them, backward and forward. Except one. The documentary *March of the Penguins* was, in addition to a worldwide smash, pure evil. A good chunk of the footage used in the film—the money shots, emperorwise—had originally been shot as "B-roll"—background footage—for your sweeping penguin epic, *Emperor Zehnder*. The world was supposed be cheering March of Richard Gere's Penguins. For two years the star had endeavored to play Bruno—studio executives tended to share one big reservation about the project: "Penguins?"

Finally, just four weeks before the first scheduled day of filming, Gere became his character. He bolted, never to be heard from again. The production died; everyone put penguins out of their minds. Except for the guys who'd shot the B-roll. Two years later, penguins were getting Oscar buzz and merchandising tie-ins, thanks to your brain-child and Morgan Freeman's voice:

> *For millions of years, they have made their home on the darkest, driest, windiest continent on earth. And they have done so pretty much alone. So, in some ways, this is a story of survival. A tale of life over death. But it's more than that, really. It's a story about love.*

Fucking Hollywood.

In the morning, a second stranger drove you four miles west, to the town of Belmont. The car approached a stately, well-groomed campus that suggested a small New England girl's college, circa 1957; it was dotted by a couple dozen houses and buildings of various styles (Tudor, colonial), sizes (standard to mansions), and eras (1800s to contemporary) but with a uniting theme: old-school blue blood elegance. Grounds by Frederick Law Olmstead, designer of Central Park. One of the houses, a two-story red-brick colonial, matched a photo in the brochure, which you clutched firmly:

THE PAVILION

at McLean Hospital

is a private-pay residence for adults seeking highly specialized, comprehensive psychiatric evaluation and treatment. Clinicians at The Pavilion excel at caring for individuals whose illnesses are diagnostically complex or who have not responded to previous treatments.

McLean Hospital

A HARVARD MEDICAL SCHOOL AFFILIATE

Ranked first among the nation's freestanding psychiatric hospitals . . .

U.S. NEWS & WORLD REPORT

Exiting the car, you passed through the four white pillars astride the Pavilion's modest front porch. The interior, in keeping with the McLean style, was warm, demure, a tad granny's house. Twelve-foot ceilings and pastel walls. Modest library with old trade paperbacks and a large dining room with fireplace and eight-seat table. All those old mahogany furnishings. That fusty Old New England Smell.

In short order, you were greeted by Dr. Six, a genial fellow with wire-rim glasses and the tweedy authority of the Harvard professor he was. Six would be, in essence, the head coach, overseeing your progression through a gauntlet of assistant coaches and specialists—from neurologists to nutritionists—who would be handling the on-field duties, alongside a talk therapist you'd see most every day.

The Pavilion was the Hong Kong of McLean. The larger body was mostly accessible to the public; it was Massachusetts General Hospital for mentals, in the only state decent enough to provide universal health care. Pressures being what they were, McLean welcomed additional revenue streams. Hence the Pavilion, where the patient with everything would receive commensurate treatment, psychiatrywise.

Minimum stay: fourteen days. Cost per same: forty thousand dollars. Payment in advance, in full. Checks accepted; insurance, not.

It was by far the largest lump-sum hit you'd ever taken (excluding the down payment on your house, which amounted to an investment). Evidently, though, you were happy to pay it, despite the fact that Cedars was right around the corner; that UCLA was Five's hospital of choice; and that both *accepted insurance*. Also concerning: "The Pavilion" rang not a single bell, and "McLean" was only nominally familiar. These issues would require further investigation, once you dealt with a more pressing concern.

The accommodations.

"Everything okay so far?" Six asked.

"Fine."

"Tired?"

"Fine."

History of Present Illness: Patient is self-referred within the context of an extended history of depressive illness. He is concerned about an approximately one- to two-year worsening of fatigue, loss of concentration and energy, and an inability to engage in creative pursuits. He has been concerned that he might be suffering from a degenerative neurologic illness.

At the time of his Pavilion admission, he presented as a well-dressed and groomed gentleman who showed no agitation, psychomotor retardation, tics, or tremors. He made good eye contact and spoke a bit softly. He described a syndrome of depression with hopelessness, but not suicidality. He acknowledged significant lethargy, severe sleep disturbance, and difficulty concentrating. He denied obsessions, compulsions, delusions, or hallucinosis, was cognitively grossly unimpaired, and appeared to be of superior intelligence. His insight and judgment were not limited.

By noon you were blinking up at your attending therapist, Dr. Seven. She was dark haired, late forties, and evoked a subset of East Coast Jewess you'd first come across in Ann Arbor. The anti-Jap. Equally laid-back, no-bullshit, and irony-rich. Junk bond dad. Socialist mom.

"Has therapy helped?" Seven asked.

"Kinda soon to tell," you said.

She smiled. Sort of.

"Yes and no," you said.

"What's that mean?" she said.

"Talking's better than not. Meds, too. But . . ."

"You still feel like crap. And can't write."

Nod.

"If there's an underlying neurological problem, we'll find it," she said. "Meantime, let's see what talking can do."

You recited, in seamless fashion, the standard chronology. Born anxious, shy, self-conscious. Loving family, friends. Things get better. Things fell apart. Isolation and rumination, shrinks and meds, Mimi and Rachel.

Seven nodded, wrote something down. "Sounds like you've thought this through," she said. "Sounds pretty thorough." She leaned forward and asked, "What's been your main frustration with therapy?"

"It hasn't cured me."

"It isn't an antibiotic. You know that?"

Nod.

"How aggressively have you participated in therapy?"

"I go regularly. Mostly. Pretty much."

"Great. But I'm asking about your degree of participation—how often you've felt comfortable enough to open up and say anything."

"I try to be honest."

"I'm sure. But let's see how far we can go. I'm gonna push you a little, okay? Might make you uncomfortable at times. But if you don't want that, we won't get very far."

"I actually like being pushed."

"Really? Who pushes you?"

"My friends. Ben, Lizz—"

"Hard?"

"No."

"How about your therapist?"

"Not really."

"Have you raised this issue with her?"

Shrug.

"Interesting. Coming from a reporter."

"That's different. Clinical. And I'm not a confrontational reporter."

"Then how'd you get to where you are?"

"Two kinds of reporters. There's the confrontational ones, who beat stuff out of people. And there's the friendly ones, who put people at ease, gain their trust, and dance around the subject until they get what they need. I'm the second kind. The nice guy. Honey. Bees."

"Well, you do seem very nice."

"Thanks."

"Nice gets you so far." She nodded. "Great most of the time. But for people struggling with anxiety and depression, it can be a sign of something else. And I think you know where I'm going with this."

"A wall. Minimizes risk. Keeps shit at bay."

"Does the pattern apply to you?"

"Every second."

"Does it help?"

"Sometimes. Turns down the noise."

"What happens most times?"

"Noise comes back. Or never leaves."

There was a pause.

"What are you keeping at bay?"

"People."

"All people or specific types?"

"All but a few."

"Tell me about the few."

"They know me. They like me."

"You're not self-conscious around them?"

"And not bored."

"Most people bore you?"

"To death."

"How can you be interested in them if you don't know them?"

"I manage to find plenty of interesting friends."

"Yet you're often bored?"

A nod. She scanned your admission summary.

"And there's a 'sort of' girlfriend," she said. "What's the story there?"

Things got quiet.

Glimmers of Caitlin:

Seated in the bar of her favorite local dinner place, a glorified fish shack overlooking the Pacific. Back in her hometown, just south of Los Angeles, in one of those tidy sea-and-tee communities where everyone smelled like warm laundry and died of melanoma. Spring 2007, a year removed from Hurricane Mimi.

The two of you rehashed the past five years over broiled trout. Her career change. The eastward migration, to start fresh. The fiancé-turned-ex-fiancé. The Decision.

"Best decision I've ever made," she said.

Lucy. Just turned two.

Photos, then and now. Same golden tendrils. Same Master Race skin, nose. Same damn-glad-to-meet-ya smile.

Girls From Brazil.

"She's spectacular," Caitlin said.

"Seems redundant," you said. "Was her father the secret twin brother you kept in the basement?"

She half laughed.

"Sorry," you said. "Bad joke——"

"No," she said. "Just thinking. Can't remember if you're a kid person."

"I love kids."

In principle. On TV.

"Kids love kids," Caitlin said. Immediately, she covered her mouth and loosed a gasp of half-feigned outrage. That was one of her things; it signaled that a person devoid of mean-spiritedness could neverthe-less appreciate its charms. "I meant it in the nice way," she said.

"Shouldn't have," you said.

"Oh, stop it."

"You can say it. I was childish."

"Boyish. Let's call it that."

"You can call me an asshole, too. Let it out."

She grinned. Sheepish.

"No need. Already did. Plenty."

A wash of relief.

"You know I'm sorry," you said.

"You didn't do anything *wrong*," she said, and smiled. "Just stupid."

"So you don't hate me?"

"I never hated you. Wanted to strangle you, maybe. But you've never been anything but nice to me."

"Likewise."

"That's why we're here now. And why you'll be picking up the check."

"So, then. Do I get to meet Lucy?"

She thought about that.

"You'll need to bring cupcakes," she said.

Lucy. A tough sell, at first. Legs a little wobbly, eyes level with your kneecaps, the wee mop-top inspected every inch of you. This went on for some time, in silence.

"Can't fool her," Caitlin said. "Don't even try."

While Lucy inspected the gift you'd presented, a few thoughts occurred to you. The first thought was that, were you to split the difference between mother and daughter, you would now be standing across from Kirsten Dunst on prom night. The next thought was that, in the event that Lucy rejected the offering, you would have no shot with Caitlin. The next thought was that, in addition to your general need to be liked, there was a sudden and burning need to be Lucy's father.

"*Cupkay,*" she said.

By early summer, a structure was in place. Once a week, you made the seventy-minute drive to see Caitlin A and B, if only for a quick dinner before the latter's bedtime; they had neither the time nor space for much else. They were temporarily living with Caitlin's parents, who pitched in with child care while Caitlin saved to buy a house. Rather than return to her beloved foodie world—late nights and motherhood didn't match—she earned a modest wage at a nonprofit organization. She raised money on behalf of physically disabled people. She was selfish that way.

Occasionally she and Lucy stole twenty-four hours at your house; most were spent in the backyard, as Lucy variously ran in circles, drew in her Mess-Free Enchanted Tales Coloring Pad, and inquired as to whether it would be possible to ride horshees or go wimming. She had a tendency to climb you. She had a tendency to be idealized. A ready-made child, minus the muss and fuss. Spoon already included.

The pace proved agreeable to you, in the slow-and-steady-wins-the-race sense—the *Sid and Nancy* days were over. The situation gave you something to look forward to, while also affording you ample opportunity to fall apart.

The Fear returned.

By August, you were halfway gone, holing up for days at a time. Diet limited to oranges, apples, and the occasional pizza. Sleep schedule staggered: thirteen hours one night, two the next. Communications restricted to email only. Unless or until one of the friends threatened to come over—in which case, you were all ears.

The parameters proved especially challenging for Daniel. Together you were writing on a tight deadline, in advance of the looming writers' strike; if you didn't hand in the script soon, you wouldn't get paid till god only knew.

But you were producing, at best, one page per day. Concentration was an issue. You'd write, "The water was warm," and suddenly a shower seemed like a good idea. Then maybe a nap. Couldn't be expected to write till you were fully rested. Then again, what if you overslept? You'd be awake all night, worrying about how you wouldn't be able to concentrate tomorrow. Then you'd lose another day. Then Daniel would get even more pissed off, say, "I can't carry your sorry ass any longer," and leave you for a better partner. And everybody would find out. And there goes the income, then the mortgage and medical benefits. And, boy, you'll really be catnip to the ladies then.

Other times, you overconcentrated. That was the Adderall talking. *The water was warm. The water felt warm. It was warm water. They were warm waters.* Wait. *It* or *they*? Wait. Stop. The words needed to be evenly spaced. Lines and paragraphs required symmetry. If the text didn't sit right, geometrically, words had to be added or deleted until squared. No single-word lines. No orphans.

One sentence, four hours.

"I've got a few questions," Daniel said, daily, via voicemail. "Call me."

"Where are you?" read his follow-up emails. "Are you okay? Need anything?"

"Fine, thanks," read yours. "Just under the weather. I'll call soon."

Eventually.

He never scolded you. Never complained. But the strain in his voice was evident. Naturally, this made you even more petulant than you already were.

"I've got some thoughts about act two," he would say.

"Uh-huh," you would grunt.

"What would you think about an underwater sequence?"

"I'll think about it."

Or not.

Doug called. Doug emailed.

"How's the story coming?" he asked.

"Almost done," you said. "Gotta run."

Three days, one paragraph.

Caitlin, by now, was a screen name.

On Aug 22, 2007, at 9:44 P.M., penguinman@yahoo.com wrote:
Need a little time, please.

On Aug 23, 2007, at 12:52 P.M., CaitLucy@aol.com wrote:
I know what happens when you say you "need time," Ned.
I'm saying I'm not holding my breath for you.

On Aug 24, 2007, at 11:48 A.M., penguinman@yahoo.com wrote:
I think you're being a bit provocative and unfair to me.

You wanted her to stay and leave you alone—to be a girlfriend by proxy. The reasons had long since been established in therapy:

1. You were still a child.
2. You still feared conflict.
3. Caitlin consistently failed to be as insane as Mimi, and therefore left you with nothing to be enraged about.
4. There was no girlfriend so flawless as the one in your head.
5. The girlfriend who couldn't see you up close was the girlfriend who couldn't see the sad, sick mess you'd become.

That Caitlin stayed the course revealed that she was, at times, too benevolent for her own good. Three-legged dogs. Crippled patients. And you.

"I'm not healthy enough to be a boyfriend," you said.

"I'll help you get better," she said.

By fall, you were underground. When returning your parents' increasingly anxious calls from Michigan, you did so at times when you were most likely to get their machine; sometimes, if one of them actually picked up, you hung up. Caitlin, though technically still in the picture, proved no match for Jade, Jenni, Tauny, Stephy, Sheena, DeAnna—just a few of the twenty-five bachelorettes vying for love every Monday night on *The Bachelor* (ABC 9:00 P.M.). Though consumed by reality TV in general (*The Real World, The Hills*), you viewed *The Bachelor* as the alpha grizzly. Ah, to be thirty-five-year-old Brad Womack, a successful, self-made entrepreneur from Austin, Texas, with only one goal left to accomplish: finding his soul mate.

The weed helped. Where once you had been a garden-variety stoner, a weekend warrior, now you were all-in. Where once weed was weed, now there was *sativa* and *indica*, Afghan Goo and OG Purple Kush—all stored in an airtight container, beside the vaporizer, the bong, two pipes, a pile of rolling papers, and a grinder in the shape of a billiard ball. And it was all legal, thanks to your medical-marijuana card, obtained from a pleasant Indian doctor who accepted walk-ins, and whose office abutted a Laundromat. Your daily intake of weed, combined with the reality programming and the lack of direct human contact, made weeks pass like days. When you had something to say, the cats proved terrific listeners.

Finally, on a Tuesday morning in early November, you lay on the kitchen floor, peering up at a ceiling turned liquid, while clutching a brownie in one hand and the phone in another. You had called one of your college buddies. "Jim," you said, "I'm freaking out."

Two hours later, after Jim talked you back to earth, you emailed Ben and Daniel:

Guys: I need to ask a favor. I've not been doing well of late. Purely as a precaution—I'm in no danger or anything—I need you to call a certain hospital and see if they have any vacancy right now.

After a few days at the Pavilion, a square-jawed doctor with thick black eyebrows walked you through the results of your blood test. He pointed to a series of graph lines that measured blood sugar, hormones, and so forth. Then he pointed to the longest line. "That," he said, "is cannabis."

His recommendation that you receive substance-abuse counseling was received poorly. "Marijuana makes the withdrawn more withdrawn," the doctor said. "It ends up causing more anxiety than it relieves."

Also: memory problems.

No, you thought. What causes more anxiety is spending thirty thousand dollars a minute in this place. For one thing, your bedroom wasn't anything like the ones in the brochure; it smelled moldy, one of the walls was chipped and water stained, and the mahogany furniture was unsuitable for an Ethan Allen clearance sale. For another thing, the patients were unavoidable. From a series of emails to Lizz and Paula:

It's a little creepy. I don't need a $3,200-a-night motel room. I worried I'm stuck with a bunch of rich old people from Connecticut who burst into tears while eating corn chowder. I'm dreading this.

Four patients are sitting at the dinner table, eating in utter and completely awkward silence. Two are clearly depressed. It's the most excruciating thing I've ever seen.

Patients are singing *Grease* on a karaoke machine. I'm not kidding.

The next week was a neurological orgy. MRI, HDL, EEG, TSU. The stuff you paid for. Some results (high verbal IQ) were better than others (low nonverbal IQ). The latter, highlighted by your colossal inability to stack and sort blocks, validated your F in geometry—you had a "nonverbal learning disability."

Then came the big-picture diagnosis:

"Minor and variable difficulties with executive functioning, particularly efficiency. While these do not appear to be of such a degree to significantly impair his day-to-day functioning, they may be problematic under more challenging circumstances, such as with his work, as he has been experiencing. However, in his current state, efficient cognitive management of large amounts of verbal information may prove challenging."

"Basically," Seven said, "it's the depression."

"That good news or bad?"

"You're not dying of a brain tumor. You'll live a long healthy life." She leaned forward. "The job now is to do that."

A nod.

"And I mean *aggressively*. Every day. That means changing your lifestyle. It means forcing yourself out in the world. It means attacking not just the depression, but the reasons why you're depressed. And that can be very hard and very uncomfortable. And it's your choice."

"Okay," you said. "Thanks."

"And it means stop being so damn polite."

"Got it."

"Are you saying that to placate me or because you mean it?"

"Both, probably."

"Look, you *understand* yourself. You know the story. But, honestly, I've never met someone who understands himself with such detachment."

There was a pause.

"I'm shy," you said.

"Don't be," she said.

That night, after commandeering a nicer room, you took a brief walk around the grounds. Nice place, the Pavilion. Way nicer than UCLA. Grounds designed by Frederick Law Olmstead. Private rooms, flat screens, four shrinks for sixteen patients. No insurance accepted? No problem. What's ten thousand dollars a week to a writer who can't write? And speaking of writers, don't think expense. Think investment. McLean was where unwell writers became Eccentric Geniuses. Without McLean there is no *Bell Jar;* no *Girl, Interrupted.* Think Lowell and Fitzgerald. Sexton and Plath. David Foster Wallace and George W. S. Trow. In conjuring images of the real writers who had preceded you at McLean, you realized you had no idea what any of them had looked like (except maybe Sylvia Plath, who wasn't your idea of fun). When you returned to the Pavilion, a few patients were huddled on the porch, talking about bourbon. The youngest among them introduced herself. This was Liza.

You talked about movies. Los Angeles. Jamie Foxx.

And you talked about Mel Gibson. He was the star for whom you and Daniel had written the screenplay about bikers, a movie that had been green-lit by the studio. Shortly before production began, however, two things happened. Mel decided he would first direct an even bloodier movie, *Apocalypto*. And Mel, during a DUI stop, went apeshit. "Fucking Jews," he shouted, "are responsible for all the wars in the world!" But he later denied that he called a female cop "sugar tits." Mel's blood-alcohol level was only slightly above the legal limit. He later acknowledged that he was, in addition to an alcoholic, a manic-depressive.

At one point, you emailed Lizz and Paula:

Everything is going pretty well, I think. The patients are friendly, nonthreatening. They're two types, more or less. Half are like me. Half are bipolars. Maybe a couple addicts. The bipolars are the most difficult. They just talk and talk and talk. One of them, a college student, getting a little too affectionate, which is sad.

Then you emailed Caitlin a photo of the orchid.

"Prettiest thing here," you wrote. "Other than you."

Then you heard a knock at the door. Nobody was there. Just a package and a note. In girly swooshes.

In one journal entry, Liza recalled one of her first manic phases, marked by cocaine, promiscuity, and mayhem:

"My first memory of my predisposition toward recklessness is skiing in Utah, as a child: The ski instructor told my parents I need to be 'leashed' because I was a menace to myself or others. Since then, on other occasions, I have sprained my neck, cracked open my head, broken an arm and a leg, and gone to the emergency room four times. Now I wash my face, quickly outline my eyes with black liner. I catch a glimpse of my reflection in the mirror. I look evil, like a witch. I will never forgive myself. I am out of control. I am entirely out of control."

Accompanying the text were a series of poems, lyrics, and quotations.

Near one of the songs' third line, you made a single notation, in pencil.

"George," it read.

CHAPTER NINE

No Georges in your life. No emails to or from one. Way too broad for a Google search. The only remaining option, a hard-drive search, unearthed several dozen more reasons why you needed to get out more often ("Former Detroit Piston George Trapp, 53, Dies of Stab Wound").

The modern amnesiac is not without modern problems. Technology makes it ever harder to walk the line between memory loss and convenient memory loss. In this, The Too Much Information Age, inconvenient memories never die.

Steve Jobs is not your friend. Gmail is not your helpmate. Together they retain every ill-advised email, every hysterical letter. Dates, times, gigabytes. An email from a woman. Attached photos of your visit to Cape Town. *South Africa?* Vague recollection of chickens running through a restaurant. None of the woman.

A folder marked *VF* reveals dozens of manuscripts, story ideas, and research materials, all prioritized by size. The fattest folder within this folder contains thirty-eight files, and is labeled "TROW."

Trow. Hmm.

Click open the folder's largest file, a PDF document titled "Ten TROW Text_1G." Helvetica font plus skinny columns equals *VF* galley pages. But a byline search produces nothing besides that resentment you now harbor against all writers who actually write. The article begins:

"He spoke four languages: English, Spanish, Latin, and Trowvian. Although the last was technically English, its larger meaning and contexts were fully understood by only one person: George W. S. Trow, social critic, journalist, satirist, screenwriter, novelist, playwright, fop, snob, populist, iconoclast, bon vivant, loner, Wasp supreme, runaway, and literary mystery man . . ."

Trow, Trow, Trow. Nothing. Crickets.

Onward: Razor-wit star of *The New Yorker,* prone to outlandish statements and hijinks, authors sparkly book, *Within the Context of No Context,* 1980. Star rises, star falls. Author, once a butterfly, now cocoons. Relationships severed. Contact limited to his dog, Duke.

The article cuts to Trow's first hideaway, in Alaska:

"Friends found Trow dazed, incoherent, and extremely ill, physically and mentally. They transported him to McLean Hospital, the famed psychiatric facility in Belmont, Massachusetts. . . . The wealthiest patients stayed in a comfortable private-pay unit called the Pavilion, which today costs $10,000 per week. Trow, like many new patients, immediately wanted out."

Sometimes it all comes back to you.

Evidently, during the months preceding your arrival at the Pavilion, you had produced a lengthy profile of this mysterious writer-guy, this George Whoever He Was Trow. Evidently, he'd made his mark as a magazine writer, first as a satirist, then as a profile writer, then as a first-person essayist, before authoring a book that became semifamous, and placed him, in his late thirties, at the center of a world in which he had everything he desired, professionally and socially.

Then he ran away to hell.

Near the top of the article, you quoted a friend of Trow's named Dick MacIntosh. "I bet you, dollars to doughnuts, that when you're all through with this story, you're going to say, 'It remains a mystery.' George was the ultimate elusive. His story is about the ultimate elusiveness."

———————

The story idea originated with *VF*'s chief copy editor, Peter Devine, who, like many staffers, deemed you unrivaled in the field of Disastrous Missteps By Erratic Fools.

"Perfect assignment," Doug said.

"Maybe," you replied.

"They all can't get eaten by penguins."

"What went wrong with the guy?"

"That's your job."

Two months spent shuttling around the East Coast, chasing down George's friends and colleagues. Initially, the relationship remained purely professional. George, though a fellow magazine writer, had inhabited a gilded but repellant era: the last days of martinis at the Harvard Club and lunch at the Algonquin with "Mr. Shawn" (as *The New Yorker*'s longtime editor, William Shawn, was called). *The New Yorker* was to Harvard, during this period, as the CIA was to Yale. If you were born of that tweedy Cheever bullshit, as George was, you were in.

George's list of friends included "modern" journalists (Hendrik Hertzberg, Jonathan Schell) and literary types (novelist Jamaica Kincaid, filmmaker James Ivory, satirists Michael O'Donoghue and Timothy Mayer). The latter two were the only ones you'd have a beer with, and they were dead. The rest of the list (Diana Vreeland and Brooke Astor; men nicknamed Winty and Ducky) read like a seating chart at a Black and White Funeral.

George William Swift Trow (rhymes with *throw*) Jr. was a blue blood by both design and disposition. Connecticut. Exeter. Harvard. Bow ties and J. Press blazers. He sat at pianos, in black tie, singing "Sad Movies Always Make Me Cry." As a teenager, he bemoaned the fall of the Hapsburg Empire and said things like *"Darling,* you absolutely *must* learn how to mix a *proper* Manhattan." He was a preppy, showy, snotty, gay, pampered, white-glove, bridge-playing, ballroom-dancing, glad-handing little yap-dog from a dark alternate universe.

And yet.

George, it seemed, had been a rather anxious boy, prone to jangled nerves and whirling thoughts. He had trouble sticking with the program, unless the subject *really* interested him—in which case, he had trouble unsticking. (See: math and lit, respectively). "He was not your average Exeter kid," MacIntosh said, during an interview at his workplace, the Frick museum. "It was a sink-or-swim environment, where he had to use his wits to survive. Wit and cleverness. I never heard him tell a joke. He just observed. Made turns of phrases. George was a gadfly, something of an outsider. And it was always clear he was going to be a writer."

George fell in with a snide bunch called "the negos," as in "negative attitude," but always leavened his sarcasm with equal parts wink, amiability, and self-parody. He wanted points *and* love. College was the daily double; it was all downhill from there. George was a driving force behind *The Harvard Lampoon's* return to glory, as the country's best satirical magazine. A parody issue of the school newspaper was an exact replica but for a few squibs, such as the one noting that LBJ had cancelled the Harvard-Yale game because India had exploded a nuclear device. George, in separate issues, described the travails of "immigrant Wasps" and authored a Q&A with "Dr. Randolph R. Randolph, Resident Psychiatrist, Bubbling Brook House, Ferretsberg, Miss."

George's first professional writing job was at the crown jewel of magazines, *The New Yorker*. He was twenty-three.

The task was to inject youthful pluck into the short articles featured in the magazine's opening section, The Talk of the Town, which had become fusty and tired. He, more than anyone, brought irony to *The New Yorker*—"George was ironic before anyone was ironic," said his friend Tony Hiss—and did so by way of his uniquely arch tone and his mega-Wasp subreferencing and fetishistic embrace of capitalization and italics. "We set off the other day to see if we could find among the Hundred Most Significant Technical Products of the past year *something* to raise our spirits," began his first story, about industrial novelties "assembled for one day in the [Hilton's] Sutton ballroom. Gilded memories, it brought to mind, of the soirees of the late Mrs. William [Caroline Schermerhorn] Astor."

He proved especially adept at deconstructing show-business types, from Bob Dylan to the then Cassius Clay. In a dispatch about the closing of the Fillmore rock club, George couldn't resist an aside about Sid Bernstein, a concert promoter: "Bernstein's outfit was, I think, less striking than the blue-blazer-yellow-socks combination of [record-company executive] Ahmet Ertegün. I mention Sid Bernstein and Ahmet Ertegün right away because I want to make clear that the Fillmore last Sunday night was not crawling with a lot of musicians and singers. The Fillmore was crawling with people more important than that."

In 1981 came *Within the Context of No Context,* a book that had begun as an essay in *The New Yorker.* Part essay, part memoir, part rant, part post-McLuhan media critique—George reserved special contempt for Stone Phillips—the book careered circuitously, tightroping between sobriety and satire; short on science but big on conclusions; with few, if any, structural or narrative lines. "That was one of George's trademarks," said one of his editors, Charles McGrath. "He never came right out and said something."

The book became a sensation (among highbrows) for the same reason George himself did (at their cocktail parties); it crackled with a kind of half-mad cerebral exuberance, a magical glibness:

Television is the force of no-history, and it holds the archives of no-history. The power behind it resembles the power of no-action, the powerful passive. It is bewitching. It interferes with growth, conflict, and deconstruction, and those forces are different in its presence.

"Entertainment" is an unsatisfactory word for what it encloses on projects or makes possible. No good has come of it.

That's the way George spoke, often punctuating remarks via a trademark laugh ("Ha-HA! Ha-HA!") that once prompted this reportage from his famed office neighbor, E. J. Kahn: "He sometimes laughs into a telephone nonstop for twenty minutes at a stretch. He does not say anything; he just laughs, a loud, carrying, braying laugh that beats against our connecting walls like the ocean surf after a hurricane."

Friends had always described George as "effervescent," "antic," "frenetic." Talked fast, walked fast. One of his Harvard classmates, Steve Cotler, recalled George's writing method. "Give me a phrase, *any* phrase, to help me get started on this paper," he once said.

"Neon-green lights," Cotler replied.

"Perfect!" George frantically typed his opening sentence: "In Anton Chekhov's *Three Sisters,* the past, the present, and the future come together like the neon-green lights of the not-too-distant dawn."

Forty-five minutes later, Trow said, "I need a convincing name for a nineteenth-century Russian critic!"

Cotler manufactured one.

"Perfect!" George said, typing along: "As the obscure Russian critic Tudrus Zlutchin once wrote, 'We are more products of our environment than we are of our parents.' The End. Let's play bridge!"

As a professional, George churned out three plays, a collection of stories (*Bullies*), a radio program (for *National Lampoon*), and the screenplay for a Merchant Ivory movie (*Savages*) popular among the nine people who saw it. Always George found time to mentor younger or newer writers, including one named Alison Rose. When profiling someone, George advised her, "look for poignancy in the noble thing, the optimistic thing. Glimpse genuine joy, in a way, in the middle of world horror. Be a servant of his energy. Allow him to take delight in his own life. His life is your life."

You paused, halfway through your "first" reading of "10 Trow text," to acknowledge a few things, namely, that the commonalities between reporter and subject were starting to outweigh the differences. A little aloof. Needs his space. Don't expect him to open up. Or settle down. Skinny nervous wreck smirks way to college, then New York; writer of cruel satire becomes profiler of showmen, happy idiots, in the employ of Condé Nast. Screenwriting beckoned.

Aside from matters of appearance, and setting aside the Noel Coward act and the sex with men, and notwithstanding George's decided advantages in intelligence, productivity, and popularity, in addition to the whole "celebrated author" thing, you were basically the same guy.

Profiler becomes profiled.

Profiled becomes profiler.

Profiles in Profiles.

His life is your life. A bit sentimental for your tastes. A tad idealized. You never deemed it necessary to *be* JLo, or to see the world through the eyes of Keanu Reeves, in order to accurately portray them in print. If anything, the world needed less of that crap. *People don't understand the pressures of celebrity. I'm a prisoner of the media.* Reporters ought not service the energy of Madonna's publicist, and cannot access the internal lives of those who have no internal lives.

The key, in each of these cases, was to keep The Celebrity at a cool remove—to just step back and be The Reporter, in the god-awful Columbia J-School sense. A stenographer. A typist. *So you really* are *just "Jenny from the Block"?* Any additional involvement would amount to a tacit endorsement of The Celebrity, and would therefore betray both The Reader (who needed to see The Celebrity as he/she really was) and The Reporter (who needed to establish the degree to which he was smarter and cooler than The Celebrity).

The three resulting profiles revealed who the real idiot was. They were tedious, crimes against humanities. Maybe if you'd pushed things a little more, if only for amusement value, possibly The Reader wouldn't have felt so violated. Instead, you produced random streams of movie titles, quotations, and half smirks collectively signifying nothing except your failure as a journalist and the magazine's contractual obligation to put *something* between the Lincoln Navigator ad and the Kate Spade ad.

At the root of the weepfest was insecurity. You needed George to respect you. To view you as, at the very least, a peer. But the odds didn't look good, given that even you didn't like you, and that George was dead. There was a chance he'd come across one of your better efforts. But the thought of him reading "Zen and the Art of Keanu Reeves" was too much to bear. You would be remembered, if you were remembered at all, as manqué, a knock-off. George Trow Lite.

And that was the good news. George, upon entering what should have been the prime of his life—his forties—started falling apart.

From the article, in part:

There had always been warning signs, albeit of the kind that become obvious only in hindsight. "Even when at Harvard, there were elements of compartmentalizing his life," says a friend, Winty Aldridge. "Sometimes he wanted to be with us and sometimes not."

Increasingly, loneliness found Trow (who had no long-term partner). He had always been anchored by his work and his friendships, but now both were melting away."

Several died, among them Mayer, O'Donoghue, Vreeland, and Bobby Wagner, son of the former mayor of New York. In 1994, illness felled Trow's father, George Sr., whom George had viewed with equal parts admiration and fear.

When O'Donoghue's biographer, Dennis Perrin, interviewed Trow about his late friend, Trow dissolved into tears. "I can't . . . I can't," Trow said, sobbing harder as he walked out the door. "I worried about him," Aldridge says. "I think he was drinking a little more and smoking too much. He was clearly depressed."

Another friend, Tony Hiss says: The New York he had known was metamorphosing into something else that he felt less sympathy for."

And so was *The New Yorker,* where the Old Guard was in full retreat after the departure of editor Robert Gottlieb, in 1991. "George had made, as they say in psychiatric lingo, a very strong transference to Gottlieb," says one former colleague. "The father fixation—Shawn, then Gottlieb."

Anxiety gnawed at George. There were scattered outbursts of anger, flare-ups at work, grudges based on slights real and less so. He spent less time writing and more time fretting, pacing. He had trouble with concentration and focus, except as they pertained to negative thoughts. He saw the magazine's new editor as a harbinger of the End Days:

Tina Brown, fresh off her highly publicized reign at *Vanity Fair,* had arrived with great fanfare and a clear mandate from corporate: get *The New Yorker* out of the red and into the twentieth century. No more fourteen-thousand-word histories of paddle tennis. The magazine would henceforward be lean, topical, edgier; it would generate something called "Buzz."

With cool precision, Brown reduced or declined to renew dozens of writer's contracts; one by one, stalwarts who didn't "mesh"—Hiss, Frasier, Kincaid—found themselves seeking employment elsewhere. Trow became a ghost, appearing only fleetingly, writing less and less. He loathed Brown's autocratic style, described by critics as Stalinist, and was enraged by how his friends had been treated. "The Anti-Christ," he called her.

Then came word that a special issue on women would have a guest editor: the TV comedian Roseanne Barr. That the rumor was overbaked was hardly relevant to Trow. By way of a letter to Brown, he went down in a blaze of glory. "Your noxious indifference to those who have long made the magazine great—Tony Hiss: remember him?—compels this," he wrote. "One can only wonder why you would sell your soul this way; it reminds me of someone trying to get close to the Hapsburgs, circa 1913."

To which Brown wrote back: "I am distraught at your defection, but since you never actually write anything, I should say I am notionally distraught."

By now Trow had forsaken Manhattan for Germantown, an idyllic hamlet on the Hudson River. There he had designed and built a striking hillside cottage that faced out on a lush apple orchard. At some point, though, Trow stopped furnishing and finishing the interior. Some rooms sat empty; some walls remained unplastered.

He entertained only his German shepherd, Duke. He grew hermetic, ignoring phone calls and generally going incommunicado for long stretches. During his increasingly rare visits to Manhattan, he looked and sounded different, partly because he no longer dressed as if he were en route to the Stork Club, preferring jeans and T-shirts. "I found conversation with him very difficult," says his old Harvard friend Andrew Weil, the self-help guru. "There was a remoteness and opaqueness in interactions with him."

His Trowvianisms, once so delightful, now rang differently. "I wish I could take the sunlight at face value," he told Rose. "The sun going down. God goes to the other side of the earth and leaves you with the humans." At another point, unbidden, he announced, "The ongoing of it is, frankly, a real problem."

During one of his rare appearances, at a dinner with two banker friends, Trow confessed that he envied them. "Here was this successful, deeply creative person, and *he* was envying *us*?" recalls one of the friends, Henry Lanier. "Two mainstream guys. We had wives, families, that sort of thing. We wondered if he was regretting a lack of emotional stability in his life."

One by one, Trow began cutting ties; to most friends, he offered no complaints, no explanations, no hints. Unbeknownst to anyone, he quietly packed some clothes, personal items, and writing supplies into his old red truck and drove away.

To Alaska.

He said he "needed to clear his head," to "get away from things." He told neighbors that Alaska "seemed so beautifully remote, so welcoming in its way." He stayed for several months, alone in a modest cabin with no phone. Neighbors considered him friendly in a removed sort of way. He took long, solitary hikes to nowhere in particular.

And he tried (and tried and tried) to write a book that wouldn't come together. His previous two books, one of which served as a kind of sequel to *Within the Context of No Context,* had tanked. But he saw his new project, *The Gold Chair,* as his magnum opus—a sprawling essay about everything under his sun: the death of New York, the evils of television, and so forth. Occasionally he mailed pages to his agent, Lynn Nesbit, and to Robert Gottlieb, who had become his book editor. "It was just pages and pages," Nesbit said. "There was no 'it.'" "I certainly felt that his moorings were looser," Gottlieb said. "He was less anchored to our kind of normalcy."

He did manage to get one essay published, in a fringe publication called *First of the Month,* a self-described "newspaper of the imagination." The article featured the following passage, beneath the title "Is Dan Mad?":

Journalists ought to get off their over-paid Huck Finn raft. Journalists ought to make of themselves a prideful guild. . . . Stand a little apart from this troubled world of ours. Identify the stories which will affect the lives of our children. And cover them.

He would never again be published.

One day, in Alaska, neighbors noticed that George's dog, Duke, was looking sickly and malnourished. And, come to think of it, they hadn't seen George in a while. They called two of his friends down in the Lower 48. After racing to Alaska, the friends found George dazed, incoherent, and every bit as wrecked as Duke, physically and mentally.

They transported him to McLean Hospital, the famed psychiatric facility in Belmont, Massachusetts. McLean had long been the hospital of choice for troubled creative types, among them Sylvia Plath, William Styron, John Nash, Ray Charles, James Taylor, Robert Lowell, and Susanna Kaysen, author of *Girl, Interrupted*. During much of this time, Trow stayed in a comfortable private-pay unit favored by wealthy patients; it was called the Pavilion.

Trow, like many new patients, immediately wanted out. But that really wasn't an option, and in due course his diagnosis became official: bipolar disorder, that insidious psychiatric affliction characterized by pendular swings between mania and depression. He remained hospitalized for four months—an unusually long stay for a patient who did not require lifelong institutionalization.

At the Pavilion, he received individually prepared meals and staggering medical bills. With his finances dwindling, he grudgingly called on his mother, Ann, who helped with the payments. But he refused most other offers of assistance, even from his oldest friends. "I sent him a note saying, 'I'd like to have a chance to check on you,'" recalls his friend Winty Aldridge. "He sent back basically one sentence, but it was not encouraging. He said he was 'on to something else.' And that was it."

So this explained a few things:
The "Ten TROW Text" galleys were dated July 30.

The Pavilion brochure was dated August 4.

The article was slated for the October issue.

The article was cut from the October issue.

You entered the Pavilion in November.

You exited two weeks later.

You flew straight to Michigan—just as you had while recuperating from the 9/11 attack. Mom's home cooking was always welcome in times of recuperation.

This time, though, home felt different. That you were now a two-time loser, a recidivist, had something to do with it. The 9/11 attack had been spun as a one-off Hollywood rite of passage: the brief hospitalization due to "exhaustion" or "an adverse reaction to prescription pain medication." But now, credibilitywise, you were approaching Matthew Perry territory, en route to Charlie Sheen.

You kept trolling for that Pat Conroy moment. There had to be some sort of shattering childhood trauma, or series of traumas, that precipitated your eventual downfall. That nothing jumped out at you, at present, probably meant the trauma was of the repressed-memory variety, which made the task trickier, but which played into your professional skill set.

David, the middle brother, met you at baggage claim. He smiled in the slightly fretful style (head tilted, good soldier) he'd mastered during his years as the family's primary worrier and fixer. David had a wife and two children, and spent sixty hours a week at the *Detroit Free Press*, where he worked as an editor. But he, like his parents, never talked about his own needs, because he was too busy worrying about everyone else's. If Mom sneezed in another state, David grabbed a Kleenex. If you were depressed, he just knew it. Naturally, on the ride from Metro Airport, David shrugged off your questions about the paper's latest wave of layoffs and angst. "How are you doing?" he said. "What can I do to help?"

The refrain was a constant one. The eldest brother, Peter, had a different delivery, though. Ironic by half. During his college years, at Columbia, he ruptured a disc in his back. The injury defied a series of surgeries over three decades, during which he married, had a child, and became a financial advisor. He managed your investments for free, and changed the subject whenever you offered to pay him. While chronic pain had done little to diminish Peter's disposition—no whining, ever—he had come to appreciate the limitations of questions like "How are you doing?"

"Fine," you said.

"Got it," he said.

The exchange took place in your hometown, Franklin, a secluded idyll located twenty minutes from downtown Detroit, amid a cluster of affluent suburbs. Franklin, in autumn, smelled of turning leaves and crushed apples; it embraced its status as the state's first historic district, replete with a cider mill, strawberry socials, and an abundance of wagon wheels. Franklin called itself "The Town That Time Forgot."

You were the family's only native Frankliner, born three months after the rest of them moved in. Franklin, in 1965, was lacking in lefty Jews and their weirdo "California Modern" architecture. But your parents, though born of old-world traditionalism—their childhood neighborhood in Detroit made Brooklyn seem goyish—were more new school than they seemed. Mom became an art dealer specializing in prewar modernists and degenerates. She and Dad joined the country's first "humanistic" synagogue, led by a rabbi who was atheist, gay, and *fierce*.

The house, with its sloped angles and floor-to-ceiling windows, was conventional in one way: square footage. Three bedrooms for a family of five. So everyone had to double up. Except the baby.

You were special.

Peter, your senior by seven years, was the cool customer. He had a dreamy, occasionally monkish quality, and could spend forever fiddling with stereo equipment and listening to *Dark Side of the Moon*. But there was a hardiness to him. He stood six feet two, with forearms larger than your thighs. He played varsity basketball, tarred roads in the summertime, and ate cereal with a soup ladle. His high school classmates headed to Ann Arbor or East Lansing; he went to Manhattan.

David, who had your mother's black hair and doe eyes, embraced the role of middle brother. He was the center of attention, even when he wasn't trying. He arrived two years after Peter, but had Big Personality at conception. He was the most outgoing and gregarious member of the family. Also the feistiest. He could be a hothead, a door-slammer. But mostly he shined. All-star outfielder. Puka-shell necklace. Girls, girls, girls.

David was Mick. Peter was Keith.

And you were Nervous. Also pale, bespectacled, and bone-skinny, with a chest bordering on concave and the posture of a seventy-year-old cabdriver. The hunch stemmed partly from your "physique," but mostly from your asthma. Young wheezers tend to hunch in an effort to draw air—a process that drains the face of blood, in much the same way that anxiety does. That you took in about 30 percent less than everyone else did was nothing compared to what happened during bona fide attacks, which tended to come in the middle of the night, and which tended to take anxiety up a notch.

The Fear is endemic to anyone who's perpetually one step—or one dust mite, or one peanut—away from acute respiratory distress. In your case, exposure to any number of allergens—dust, mold, pollen, ragweed, grass, feathers; carrots, melons, bananas; dogs, cats—caused airways to constrict into pinholes. It was like breathing through a loofah. Hence the panicked midnight runs to the Henry Ford Hospital. The best defense, in the days before fast-acting inhalers came along, was behavioral.

Avoid exposure.

208 | NED ZEMAN

Nailed that one. Took it to heart. For a decade, Mom walked around with a child clinging to her ankle. External threats were obvious (big dogs, mean kids) and less so (torn linoleum, holes in seats). So why risk it?

The world beyond was a thicket. At summer camp, your main activity involved sitting on the director's desk, alternately sobbing and demanding phone calls. The director, when talking to your parents, said he'd never seen a camper so committed to homesickness.

The next summer, in consultation with a child psychiatrist, Mom and Dad determined that another go around would do you good. You, in turn, determined to charge them the price of betrayal. Buried them in letters. Baited them. The clincher was a one-line postcard that read, apropos of nothing: "They took the splint off today." You were home by Monday.

Nobody, in your experience, made a persuasive case for why you would be foolish enough to leave the safe embrace. You had plenty of friends—the same kids since kindergarten. You had brothers who let you win at Nerf basketball and who didn't laugh when you dropped a fly ball. And you had Mom and Dad, who called you handsome and smart, protected you from evildoers, and rubbed your back while you wheezed all night or cried like a little bitch.

High school, although predictably awkward and occasionally soul-crushing, was devoid of bullying or buggery. There was a cute girlfriend named Jenny, who was a sweetheart every time she dumped you. You ran with a tight-knit group of friends, who were welcomed at most keggers, but who spent most of the time huddled in a corner, mocking the hosts and counting the days until the gods of higher education banished them to MSU and you to U of M.

The latter would have been a foregone conclusion, were it not for the spells. They appeared in tenth grade. Mondays, Wednesdays, and Fridays—the days you took geometry. Until this point, you had been a solid, if unspectacular, student. Humanities-type classes (English, history) came fairly easy, although teachers frequently noted your inattention to detail. You "drifted," "lost the thread," "failed to apply yourself." Verbal skills, high; reading-comprehension, less so. You'd be reading *Moby-Dick* but quit at the first mention of longitudes or latitudes, which you couldn't comprehend, except to the extent that they had something to do with geometry, which you failed.

Geometry was taught by a mustachioed prick in Sansabelt slacks. Again and again, he would reveal to the class some sort of *thing* he'd drawn on the chalkboard. Some hecta-this or octa-that. They all looked the same to you—which is to say, like lines and pointy stuff signifying nothing. Like origami cave drawings. The students sure seemed to know their poloyoctahoozits from their hectawhatnots. But Sansabelt sensed fear in one of you. "Hello," he'd say.

That's when the spells began. There would be a stiffness of extremities, then a low ringing sound, then breakdowns in the areas of swallowing and sight. Colors faded, washed out; everything quickened, except for your cardiovascular system, which slowed in an audible way—like underwater sonar.

Then, vapor lock. You remained conscious, and conscious of being conscious, but also senseless and immobilized. And neutral. That was the main thing: There was no main thing. Which was all well and good—or, at least, neither here nor there—until the spell broke, typically after a period of one to three minutes. The first time this happened, you vomited in your lap; most times, you fled the room. The latter outcome, although preferable to the former, was less than ideal, socially speaking.

The spells, coupled with your brain's general state of disrepair, alarmed your parents. They took you to a neurologist, who put you through a battery of tests, scans, probes. "We found the problem," the doctor announced. "It's a condition called *you're just very nervous*."

During the drive home, Mom sensed that you were rather less relieved that she was—that "it's all in your head" did little to soothe her young head case. Didn't give you much to work with, excusewise. Not to mention what it implied about your intelligence. "Guy walks into a psychiatrist's office," she said. "Guy says, 'I spend all day tearing paper into little pieces, and I can't stop. Please, Doctor, what do I do?' Doctor nods, leans forward. 'Schmuck,' the doctor says, *'stop tearing paper.'* "

Mom was funnier, and altogether more fun, than other moms, who spent entirely too much time talking about humidity. She had, in addition to impeccable manners, an impish, understated warmth. And she, like everyone in the family, knew the best way to bring you back to earth was to lighten you the hell up. All four of them were gifted in this regard, but Mom had the toughest draw. Because she was in charge of day-to-day operations, also had to play good cop *and* bad cop; she was the one nobody wanted to mess with. Woe was the kindergarten teacher who taught you the Lord's Prayer; the guidance counselor who suggested community college was never seen again.

That Mom was the enforcer always amused people, given that Dad was the decorated soldier. Army. World War II. Italian Front. Twice injured: months in body cast, multiple surgeries, chronically damaged knee. His Purple Heart lay in the pocket of an old jacket he never wore. In secret, you and your brothers would liberate the medals and hang them around your necks. Whenever you asked about them, Dad would shrug it off. "Not much to say," he'd say.

Dad couldn't fathom why anyone would glory in war stories, because he was congenitally peaceable—a man without enemies, grudges, or agendas. Sometimes people took advantage of it. You certainly did. You knew the briefest flash of disappointment, on your part, would turn "no" into "oh, all right."

Dad grew up in a cramped apartment above Zeman's Bakery, a stark but popular place he described as "world-famous in Jewish

Detroit." After the war, he and his brother Bob started a wholesale business called Allied National, which sold sewing-machine parts, and which provided them with solidly upper-middle-class incomes.

Dad worked hard, even when he didn't have to. He shunned retirement, even in his eighties. But he didn't want you to misinterpret that. There was a difference, he said, between working all your life and working your life away. Without family and fun, he said, what was the point? "Please don't take the rest of it too seriously," he would say. "Just go outside. Have fun."

Living. That was the point. He was forever in motion, like a Little-Leaguer in a man's body. Walking, playing, baking: They kept him looking and feeling impossibly young. He'd spend Sunday afternoon baking apple pies, then all evening distributing them to friends and relatives. He gave to the point of absurdity. His sons learned to never compliment anything he was wearing. To do so would to see him peel off the item—his shirt, his watch—and thrust it into your hands.

"Miles," Mom would say. "Try not to do that."

That was as rough as it got between them. Neither you nor your brothers ever witnessed anything approximating parental discord. Not a single clipped reply or passive-aggro silence; no tight *Ordinary People* smiles. They were freaks of love. It was impossible to imagine one without the other, because they were always together. Every evening, for more than a half-century, they could be found side by side in the den, trading sections of *The New York Times*, watching interminable PBS documentaries about Stalin, and sharing pie. When they looked at each other, they *giggled*.

So then: what the hell was *your* problem?

Seriously. All your friends managed to keep it together, settle down, start families. And half of them, at least, had come from families full of rage, shame, and betrayal. Cheating moms; pervy stepdads.

Your family's darkest shame?

Misdemeanor hovering.

Worst you come up with, and even that was iffy. Your relatives hovered and monitored—and fretted and fixed—the way others fought and drank. And, sure, sometimes the worrying could be . . . worrying.

But jeez. A Jewish family stops hovering the day they become Presbyterian.

Anxiety. A people.

Sudden noises made Dad whirl and wince—another wage of war—and bad restaurants turned him to stone. If he didn't like how the bread was baked, dinner would be a silent siege for everyone. And to watch a tight Michigan game with Mom and Peter was to form a trio of cuticle-worriers. Whom David worried about.

Ran in the family. But only up to a point. More than once, when Mom and Dad asked about your condition—and they did so frequently—you emphasized the genetic component. Sounded more clinical, less pathetic. Although they themselves weren't depressives, surely there must have been one or two "excitable" aunts or "eccentric" uncles. "Not really," Dad said. "We were too poor."

"Nobody?" you said.

"Well, not that we knew about," Mom said. "It was a *very* different time."

"The Depression," Dad said.

They had theirs and you had yours. That's how you saw it, initially. The greatest generation versus the generation of whine. Mom and Dad didn't speak Therapy, and were naturally averse to anything that smacked of psychobabble. Dad, after a rough day at work, would take a hot shower, drink one scotch, and instantly look like new. "All better," he'd say. "How's my boy?"

Now, all these years later, he asked the same question.

"Good," you said. "Much better."

"Really?" he said. Like a teenager.

"Really," you said. Like a dad.

He was eighty-seven. And, for the first time in his life, he was beginning to look his age.

This was the main reason why everything felt different.

Some five months earlier, during the summer of your discontent, Dad had grown uncharacteristically fatigued. A trip to the hospital revealed a condition called myelodysplastic syndrome, a kind of cancer/anemia hybrid commonly known as "preleukemia." Treatment involved blood transfusions and chemo-type therapies; most could be administered on an outpatient basis, as long as his health held up. Usually, though, MDS presaged acute leukemia, typically by two or three years. Which meant that Dad stood to die by the same disease that had killed his sister, Nettie—your namesake.

You visited regularly. You and your brothers left no stone unturned. You told friends everything.

And yet.

You didn't talk about it. Not really. At McLean, where you got the best talk therapists money could buy, you talked about . . . talking. And careers. And *penguins*.

But not about *it*.

Just couldn't. Or wouldn't.

Even now, when things were looking good. He remained fatigued. A little gaunt around the edges. But the therapies were working. He was running errands. Baking. Accomplishing more in an hour than you had in a month.

But still. To talk about it would be to legitimize it. And to legitimize would be to make it real. And to make it real would be too much for your little heart to bear.

It was Thanksgiving 2007.

CHAPTER TEN

The moment you broke with the Church of Pharmacology was the moment that doomed you to the electric chair. The seeds of the case had been planted by Shrink Number Five, in the weeks prior to The McLean Experiment. More like seedlings, actually. A tiny handful of them, sprinkled over fallow soil.

"I still think meds will help," Five said. "But if the slide continues, there are other options. So don't worry—"

"Like what?"

"Like ECT, for one. Know what that is?"

"Oh, God. My friend Barry did it freshman year."

"Oh, okay. Did it help him?"

"Self-empowerment? No talking or urination?"

She smiled sweetly.

"I think he did *EST*," she said. "EST isn't ECT."

Whatever.

"Electroconvulsive therapy," she said. "Stimulates the brain through tiny electrical currents. It's safe, effective. You hardly feel a thing." That smile again. "It's not what it used to be. It's what they used to call 'electroshock' therapy."

This therapy was going nowhere.

"*Shock treatment?*" you said.

"What are you thinking of?" she asked.

"Jack Nicholson," you said.

Ninth grade. Girlfriend's TV room. *One Flew Over the Cuckoo's Nest*.

You gloried in every frame in every scene except one. That was Nicholson's ECT moment: when McMurphy, the insurgent voice of sanity, gets the juice. And gets it. Until he's a potato. No gore. No decapitations. But all that jerking and biting—without a soundtrack—seemed a bit too *real*.

"Okay," Five said. "Forget Jack."

Stop tearing paper.

The subject was tabled for the rest of the session. But it remained in the ether. All that Sylvia Plath unpleasantness, at McLean—*weeeeeeee!*—proved to be part of a larger piece, shockwise. This you determined around Christmastime, about a month after returning from Boston. You were fast becoming a teenage girl, forever clutching *The Bell Jar*. By the time you were midway through the novel, you were fully invested in the author's alter ego, Esther, a college-age gal with a knack for attempted suicide. With each gambit—drowning, pills—you rooted ever harder, hoping that this would be the attempt that finally finished her off.

With each page you turned came a newfound appreciation for Plath's husband, the poet Ted Hughes, who himself was no walk in the park; his philandering and all-around prickishness were said to have driven Plath to shove her head in the oven. By your lights, though, it was a miracle Hughes hadn't broiled himself. Plath, like Esther, was a humorless wretch who should have called the book *The Sender*.

Turned out you wanted only one thing from the little mope. You wanted further information about ECT.

You found satisfaction elsewhere, in dozens of books, articles, and crackpot websites. Most established one thing straight off. Shock therapy was not, nor had it ever really been, *shock* therapy. The former was a corruption of *l'elettroshock*, an Italian term meaning "the electric stimulus." The procedure—Italy's lone contribution to civilization during the World War II era—induced seizures, which had long been known for their salutary effects on misfiring brains. The ancients didn't wear eels and torpedo fish on their heads in order to be fashion forward; electric currents seemed to relieve headaches. Also, epileptic seizures seemed to guard against schizophrenia. ECT, when combined with certain drugs, could jump-start catatonics and reset yard-barkers to their original settings. Human hard drives, rebooted.

Admittedly, the shockheads of yore faced a number of challenges. As if being bat-shit wasn't hard enough, they were transformed into de facto guinea pigs. The procedure was generally reserved for worst-off patients, who had few legal protections and little say in whether or not they would receive 125 volts to the brain (by modern terms, enough wattage to run a thirty-two-inch plasma TV). Often they received little or no anesthesia; they just rode the lighting, again and again. Screams. Fractures. Defecation.

Leeches.

Lobotomies.

Electroshock.

Enter *One Flew Over the Cuckoo's Nest*. Ken Kesey's novel, published in 1962, exposed *Mad Men* America to Madhouse America, with its troglodyte orderlies and abused mute Indians. ECT was, in Kesey's words, "a device that might be said to do the work of the sleeping pill, the electric chair, *and* the torture rack."

Director Milos Forman won an Oscar for his movie version in 1975. Louise Fletcher, as the wretched Nurse Ratched, became the first in a line of actresses would take the trophy for Best Actress in a Supporting Role Opposite a Shockhead: Kim Stanley (*Frances*), Jennifer Connelly (*A Beautiful Mind*) and—twice!—Angelina Jolie (*Girl, Interrupted, Changeling*).

Electroshock: Oscar bait. Stars loved shockheads even more than they did legless war veterans and happy idiots; actors weren't Actors until they were convulsing on a gurney, eyes bulging, mouth frothing, teeth clamped hard on a thick rubber bit, while orderlies shouted "Who's laughin' now, freak!" and "Take it like a man, Nancy!"

And the nominees were:

Jack Nicholson, *One Flew Over the Cuckoo's Nest*
Jessica Lange, *Frances*
Geoffrey Rush, *Shine*
Russell Crowe, *A Beautiful Mind*
Ellen Burstyn, *Requiem for a Dream*

Crowe's character, the schizo math whiz John Forbes Nash Jr., wasn't even the real deal. In about 1960, he received "insulin shock therapy," a kind of poor-man's electroshock. A year or two later, IST was discredited and discontinued. But Nash balked at ECT. He feared memory loss.

Such a paranoid, that one.

Finally, in the mideighties, it occurred to someone that *One Flew Over the Cuckoo's Nest* was fictional; that, though the novelist had once worked at a mental hospital, he had concurrently ingested huge quantities of LSD, mushrooms, and mescaline; and that he had done so while volunteering for a secret mind-control experiment administered by the CIA.

In fact, the Medical Establishment had long since deemed ECT the safest and most effective treatment for certain acute stages of schizophrenia, mania, and depression. By the early 1990s, virtually every major psych hospital, med school, and government agency in the country endorsed ECT, deeming it a vital defense for otherwise "treatment-resistant" patients: the ones for whom drugs and therapy hadn't done the trick.

Also, ECT was an *elective* procedure. Doctors required a patient's informed consent (except in the rare case where the patient was declared, by both his guardian *and* an outside judge, a batso who would otherwise savage himself).

Still, most celebrity shockheads remained forever unidentified: publicity agents and studio executives seemed to find the term "shock treatment" incompatible with their marketing strategies.

In recent years, however, lips had grown looser. One night you came across articles about two recent shockheads. The first was the professional talker Dick Cavett. He rode the rails in the early 1980s, following a long depression. "In my case, ECT was miraculous," he said. "My wife was dubious, but when she came into my room afterward, I sat up and said, 'Look who's back among the living.' It was like a magic wand."

The second was Kitty Dukakis, wife of the loser you voted for in 1988. She took the plunge in 2001, for similar reasons. She recalled the first time she awakened, postprocedure: "I feel good—I feel alive. Michael is standing there next to the nurse as I struggle to keep my eyes open, and I give him a big grin. That surprises him right away. After a bit more dozing I am awake for good, and get dressed. Michael takes me to the car. . . . I have been warned not to expect too much from any single ECT treatment, especially my first. . . . But I already can detect a difference. Feeling this good is truly amazing, given where I am coming from, which is a very dark place that has lasted a very long time."

ECT still had critics—a vocal minority that fretted about brain damage and death risks. The loudest opponents were Scientologists, who also believed that psychiatry was evil, that autism was a lie, and that mental illness could be "erased" via a small electronic gizmo called the Hubbard Electrometer. This from the people who brought you *Battlefield Earth*. If they hated ECT, it had to be good.

Then again. You did have something in common with the average Scientologist, in that you were both star fuckers. You were sold on ECT the instant you determined that it was basically the only thing standing between you and immortality:

Hemingway.
Styron.

Lowell.

Artaud.

David Foster Wallace.

Vladimir Horowitz. Cole Porter. Bud Powell. Lou Reed.

Townes van Zandt. Oscar Levant. Tammy Wynette.
Michelle Shocked.

Paul Robeson. Gene Tierney. Vivien Leigh. Edie Sedgwick.

Dick Cavett. Carrie Fisher.

Yves Saint Laurent.

Jimmy Piersall.

That the list was chockablock with creative types was notable, in part, because artsy types were simply more likely to acknowledge this sort of thing, if only because they were too drunk, broke, or bonkers to care. Plus, it never hurt to add a few extra Tortured Artist Points. Might get a Penguin Classics series/Grammy Lifetime Achievement Award out of it.

Regardless, the clichés about tortured, depressed writers were clichés for a reason. Many or most of the best ones were, like George, manic-depressive. Were it not for mania, and the works it fueled—*The Norton Anthology of English Literature* would be half as thick and twice as dull—nothing but sonnets and Ode to a Grecian Fucking Urn. The two most electrifying poems of the Romantic Era—Byron's "Don Juan," Coleridge's "Kubla Khan"—could only have been produced by opium-sniffing maniacs. It wasn't the depression that inspired Byron to produce an epic ode to hypersexuality. A depressed poet would not be apt to write, as Coleridge did:

> *The shadow of the dome of pleasure*
> *Floated midway on the waves;*
> *Where was heard the mingled measure*
> *From the fountain and the caves*

It was a miracle of rare device
A sunny pleasure-dome with caves of ice!

A depressed poet would not be apt to write *anything*. McLean's bipolar laureate, Robert Lowell, tended to feel flattened and useless when depressed. But mania, though brutal in a thousand ways, prompted something beyond creativity. To experience it, Lowell said, was to behold "a magical orange grove in a nightmare."

Fittingly, the most noted textual source on famous bipolar writers was authored by Kay Redfield Jamison, the famous bipolar writer. In the book, *Touched with Fire,* Jamison sites a study of writers who attended the famed Iowa Writers' Workshop. Eighty percent of them had a mood disorder; nearly half were bipolar.

In purely creative terms, at least, maniac depression offers double the flavor. "Depression prunes and sculpts," Jamison wrote. "It also ruminates and ponders and, ultimately, focuses thought." Manic states, by contrast, "generate ideas and associations, propel contact with life and other people, induce frenzied energies and enthusiasms, and cast an ecstatic, rather cosmic hue over life." The title of Jamison's evokes Byron's theory about writers: "Some are affected by gaiety, others by melancholy, but all are more or less touched."

PANTHEON OF EXTREMELY MOODY WRITERS

Andersen. Balzac. Baudelaire. Berryman. Blake. Boswell. Burns. Byron. Clemens. Coleridge. Conrad. Coward. Crane. Dickens. Dickinson. Dinesen. Eliot. Emerson. Faulkner. Fitzgerald. Goethe. Gogol. Greene. Ibsen. Hesse. Hugo. Inge. James (Henry and William). Keats. Lamb. Lowell. Melville. O'Neill. Pasternak. Poe. Pushkin. Roethke. Sexton. Shelley. Strindberg. Styron. Thomas. Tolstoy. Tennessee. Tennyson. Thompson. Turgenev. Whitman. Woolf. Zola.

Trow.

Chipper, well-adjusted people don't write "The Raven," *To the Lighthouse,* or *Heart of Darkness.* (Or "Is Dan Mad?" Or ten zillion affirmations about flightless birds.) Writers, *creatives,* were different from everyone else.

So things were looking up, careerwise.

Shortly before the holidays, at your request, Five pointed you to an ECT specialist, Dr. E, a bearded fellow wearing wire-rim glasses and a yarmulke. He had been at the switch, in one way or another, since the Cuckoo Seventies.

"Oh," he said. "That movie."

"Comes up a lot?" you asked.

"Now and then."

"Didn't care for it?"

"The acting was good."

He reviewed your records, including the results of a "QIDS-SR" test, a sixteen-question "quick inventory" of a patient's general state of mind. Your score (eighteen out of a possible twenty-seven) indicated "severe depression." He ascertained all the relevant information: background and medications, anxiety and OCD.

"And you saw neurologists," he said.

"Problems writing," you said.

"How bad is the decline?"

"Shadow of what it was before."

"Can you put a number on it? Fifty percent of your capacity? Twenty-five?"

"Ten."

He noted, in your chart, that you presented as alert, cooperative, oriented, and appropriate—but also visibly anxious, depressed, and somewhat slow to speak. He diagnosed "major depression, recurrent with melancholia," "obsessive-compulsive traits," and "concomitant possible anxiety disorder."

"So here's what I see," he said. "I see a person who is seriously depressed, who isn't responding to medication, and who is getting more withdrawn and less functional. Does that sound right to you?"

"Uh-huh."

"Then I recommend ECT."

"As in have-to-right-now important."

"No. There's no have-to. I'm saying ECT is a treatment option you should strongly consider. But it's not the only one. You might prefer to try additional drug therapies instead.

"It's not?"

"Drastic is feeling worse and being hospitalized. ECT is safe. It's outpatient. And I think it will help."

"Think or know?"

"It's impossible to *know* how a person will respond. But, based on all the information, the odds are favorable."

"As in?"

"About seventy percent."

"And the risks of ECT?"

"Ever had anesthesia?"

"Yes."

"That's the riskiest part. An ECT patient faces no more danger than anyone who goes under."

"So the Jack Nicholson thing . . ."

"I've been doing this for decades. During that time, ECT hasn't caused a single death. It hasn't caused any brain damage. The worst pain you can expect is a tension-type headache for a few hours. Nothing Tylenol won't fix."

"So why don't people just do this all the time?"

"There's usually one main side effect," he said. "Memory impairment."

Almost certainly, he said, you would suffer some degree of amnesia. The surest bet was short-term memory loss, a.k.a. "anterograde amnesia." You'd forget, in addition to the event that caused the amnesia, events occurring from that point forward; new memories just wouldn't stick. You'd forget phone numbers, lose your wallet, tell the same joke you told twenty minutes earlier; you'd get lost en route to destinations unknown. You'd be, to some degree, a sober drunk person or a young old man. The impairment would likely be cumulative, materializing gradually and increasing somewhat with each treatment. Or not. Or just little.

"Differs from person to person," he said. "The more treatments, the more impairment."

The average patients receives between six and ten treatments. Sometimes they need more. Sometimes three or four suffice.

"Expect some problems with everyday things," he said. "You'll need somebody watching you on treatment days. And you definitely won't be allowed to drive."

But it would be temporary. Once the treatments ended, the short-term memory would gradually return, becoming fully functional in a month or two.

Somewhat less likely were long-term memory problems, a.k.a. "retrograde amnesia," an inability to recall events occurring prior to the inciting event. Days prior. Or weeks. Or months. Some patients—usually those who receive the most ECT—experience losses (whole or partial) spanning upwards of a year. Retrograde amnesia might take longer to resolve—six to nine months, at worst. Probably some of the lost memories would remain that way, while others would return, wholly or partially.

Patients often experience some retrograde amnesia. But reporters of larger losses are less common. "That's the worst-case scenario," E said. "But I should note that a few patients have reported some longer-term losses."

"How few?"

"*Very* few."

"So, basically, my memory sucks during ECT, then starts clearing up in a month or two?"

"Basically, yes."

This day marked the beginning of a pattern that lasted for weeks. Whenever *ECT* entered the conversation, you experienced a slight power surge. "I think it's the right thing to do," you told Five. "I think it's time for ECT."

At which point, almost imperceptibly, a body part (ear, nose, armpit) would, for a period of three to five seconds, tingle, tickle, pulse, pound, itch, or quiver. Also, simultaneously, came a slight sharpening of vision. An awareness of shutter speed. The boomlets, though distinct little snowflakes, arrived with increased reliability. And with that volume came a cascading therapeutic effect lasting upwards of a minute; it translated into a sense of optimism, resolve. If Adderall was epinephrine minus the needle, then ECT—the mere *thought* of it—was the smart drug of all time.

The only remaining task, at this point, was a biggie. Selling friends and family on ECT would be akin to selling the Church of Jesus Christ of Latter-day Saints on transgender marriage. Electroshock didn't poll well *anywhere*. The voters in your area, in and around Hollywood, were well.

"I know what you're thinking," you told Ben. "Jack Nicholson."

"No," Ben said. "Jessica Lange."

Your two motives were somewhat at odds with each other. On the one hand, you didn't want to freak anyone out, if only because that would freak you out. You didn't want them thinking you'd gone off the deep end. Yes, ECT was indeed considered The Treatment Of Last Resort. But how many treatments were there, really? Two. Meds and ECT. So the leap wasn't a life-or-death one. And you'd already laid to waste most pharmceuticals.

Buspar.

Cymbalta.

Emsam.

Effexor, Paxil.

Prozac.

Seroquel.

Serzone.

Wellbutrin.

And Zoloft.

On the other hand, you didn't want to underplay the situation. Because you wanted it known that you weren't diddling around anymore—that this wasn't some sort of experiment in alternative lifestyles. This was serious. You were serious. It was time people understood that you were Really Sick and Totally Deserving Of A Little Fucking Attention.

These people had to be finessed, at the grass roots. They'd be nodding along, studiously digesting your little preamble about The Limits Of Drug-Therapy and Advances In Modern Science and blah, blah.

"ECT," you'd say. Leading with the acronym. Sounded so corporate. "Electroconvulsive therapy."

Nodding.

"It's like getting an MRI. Little high-tech doodad."

Nodding.

"Stimulates the brain. Tiny electrical currents."

Nodding.

"Here's what it's not," you'd say. What came next amounted to a calculated gamble on your part. Couldn't let them think you were ducking the subject. Better to get out in front of it. Deflate the thing. "It's not electro*shock*."

Abruptly, the nodding would cede to a slight but sudden jerking of the head: backward, then forward, then stop. Chin at five o'clock; eyes narrowed.

"Wait," they'd say. "As in shock treatment?"

Crisis point. Some people fell silent. Caitlin's eyes welled.

"That's what it used to be," you'd say. "It's totally different now."

"I didn't even know they still did shock."

"They don't really. This is like an MRI."

"Oh, so it's not shock treatment?"

"No. Forget Jack Nicholson."

The campaign slowly made inroads. The key was to project an air of studied calm. ECT, you said, was the future, not the past. High-tech. Increasingly popular. More than two hundred thousand patients got it every year. *Carrie Fisher*. She referenced the Nicholson stigma during the stage adaptation of her memoir *Wishful Drinking*. "It's not like that anymore," she said. "Now it's really *fun*."

During the lead-up to your first ECT session, you emailed repeated updates and assurances, i.e.:

> No need to be super-secretive about this; it's truly not such a big deal. A few memory problems—that's it. But kindly refrain from emailing this note to anyone, since we all know how that can go. Ideally, this stays within the family. ECT still freaks people out, and I'm trying to spare my parents needless worry. I'll keep you posted, thanks for everything, and forgive me if I greet you as "Brenda."

Sleep came fitfully on the eve of your electrocution. The date was March 7, 2008. You sat up in darkness, shoulder blades flush against the headboard, gaze pivoting between the alarm clock to the left and the window more or less straight ahead—the easternmost window, where the first flickers of dawn would appear, at 6:00 A.M.

The suspense was almost too much. There were dicey moments. Periods of doubt and fear and gastrointestinal challenges (although possibly that last bit had something to do with your nutritional choices, which by then were down to McIntosh apples, Martinelli's sparkling apple Juice, and apple Jolly Ranchers—the Michigan Diet). But you endured worse cramps every time Michigan kicked off to Ohio State. Then, as now, nervous excitement signaled "Big Game," and therefore heightened the overall excitement experience. It was value added. As Jay would say.

At first light, a telltale rattling drew your attention to the bedroom door. Beneath it, in the inch-high gap beneath the door and the floor, two furry appendages (one gray, one calico) repeatedly breached from beyond, in grand sweeping motions, "palms" alternately up and down. The cats did this every morning, hoping in vain that this would be the day when love and breakfast arrived early.

Their day had come.

They were stunned, at first. They thought maybe it was a scam. They just sat there, saucer-eyed, as you scratched their whiskers and backs. Normally, the three of you headed downstairs together, with the cats darting between your legs, in a weaving pattern of the sort seen at JV basketball practices.

This time, though, two minutes elapsed before the cats descended, tactically, the way they approached insects, suspicious shadows, and their own reflections.

By this time, you were reading email in the office. It was a fine crop. The four usual suspects, individually, offered warm encouragement. So did the lifers back East—Matt, Jim, David, Mark, Barry. The latter wrote:

My heart is with you for having to continue to pursue curatives for your condition. May this next step bring longer-term hope. I'll leave many disorienting voicemails in the weeks ahead.

The five of them produced a group-email containing an MP4 track by Crosby, Stills, and Nash: "Just a Song Before I Go."

Next came emails from your siblings Peter and David, who did their damndest to sound unlike fretful, codependent big brothers. Everything proceeded nicely until you came across the following bit, from David:

> Have you made a decision about whether to tell mom and dad? I ask because mom just asked me this morning if I had heard from you lately.

You wrote back:

> Okay, so I "finessed" mom and dad, by saying I'm getting a "neuro-stimulation treatment" that's well accepted, basically harmless, and outpatient. It's a white lie, in that there are indeed many forms of "neuro-stimulation therapy," most of them benign. ECT just happens to be the most extreme form. I never mentioned "ECT" or "electroshock." They seemed totally unfazed.

To which David promptly replied:

> It sounds like you're getting a nice massage.

Finally, you reviewed the traffic with Caitlin, which had begun a day earlier:

> Caitlin: I hate to sound pedantic, but I'm VERY proud of you for taking this step. I think it is incredibly brave and powerful. Xx

> You: Means a lot to me.

> Caitlin: Please let me know how I can be there for you.

> You: Will do. Staying with B and D. Come any time.

When Paula arrived, at 8:30, you were already halfway down the driveway, in your jeans and T-shirt, as if awaiting an ice cream truck. She had the look on her face: half bemused, half maternal. Same look she'd had the last time she'd served as your psych-ward chauffeur. Same one she had whenever she felt embarrassed that you would ever feel embarrassed around her.

Paula had long since attained platinum-elite status, having spent endless hours in your company, trading stories of indignity and shouting at reality TV shows.

This was the plan:

Most of the ECT duty would fall to Paula, who purported to be the team member possessed of the most operational flexibility. Although this wasn't exactly *un*true—she was on a year-long hiatus from acting—it would have been more persuasive had the hiatus been prompted by drunkenness or unemployment, rather than by 24-7 childcare responsibilities.

Occasionally, the job would fall to Daniel. Daniel was stuck finishing your latest "collaboration," a self-generated script that would have been finished by this point, had you not conked midway through act 2. Which wouldn't have been the biggest deal, had screenwriters not spent the preceding four months on strike, and therefore unpaid. Which wouldn't have been the end the world, either, had Daniel been a shut-in bachelor like you, rather than the father of two kids whose preschool tuition fees exceeded your yearly mortgage costs.

Enter Ben, who, during standard business hours, functioned as Primary Caregiver (whatever that meant).

Lizz was the only team member (and possibly the only Angeleno) who had A Real Job, in a real office full of real bosses. So she would function as the Oz figure, unseen but ever present, shaping and monitoring every operational detail, strategy, and communication, no matter how small or tedious. She worked out scheduling; she disseminated information to your brothers and your friend Jim up in Palo Alto, who then passed word to your friends back East. All of which reflected her propensity for (a) loyalty and (b) control issues. "I need to know *every-thing* that happened," she would say. "And if you don't tell me *every detail,* this relationship is over."

But, hey. In all likelihood, you were looking at a total of six to eight reboots. And quite possibly fewer. You weren't one of those barking-at-fire-hydrants cases. Probably drained the system, those people. Skewed the averages. Plus, sessions would be spread over three weeks: Mondays, Wednesdays, Fridays. Same time each morning. Ninety minutes a pop.

Paula would be free by noonish, having deposited you at home, where you would spend the afternoon napping, watching TV, and tossing squeak toys to the cats. Then you would make your way to The Ben And Daniel Suites for a well-deserved night of pampering, luxury bath products, and fine dining experiences (free of charge, except to them). Doctor's orders: Patients needed someone looking after them on treatment days, lest the patient accidentally wander into traffic, leave the stove on, or lose his pants. Everyone was clear about that.

Paula's life, unlike yours, had gone somewhere. She was married now, to a writer named Mike, whom she'd met during a paintball match organized by Daniel. Her Porsche was long gone, replaced by a mini-SUV, which proved a more suitable form of transport for her five-month-old infant, Charlie, who could now be found in the backseat, cooing.

It occurred to you that the current situation was, by infant-rearing standards, a less than ideal one.

"You're a saint," you said.

"You're ridiculous," she said.

Charlie made squishy baby sounds.

"They say babies love shock treatment," you said. "Soothing."

"What if they really did love it?" she said.

"I'm making a mother and infant go to an insane asylum."

"It's part of a regular hospital."

"Well, it's our tradition."

She took Beverly Boulevard, westbound, through a two-mile stretch of burrito stands and Thai catch-and-release massage parlors.

"*Are* you nervous?" she asked. Paula, when asking uncomfortable questions, always emphasized the first word, rather than the operative one; it was a warning flare. "I apologize."

"She finally acknowledges how rude she is," you said, to Charlie, before addressing the question. "A little nervous. But fine."

"*Are* you being completely honest?"

"Yes." (And no.) "I'll sleep through the whole thing," you said. "You're the one who should be nervous."

"I'm sorry?"

"You'll be the one carrying me home in a bucket."

"What if I really did have to do that?"

"What do you mean *what if*?"

"What if you wake up and think I'm your mother?"

"What if you keep insisting I'm Charlie?"

"Okay, enough."

"Or what if it's not amnesia, but something weirder?"

"Oh, jeez."

"I'll seem exactly the same, but with an intense passion for baroque furniture."

"And the next time I pick you up, you've refurnished the entire house like Versailles."

The conversation tailed off a bit as the car moved through West Hollywood, a swankier territory dotted by vintage furniture stores of the sort that slapped varnish on discarded footstools, labeled them "classics," and sold them for seven thousand dollars to Jennifer Aniston.

"How much do your parents know?"

"The basics," you said. "Not really."

"*Have* you talked to Caitlin?"

Same delivery as above.

"Yes."

"*Directly?*"

"Well, email."

A look. "*Is* she angry that you've chosen to go to ECT with an infant instead of her?"

"She doesn't get angry."

"Because she's *lovely.*"

Silence.

"I apologize," she said.

Conversation trailed off.

The iPhone rang. Lizz.

"*Are you nervous?*" she asked.

Maybe a little.

"Not at all," you said.

Paula took a right on Robertson, then parked on the street. The block was a familiar one; every year, at about this time, you made your way to a restaurant near the corner. Morton's steakhouse was home to the A-list's annual ritual of self-gratification: the *Vanity Fair* Oscar Party. Nobody got into that party unless they were unreasonably famous, dangerously powerful, or related (by blood or blackmail) to Graydon. The rare exceptions were the few poor grunts he felt obliged to squeeze in, because they lived in Los Angeles, and because they needed validation more than he needed the stars of *Good Luck Chuck.*

But now, minus the black tie, you headed in the opposite direction, squinting. Sun, too bright; mood, darkening. To the left loomed Cedars-Sinai Medical Center, a squat brown colossus topped by a shiny Star of David. Cedars, like Hollywood, was built by Jews. All the legends died there, from Frank and Lucy to River and Biggie; the hospital felt like a safe haven, because there was always celebrity watching over you, whether it be at the Steven Spielberg Pediatric Research

Center, the Burns and Allen Research Institute, the Johnnie L. Cochran Jr. Brain Tumor Center, the Gilda Radner Hereditary Cancer Program, or the Sharon Osbourne Colon Cancer Program.

Cedars offered practical advantages over UCLA, being both closer to Los Feliz and composed entirely of private rooms. The key thing was to avoid being on display, in front of strangers, let alone diseased colostomy strangers. That you were presently scheduled to receive outpatient treatment only served to heighten your vigilance in this matter. Anxiety, like chess and scouting, was about thinking three steps ahead.

Together you headed past the Spielberg building and entered the psychiatric hospital, which was located west of the Max Factor Family Tower, and which was conspicuously lacking in boldface namesakes. The best it could offer was "Thalians Mental Health Center," a section of the hospital to which you were headed. Thalians had been funded by a group of Hollywood benefactors, among them the lovably batty Debbie Reynolds. The mental-health center owed its name to the Greek goddess Thalia, Muse of Comedy.

By the time you alighted the elevator, however, laughter proved elusive. And so did everything else. You were on the third floor of Thalians, in a linoleum hallway unfurnished but for the three flat blue sofas, in a semicircle. No people. No sounds. To your left and right were reinforced steel doors of the kind favored by psych wards and detention centers; the entryways featured electronic buttons and locks, an in-house phone, and a sign the size of a license-plate: ELOPEMENT RISK. NOT THE GOOD KIND.

A kind of muted panic set in as the three of you hovered near the sofas, waiting for signs of life. A nurse appeared. This was Nurse K. She had a soothing manner and slightly golden features, in the Californian sense. "We're all ready," she said.

"I'll be right here," Paula said.

She smiled. You smiled. Everybody smiled.

234 I NED ZEMAN

It was *Ordinary People*.

The last you saw of Paula, she was sitting awkwardly on one of the blue sofas. She smiled, as actresses do.

The ECT room looked like an ER in heaven, in miniature; it was the size of a high school classroom and included four berths replete with standard-issue beds, IV stands, monitors. But the fluorescent lighting amplified the dominant colors—white, sky blue—and gave the place a dreamy, cocoon-like feel. Noise was at a minimum, rarely exceeding the low hum of the high tech. The ECT machines, though state of the art, were benign-looking rectangular boxes; they looked like the Magnavox stereo-receiver you'd once traded for Bob Seger tickets. This was oddly comforting.

"It's gonna be easy," she said. "Promise."

After helping you negotiate a medical gown, Nurse K checked your vitals, and ascertained the basics. "Mood," she said. "Any changes in the depression?"

"About the same," you said.

"Thoughts of suicide?"

This again.

"Not seriously."

"Meaning?"

"Only in the somebody-shoot-me sense."

She marked a box indicating "suicidal thoughts," and noted your "blunted" affect. Everything else, she said, checked out fine. She marked you as alert, steady, appropriate. Your memory, she noted, was "intact."

Dr. E appeared shortly after 10:00 A.M., cheerful as ever. "Good morning," he said.

"We'll see," you said.

"Anything you'd like go over?"

He encouraged questions more than he did remarks. He reminded you of (a) your old lit professors, whose cheerfulness was born more of necessity than nature, and (b) your old relatives, whose traditions would die with McJews like you.

With a quick needle poke, Nurse K attached an IV line to your right forearm. She wrapped your arm with a blood-pressure cuff and popped a blood-oxygen monitor one on of your fingers. Then came the electrodes. A few were affixed to your chest (via standard adhesive glop) and linked to the cardiogram machine; the remaining six electrodes went upstairs. One on each temple. Four across the forehead. An EEG machine would record your brain activity; the ECT machine would administer the money shots.

The professionals ran through a series of checks and tests before injecting into the IV a standard dose of methohexital, a short-acting anesthetic similar to sodium thiopental. You were out within about three minutes, breathing through an oxygen mask, while a muscle relaxant, succinylcholine, rendered you motionless.

And so it began. The machine transmitted to your brain a series of "brief pulse currents": intermittent electrical charges, each lasting between one and six seconds. The currents measured some eight hundred milliamps—equal to the units required by a cell phone battery charger. But you slept peaceably, reacting in only the slightest way. About five minutes into The Procedure, your toes fluttered and curled, as if tickled by a feather.

Simultaneously, the EEG indicated a spike in brain activity, which indicated the beginnings of a seizure, which precipitated a kind of neurological reboot: neurotransmitters firing, serotonin surging. This was your brain on electricity.

Or something like that. You had trouble explaining precisely how and why the brain took to ECT, because the doctors had never told you, because they didn't know, either. They had plenty of hypotheses, most of them involving various permutations of the computer-reboot scenario.

Meantime, though, ECT remained a conviction based on circumstantial evidence. There was plenty of that. According to most experts, between 60 and 70 percent of all ECT patients saw a marked improvement, often within a week or two. The typical shockhead required six to eight sessions, three times a week: sluggish brains, like sluggish motors, usually required repeated revs. ECT wouldn't eradicate the disease(s) that caused the symptoms. Relapses were to be expected but often could be forestalled or minimized by way of periodic "maintenance" sessions.

Within ten minutes or so, The Procedure was over.

Forty minutes later, you were changing into your street clothes, clutching discharge instructions, and mulling whether to stop for sandwiches or burritos. You were a little pale, weary. But that's how you always felt. The anesthetic had run its course, and the wheelchair seemed unnecessary. But Nurse K had insisted. Regulations and so forth.

Nurse K wheeled you out to the lobby. Paula approached, tentatively. She was unsure whether you even recognized her.

"Hi!" she said.

"Caitlin!" you said. "Hi!"

There was silence.

"Hi," you said. "*Paula.*"

The hilarity eluded her. While you had been napping comfortably, she and her baby were left to kill nearly two and a half hours in the dead zone between psych wards. The steel doors. The inpatients occasionally heard but never seen. Mother and son did see one other shockhead, though. He had drool on his chin and glaze in his eyes as a nurse wheeled him toward his wife. Like a standard poodle being returned to its owner.

As if the dog tableau wasn't freaky enough, Paula had Nurse K pulling her aside and saying that Paula couldn't let you out of her sight for the next twenty-four hours, because otherwise you might wander into traffic or forget to turn off the gas stove or god only knew what, because you were a Mentally Impaired Person (one who would likely remain so until the dust settled, by tomorrow). As if *that* wasn't enough, Paula was required to sign documents that said, in essence: *"For the next forty-eight hours, this mental patient will be solely Paula's responsibility. In the event that Paula lets this doddering half-wit out of her sight, even for a millisecond, agents of this hospital will seize Paula's assets and explode her house. Seriously."*

"You're a saint," you said.

"Stop it," she said.

Already you were pissing and moaning about the wheelchair situation, which felt degrading on its merits, and which also attracted unwanted attention from strangers (which made things even more degrading). By the time a nurse deposited you at the curb, you were in fine form.

"We'll be home soon," she said.

"I could eat," you said.

The honeymoon ended thirty minutes later, in a precious lunch spot in West Hollywood. The muscles in the back of your neck had stiffened, triggering a dull, helmet-like headache; queasiness set in, followed by cold sweat, followed by mutual anxiety. You slouched over your steak sandwich, palms bracing your head. "Please take me home," you said.

Instead, Paula drove you to her house, in one of the canyons just east of Los Feliz. You crashed in the guest bedroom, while the other baby slept in his bassinette. You awakened two hours later, a bit rejuvenated, then found the two of them in the living room.

"*How* are you?" Paula asked.

"Better," you said. "Definately."

Charlie's blinky pinkness demanded acknowledgment.

"Hiiiii . . ." you said.

Trailing off. Pointing.

"Um," you said. "I don't know his name."

———

As scheduled, Ben and Daniel manned the night shift. As scheduled, they provided home-cooked deliciousness (salmon, cake), high thread counts, and HBO. They cleaned your dirty plates before you could feign interest in doing so. They let you veto their preferred show, *Project Runway,* in favor of an Animal Planet double bill: *Escape to Chimp Eden* and *Clinically Wild: Alaska.*

"Tell me what I can do right now," Daniel said.

Most people, including you, went passive in such situations: "Is there anything I can do?" or "If you need something, just ask."

Ben and Daniel went straight to active—exactly as your mother did. Help wasn't available upon request. Help was *happening.*

"Please tell me how you feel," Ben said. "Don't just say 'I'm fine' and change the subject."

That there was little talk of The Procedure itself was probably just as well, since you remembered none of it, save for the occasional postcard: the nurse's face, the doctor's beard. The hours prior to ECT amounted to a montage in *Cat Fancy*: paws beneath the bedroom door, Buck savaging his scratching post; the six hours immediately following The Procedure were gone, too. Entirely.

"Is that *so weird*?" Lizz asked, by phone.

"Not really," you said.

"Did I freak you out by asking that?"

"Not really."

You sensed, in this moment, that something special had happened. That you had lost your cherry. That those who fear amnesia are those who haven't had it.

Slept like a prince. In the morning, having shed the cobwebs and summoned the name of Paula's baby, you were cleared to return home for the rest of the weekend. By lunchtime, you were seated beneath the giant palm tree in your backyard, updating your mother by cell phone:

"In and out," you said. "Like an x-ray."

"Really?" she said.

"Really."

You turned the conversation in a more desirable direction. Dad, true to form, had rebounded nicely from his health scare. His voice was a bit brittle, owing to the meds. But he was nearly back to full health.

"So, my boy . . . ?" he said.

And the race was on.

"Dad," you said. "How are—"

"Oh, fine. Easy."

"Really? Any response?"

"Hard to tell. Maybe. Might take a week or so."

"And that's typical, right?"

"Absolutely."

A pause. The opening you needed.

"But how are *you*—"

"Much better," he said. "Almost human again."

"Doctors are pleased?"

"And pleased to be rid of me."

"Any side effects?"

"A little tired. But I don't wanna talk about me. How are *you*?"

Still the master. Even now, a few days removed from the hospital, he outdeflected the best of them.

Once the conversation ended, muffled sounds drew you to the narrow walkway leading to the front of the house. The sounds—a rattling door, footsteps on blacktop—suggested human activity, which was lose-lose even in the best-case scenario, which was really just the best worst-case scenario, which involved yet another awkward conversation with an ex-con trafficking in bogus magazine subscriptions and white guilt. The worse worst-case scenarios involved home invasion and neighborly neighbors.

What you hadn't expected to find were two pairs of girly shoes (pastel, side by side) on the front stoop. The first were simple flats, tan colored, adult-size; the second were tiny slippers, light pink, with neon-pink sparkles.

Through the kitchen window, you watched Caitlin and Lucy negotiate with the cats. The little terrorists were all over the place. Yowling. Lunging. Rising up against the blond imperialists. But Caitlin let them be, saying "Oh, *you.*" Lucy thought it was a big game of tag. The cats fled to closets unknown; the humans settled in the kitchen, unpacking bags filled with berries and baked goods.

You'd been anticipating this moment for days—which is to say, fearing it. Caitlin and Lucy had always been welcome guests. But this was the first mother-daughter overnighter in house history. Potential hazards were many; there were cats to consider. It was tricky enough handling one interloper; now you'd also have a miniature duplicate, a little stealth clone, assessing your lifestyle choices. Drawing conclusions. *Judging.*

But to see them now, in the fishbowl sense, was a relief. It seemed as if the kitchen were their kitchen, and as if you were just dropping by for cobbler. Your family's kitchen, back in Michigan, had always been the central gathering spot; all anyone did was eat or talk about eating. Mom cooked for a family of pig-boys; Dad baked habitually. But your current kitchen, during the five years you'd owned it, had housed zero gatherings. It was the place where the door was.

The house looked different with people in it. Animated. Lucy scaled your left flank, as if climbing a tree; Caitlin presented a vanilla cupcake. "This one's yours," she said. "Lucy picked it."

"Cuckay," Lucy said.

The ease with which the three of you interacted was notable, given that you were a feeble-minded loser who wasn't half as manly as all the other guys she could (and should) have been with. She was one of those for-better-or-worse people you'd heard about. And she couldn't do much worse than you. So there it was.

She asked about The Procedure only after Lucy went down for the night, in the guest room across the hall. The imp had done so without a peep; the cats, less so. The guest room was their last redoubt. Now, displaced and outraged, they battered your bedroom door, demanding justice. Caitlin invited them in, and you climbed into bed. Just the four of you.

"Does this freak you out?" she asked.

"No," you said. "Freaks her out."

"I mean this. Us. Me and Lucy."

"God, no. It's a gift."

"A little?"

Yes.

"No."

She touched your forehead.

"Did it hurt?" she asked.

"Does it freak you out?" you asked.

"Not at all," she said.

"A little bit?"

"Only a little."

"I know. I'm sorry."

"For what?"

"Being a crazy freak."

"Takes one to know one—"

"I know I'm a nightmare."

"Stop," she said.

"And I'm *really* sorry."

"It's okay. Rest."

Heads on pillows. Eyes shut.

"Everything's about to get better," you said.

That's when it first happened: 5:30, eyes open, cats baffled. The zero-to-sixty effect was refreshing—normally, there was a larval stage. The breeze, once you opened the window, felt different. *Cleaner.* Greedily, you angled your head through the opening. A terrier at the window of a speeding car. Tongue slapping ear.

Onto the roof. The rubbery shingles (slate gray, paperback size) pleased the feet, like the turf at Michigan Stadium; the give stabilized the heels and toes, while the novice house climber negotiated the roof's awkward, forty-five-degree incline. An exhaust chimney provided all the support and leverage you needed to make a successful ascent.

When you summited, ten seconds later, you naturally faced southward, toward the city: downtown to the left, Hollywood to the right, Los Feliz below. Immediately, two thoughts sprung to mind.

The first was that this was awesome.

The second was that *you* were awesome.

These thoughts arrived in step with the laser show, which was the best you'd ever seen (and you'd seen plenty); it began in miniature, with a few mottled streaks—pale yellows and pinks—inching over the foothills due west of your house. You blinked, and the downtown skyscrapers were mirrored grain silos, more peach than pink, and poised for lift-off. The skyscrapers briefly melted, then unmelted.

Then everything became a Santana album; everything was the cover of *Abraxas*: a psilocybin universe of fire-dragon reds, yellows, and oranges, with nods to cosmology, Gnosticism, and José Feliciano. This was in the early stages, when things were more rise than sun. Once separation was achieved, and the sun became a magical orange in the sky, everything morphed into the band's follow-up album. This was *Caravanserai*, whose cover featured a less vivid but more majestic image: a magical orange sun in the sky.

Magical orange.

Rolled off the tongue. Rang a bell.

Or not. Couldn't recall.

Couldn't recall most things. What day it was. Your phone number. Didn't care.

You felt yourself laughing. You felt giddy. You wondered how long you could stare at the sun without blinking.

CHAPTER ELEVEN

For seven consecutive mornings, from the exact same vantage point, you saw your first sunrise.

It always started the same way. At 5:30 A.M., in darkness, you awakened from a dead sleep. No bleating alarms. No furry incursions. The cats would be caught flat-footed; ever since they'd established a beachhead between you and Caitlin, at the beginning of the week, they'd lost their competitive edge. Now, each time you nudged them aside and padded through the darkness, they became incrementally more indignant and embarrassed. They spent most of the time either infighting or pretending to be asleep. The latter act was easy to suss out, because their eyes were open.

You opened the bathroom window, which faced the backyard. The screen was missing, thanks to one of Buck's jailbreaks. With one quick shimmy, you were out.

You'd be standing out there, legs planted firmly on the slanted rooftop. You'd be flanked by darkened treetops and facing southward toward the city, which stretched infinitely in either direction. Now it was just a matter of waiting for the sun.

Electricity, you'd think.

The circadian state of grace spanned the first full week of ECT, while you were in the care of a special-guest nanny. This was your dear old friend Jim, who normally lived in Washington, D.C., but who was spending the year in Northern California. Jim was one of the lucky few who had been preapproved for ECT duty, because he was one of the few people you didn't want to beat with a shovel.

The comfort level had existed since the first day you'd met, on the first day of college. He was an "honors student" who looked like Kevin Bacon and loved the Grateful Dead. He studied like a fiend, wrote ponderous op-eds for the school paper, and joined a "secret society" called Michigamua, which was really just Skull and Bones for jackasses who couldn't get into Yale.

But the boy had skills. He turned his door room into a kind of Zen lounge, replete with entertainment system, plush carpeting, and percussion instruments. He projected a heady, vaguely Scandinavian calm. "Just relax," he'd say whenever you freaked out. "Let's think this through."

Now a Washington think tank paid him to think about trees and pipelines or some such. Whenever people asked Jim to describe his job, he'd hesitate. "I'm an environmental economist," he'd say. "Which means I . . ." At which point, he might as well have been speaking Aramaic. His work was so wonky, even he couldn't explain it. That you had no idea what he did—that he was a Ph.D. and you were a "learning-disabled" boob immune to the most rudimentary geometry tests, block puzzles, or household appliances—spoke to the transcendent power of friendship.

Jim, though a fixture of the Peter Pan Olympics, always finished a distant second to you. He had a wife, a daughter, and Positions Of Great Responsibility—the latest being a one-year teaching post at Stanford. As if the move weren't stressful enough—uprooted family, Stanford weasels—Jim's wife, Lisa, had fallen ill. She recovered nicely, but only after weeks of misery and bed rest. (Plus, he'd spent New Year's watching you stare at the ceiling for three days.) What a perfect time for Jim to spend his vacation time down in Los Angeles, shuttling you to the bin.

"I'm sorry," you said.

"Don't be," he said.

Twice Jim was there as the swinging doors opened and a nurse rolled you out: blinkered, woozy, sounding like Jerry Quarry. But not the sad, tragic, white-patsy Jerry Quarry. The *good* Jerry Quarry. The scrappy heavyweight contender. The blue-collar hero with the brains of a hamster but the heart of a lion. In the car, you'd be chatty, dispensing wisdom about sushi rolls or Michigan's new spread offense.

"It's all about speed," you'd say.

But then, about halfway home, you would remember why you were seated in the passenger seat of your own car. This memory, like all subsequent ones, made the trip less enjoyable. By the time you reached home, you were the bad Jerry Quarry.

"I'm *really* sorry," you said.

"Really, don't be," he said. "No need to keep saying—"

He stopped. Annoyance into guilt.

"I'm sorry," he said.

"For what?"

Between heaven and hell lay the purgatory called semiamnesia.

"I'm sorry you're going through this shit," he said. "I'm sorry I'm not doing *more*."

While you slept and slept, the selfish prick spent the week fetching tacos, untangling computer wires, and facing retribution: twice a day, in hissing fury, Scrub would spring from the shadows and savage Jim's ankles. You'd awaken to a distant crashing sound, followed by a shriek—"HOLY FUCK!"—followed by keening silence. Then you'd go back to sleep until it was time for Jim to spring for dinner.

The first real action occurred on the day between the second and third ECT sessions. Late that afternoon, Jim drove you down to see Caitlin and Lucy. He was eager to meet them but didn't know what to expect, because you always changed the subject, because avoidance was bliss. "The mystery of Caitlin," he said. "The black box."

The three of them got along famously, in that Scandinavian way—by the time the salads arrived, Lucy thought Jim was her father. The three Nords were so immersed in whatever it was that those people talk about—seafaring, craftsmanship—they barely noticed your exit. "Be right back," you said. "Forgot to return a call."

The déjà vu was under way. The first wave arrived after you asked Lucy if she missed Scrub. "Buck!" she squealed. This prompted one of Caitlin's big, beautiful laughs. You were sitting there, basking in the laugh—both the sound and sight of it—when suddenly it became a different laugh from a different time. Or times. Or something. You weren't recalling details. Just *sensing* them. They were little ghosts. They seemed illusory. Conjured.

Suddenly you weren't so sure about the dinner table laugh, either. You looked at Caitlin, scanning for clues, trying to latch onto something. That's when the déjà weirdness became unbearable.

You knew everything about Caitlin.

But you remembered nothing.

Things got a little fuzzy at that point. Next thing you knew, you were out in the parking lot, iPhone hard against your left ear. "This is important," you were saying. "Just hear me out—"

That's when Caitlin appeared, clasped your hand tightly and silently mouthed the words *Are you okay?*

"*Guh!*" you said, and hung up.

"I got worried," she said.

"Why?"

"You were gone awhile."

The dinner plates were gone.

"Oh," you said. "Wow."

You were changing the subject to dessert when a voice piped up.

"Who talk?" Lucy asked.

She lunged for the phone. It happened fast.

"My family," you said. "My mommy and daddy."

She found this riotous. Caitlin and Jim just found it odd, given the cone of secrecy.

"Long story," you said.

Lucy broke into the singsong she reserved for special occasions.

"Mommy, Daddy," she sang. "Mommy, Daddy."

You were back in the car, bombing toward downtown Los Angeles, when the weirdness returned. It was 9:00 P.M.; the freeway, like the whole of downtown, evinced a kind of lunar emptiness: Los Angeles, The City That Sleeps. Jim was in the driver's seat, fiddling with the stereo and invoking *Blade Runner*. "It's not just the story," he said. "It's the atmosphere."

The words hung there. Jim knew you hated nothing so much as science fiction, sci-fantasy, and pretty much anything involving hover-crafts, time-space continuums, or interstellar Wars, Treks, Galacticae. (Also, dunes.) He was fishing.

"See, there's your problem," Jim said. "Your problem is, you don't like *Blade Runner*."

Nothing.

"Oh, I forgot you work at *Vanity Fair*," he said, with tone. "Hey, what's hot at Sundance this year?"

Now he knew something was up. Nobody rose to bait faster than you—under any circumstance, Jim would be hip-deep in aspersions about bean-counting Swedes with State Department haircuts.

"Almost home," he said. "Good night's sleep—"

"Fuck Caitlin," you said.

He laughed.

"Yeah," he said. "Fuck that bitch."

He stopped laughing when he saw your face.

"This is serious?" he asked.

"She isn't there for me," you said. "So I'm not there for her."

"What? Wait. She's not?"

"Can't deal with me being sick," you said. "The depression. The ECT. All of it."

His puzzlement was obvious.

"Really?" he said. "That's not the impression I get."

"Well, you haven't seen it."

He nodded. Due deference.

"Just help me understand," he said. "Tonight, when you were outside, all she talked about was how much she wanted to help you."

No response. Freaked him out a little.

"Ben and Daniel said she's been a saint," he said. "To be honest, I've always had the impression that you were keeping her at arm's length."

"That's bullshit," you said.

"Fine. I'm just saying let's think this through."

"I'm done talking."

Silence for miles.

An hour later, you found Jim sitting in the backyard, drinking a beer.

"This is fucked-up," you said.

You walked him through the déjà vu situation. Minutes earlier, while listening to voicemails, each voice sparked "memories" of conversations past. And now, as you moved through the yard, you moved through every yard you'd ever visited.

"That is fucked-up," Jim said.

"Actually, the yard part's kind of cool," you said. "Like an acid trip."

"You've never taken an acid trip."

"That's what makes it cool."

You both headed inside.

"Feels like something's turning over," you said.

"In a good way or a bad way?"

Fingers crossed.

All night you dreamt of golden bears. The dream was plotless, a German film-school project similar to ones you'd produced in your dreams during the post-9/11 fallout. The setting, as per usual, was a white wilderness far, far away; the "plot" was a hodgepodge of poorly lit vignettes (bears walk, bears climb) and bad metaphors (bears roar). But the performances were top-notch. They were the two grizzlies last seen from a bush plane in Alaska. The bears who loved you.

The next morning, like clockwork, you were up at 5:30, on your roof. You perched on the slanted rooftop, basking in the cool spring air, feeling blessedly awake. Seemed a perfect time to check in with friends and family back in the Eastern Time Zone. You dialed your parents' number. Or tried to. The number—the only one the family had ever had—escaped you. So did both your brothers' numbers. So did everyone else's.

Then, as if guided from above and detached from your brain, your fingers touched the iPhone and dialed. The number just came to you.

"Well, hello," came the voice.

The little, raspy bird voice. The one you hadn't heard in two years, maybe longer.

"Somebody's up early," Mimi said.

"I knew you'd be up, too," you said.

"Yeah. But I'm three hours ahead."

"But you've been up for six."

"How'd you know that?"

"Because you sleep like a bird."

The little Marlboro-bird laugh.

"I was going to call you today," she said.

Abraxas. Latin for "Abracadabra."

"*Really?*" you said.

"Well, why wouldn't I?"

"Why *would* you?"

She paused.

"Wait," she said. "Did you not leave me a message last night?"

Hard to say.

"Just wanted to say hi," you said.

"I'm glad," she said.

"See how you're doing."

"I'm a cow."

"Somehow I doubt that."

She made a mooing sound.

A sound you missed. A sound you remembered.

"Knew that was coming," you said.

"How are *you*?" she asked.

"Never better."

"How are the cats?"

"They miss you."

"They hate me."

"They hate everyone."

It was all coming so easily. The bad old days were forgotten.

"Haven't seen you in forever," you said. "I miss you."

"Aww," she said. "I'd love to see you."

And there it was. Nakedly.

"I need to hop on a conference call," she said. "But keep in touch. I'll be here all spring."

Begging for it. Between the lines.

When you hung up, the sun beamed.

Electricity, you thought. Electricity was everywhere.

That was just science.

The cityscape all around you. Electric.

The phone in your hand. Electronic.

The earth beneath you. Electromagnetic.

The sun rising above you. Electricifinity.

Admittedly, you were a tad late to the game vis-à-vis the fire-in-the-sky thing. Hats off to cave dwellers and apocalyptic cultists. Also, those little Stonehenge people. Also, the native tribal communities of Alaska (the Ojibwa, the Tlingit) and Antarctica (the penguins). All were devout sun-worshippers; emperors, when marching, seemed to follow solar (and lunar and stellar) cues.

Whereas you developed skin cancer.

Shunned the sun. Killed the switches. Unplugged.

And darkness fell.

And then you rose again. Electroconvulsively.

I sing the body.

Dylan goes.

Electric. The ultimate "up" word.

By week's end, you were buzzing with life. You, like everyone else, had spent years pretending to have read *Infinite Jest,* David Foster Wallace's titanic novel about . . . whatever it was bipolar freaks wrote about. You'd never gotten past the second chapter. All that loopy, manic, nonlinear mumbo jumbo was for shit.

Now it read like running water. Now it spoke to you.

"Are we not all of us fanatics?" the writer asks, before explicating the degree to which people generally and Americans specifically are enslaved by needless attachments to people generally and America specifically. The character who speaks these truths is Remy Marathe, an operative for a group of legless Quebecois secessionists called the Wheelchair Assassins. (Also, his wife has no skull.) Find that one thing bigger than yourself, he says. "Choose your temple of fanaticism with great care," he suggests. To do otherwise is pure madness, especially if your attachments are of the flesh and blood variety. It was all so clear now: "Persons leave, lie, go mad, have sickness, betray you, die."

You drive. The love of a good woman.

"Take the next road on the right," she said.

That voice. The velvet hammer. No dithering, no dissembling; no pity, no judgments. She had it all figured out. She's had *you* figured out.

This was good. This was *very* good.

252 | NED ZEMAN

Finally, a connection. More or less. At times like these, you couldn't be too picky. Everyone agreed on that much. If only you could remember who they were.

"Take the next road on the right," she said. "Then turn right."

Too late. You were Listening Without Hearing. There had been a few problems of late, but this one was tops. Ben and Daniel had been carping about it. (This was another problem.)

So what began as a right-turn turns into a left. Which wasn't the biggest deal until you jerked the wheel back to the right, then left again, then right, and then somehow found a nice little groove between both lanes. That gorgeous line. This clean, white broken line. God's eyes, god's ears. *Shoo-shoo-shoo.*

White over black, wheels over blacktop. Sunset, Boulevard of Dreams. Honk all you want, rubes. *Tourists.*

You hung a right near the Scientology center, then headed straight for Bronson Canyon. Unfortunately, the park's front gate was locked. Something about "regular hours." As if 5:00 A.M. was "irregular."

Over the chain-link fence. Down into the park. Where it was just you, the moon, and a few hundred coyotes. The skinny wretches always seemed shocked, *shocked,* to see another living soul. They never took their beady red eyes off you.

Headphones on. Hit "play."

"Hail to the victors valiant / Hail to the conquering heroes . . ."

You trotted. Ran. Ascended.

"Hail, hail, to Michigan, the champions of the West."

Twenty minutes later, having barely broken a sweat, you reached the giant white letters in the sky: HOLLYWOOD.

The sun was coming up. The sky was imperial blue. You caught sight of an airplane headed due east, in a beeline to New York.

CHAPTER TWELVE

The next ECT session was postponed by the Gods Of Destiny. It was out of your hands. Word came down first thing Sunday morning, midway through your diurnal tree line constitutional (which, by the way, was splendid). Session Five, originally scheduled for the following day, would now take place three days hence, on Wednesday morning.

Force majeure. Deus ex machina. Semper Fi.

So now you had three days and two options. You could either seize the moment (*carpe*) or let it seize you (*diabolus!*). So, really, there was only one option. Which made it (*ipso*) something other than an option, but this was no time to get bogged down in technicalities. The important thing, the take-away, was that you saw the postponement for what it really was. A test. A Rubicon.

Also, an opportunity. That was the biggie. The *o*-word kept rattling about, as if lodged somewhere between your cranial nerve and cerebral cortex. The echoes transported you back to the loneliest night of your career. The night you attended *VF*'s ad-sales dinner in Santa Fe. The Night Of The Blue Iguana-tinis. And the team-building exercises. And a thousand exhortations to Think Outside The Box, Push The Envelope, and find Windows Of Opportunity.

Now it all made sense. Now you flung open that window and asked for more, please. Time was of the essence; an executive decision was at hand. At the end of the day, as the sales folk say, it was all about results (ibid). Another buzzword of the moment? *Proactive*.

You emailed the A-team about "the scheduling change" and your revised plans for the day. You just needed to move fast. Move some things around. "Taking a 'personal day' tomorrow," you told the usual suspects, via email. "May be a little hard to reach."

Then, skyward. The flight took off from Burbank Airport, located ten miles north of Griffith Park, on the discount side of the hills. And the hills, as seen from an ascending jet on a baby-blue day, called to mind Sicily in the days after Michael whacked Sollozzo. You fixed on the peaks you'd visited hours earlier, near Beachwood Canyon. Could have sworn you spotted a bear.

Admittedly, the spotting may have had something to do with the little plastic mascot you'd found in your computer bag. The Mimi-grizzly, having retreated from view for two long winters, had suddenly emerged from the wilderness, in time for the spring run.

You remembered all relevant details about Mimi, about bears, and the history. You remembered that the plan was to hand deliver the bear to Mimi. The only thing you couldn't remember was where the hell you were supposed to meet her. Or when. You couldn't even recall what neighborhood she lived in, although you were certain it was a fancy one. Tribeca, maybe. Or was that Evgenia? Or both? Did Tribeca, like Condé Nast, the Ivy League, and you, have dibs on all the tiny, blue-eyed Jewesses?

But you remembered the iPhone. And the iPhone remembered everything.

"Usual place," Mimi said. "Usual time."

"Of course," you said.

Here the average amnesiac might have panicked and blown his cover. The skilled amnesiac navigated minefields.

"Say, do you recall the address?" you asked. "I might meet a work friend there later, and the poor thing couldn't find her way out of a paper bag."

Bingo.

"Great!" you said. "So I'll be seeing you in about . . . *shit* . . . damned watch died again."

Ibid.

"Great!" you said. "See you in two hours."

"Aces," she said.

Aces! Sweet relief. Initially, at the beginning of the conversation, you thought you detected something amiss. "Usual place" sounded clipped, harried—the tone reserved for telemarketers. But then, once she threw down the ace, the truth was revealed. Mimi, bless her bite-size heart, was *excited*. Her mouth couldn't keep pace with her revving brain, as usual. Her verbal communications resembled her emails. They arrived as random staccato chirps. As in: "Aces."

It all came together in the taxi, as the nice Pakistani man barreled toward Manhattan, en route to your hotel in . . . the borough of Manhattan. The specifics proved elusive. Fortunately, per the doctor's instructions, you'd written everything down. Somewhere.

"Name of hotel?" the Pakistani asked.

"No," you said.

"Street?"

"No."

"Neighborhood?"

"No."

He took a long look.

"West Village," you said.

"Just anywhere?"

"Just fast. I'm in a big hurry—"

It was about timing and preparation. Arrive early. Control the playing field. Execute the game plan.

As usual, though, Mimi was a step ahead of you. She had secured the restaurant's lone outside table—a two-seater, in a narrow patio between the entrance and the street. She sat in her standard three-point stance, simultaneously smoking an American Spirit, drinking a glass of red, and typing on her BlackBerry.

"Same as it ever was," you said.

"Ooh," she said. "One sec."

You hovered for a few seconds, as she dispatched her email. This was a do-or-die moment. Up until now, you had been operating under the assumption of sanity. Everyone in your inner circle—friends, medical professionals—had offered repeated assurances that you looked and sounded normal—that, aside from the occasional senior moment, nothing about you screamed "shockhead," "mental patient," or "amnesiac" (or all three).

And yet. There was always the possibility that these people, despite their pathological honesty, were simply trying to spare your feelings. You were, after all, a mental patient (and arguably, at this point, *an escaped mental patient*). You didn't remember much, but you remembered some of the other potato heads from the ECT ward. Their friends probably told them they looked normal, too. Oh, Jesus.

"Almost done," Mimi said.

She looked the same as ever, except for a slight alteration in hairstyle: shorter, more editrix than blogette. Same black-on-black Mimi-wear; same unlined skin and swimming pool eyes. Maybe a bit more skittish than usual. But that was to be expected, given the magnitude of her emotions.

"Well, hello," she said. Smiling. Rising.

The embrace, though brief, felt like home. Her head at your chest; her oversize wristwatch sliding and clattering down her forearm.

"You look great," you said.

"Cow," she said. "My ass fell again."

She laughed. Exhaling smoke. Sideways.

The anxiety melted away. You passed the test.

"Glad we're doing this," you said.

"Me, too," she said.

"Really? Are you?"

"Of course. It's nice to see you. It's been what?"

"Two and a half years."

She set down her glass.

"Yikes," she said.

"We've got a lot of catching-up to do," you said.

"You go first."

You leaned forward. Almost embarrassed.

"Well," you said. "Everything's been *pretty great*."

For thirty minutes, while guzzling a beer called Old Thumper, you regaled Mimi with tales of triumph and tinsel. Oh, sure, "George's" house in Lake Como *was* pretty impressive. No, "Mel" wasn't *all* bad. But whatever. They were just colleagues, really. Hardly worth mentioning.

Sort of like the ECT stuff. Which you skipped altogether. Just worked out that way.

"Anyway," you said. "Ever heard of a writer named George Trow?"

"The one from *The New Yorker*," Mimi said.

"Wow. You have?"

"He's not the one you mentioned five minutes ago?"

Pause.

"Jet lag," you said.

"Feeling dehydrated?" she asked.

"Nope. Why?"

"Never seen you drink that fast."

You were signaling the waiter for a third round.

"It's a light beer," you said. Pointing to her glass. "Chianti, right?"

She placed her palm over the glass.

"Never seen you stop drinking that fast," you said.

She tapped her giant watch.

"I've got a dinner," she said. "Remember?"

Yes and no.

"Of course," you said. "But not before you give me the rundown."

She spoke in emailese, blitzing from subject to subject. Work ok . . . friends r fine . . . kitchen redone. Life in general, she said, was "mezza-mezza." She was stir-crazy. She was tired. She mentioned—in passing, while fumbling for a cigarette—"a guy I'm seeing."

Not "my boyfriend." Not even "*the* guy."

It occurred to you, at this moment, that she was crying out. That she was doing what she always did. Planting seeds. Baiting. If she'd wanted to scare you off, she would have oversold the guy. She would have dropped the prick's name all over the place. *Brad has a little place in East Hampton, but not the fancy part. . . . Tripp runs a hedge fund, but he's really down to earth.* Instead, she was almost apologetic. She was saying, in essence, "I'm yours."

And, really, that's all you needed to hear. This was a targeted strike. Swift. Surgical. In the morning, you'd be halfway back to California. Mission accomplished.

That was the first reason.

"We'll do this again soon," you said.

"Okay," she said.

It was all between the lines.

You watched her skitter down the street, toward her favorite overpriced Japanese place. She had an extra bounce in her steps. Unfortunately, just before the clincher—the inevitable backward glance—the damned crickets ruined the moment. The problem was a recurrent one. That's because you kept forgetting the last time you'd stopped and said, "*Crickets*? What the . . . ?" only to eventually trace the sound to your iPhone. At which point, you'd make a mental note ("remember cricket ringtone!") identical in every way to the reminder you'd written the last time.

"Hello," you said.

"Just checking in," Caitlin said.

"Okay," you said. "Can I call you back later?"

"Sure. Is everything okay?"

"Fine. Just in a hurry."

"Okay, well, I'll be at—"

Click.

You hailed a cab, then barked out an address you had scribbled on your left palm. The cab headed over the Brooklyn Bridge and past the streets where you had spent your formative crack-up years, in the late nineties. The journey ended outside a restaurant on Smith Street, which was located in an area called Cobble Hill, which was the hippest section in Brooklyn, which was like being the prettiest girl in Poland. But whatever. The bar, like all bars on Smith Street, endeavored to be old-school—speakeasy meets tapas-bar—even though the previous tenant had probably been a Kinko's.

There you met, for the first time, a lovely young woman. Her name was Erin. She had dewy eyes and long, studiously mussed brown hair. She was a writer, talented but young. Late twenties. She resembled a girl who'd broken your heart many years ago.

It occurred to you, while catching her eye, that you were catnip. Increasingly, over the past week or so, women drew near. Homed. You detected, while walking the streets, telltale signs of smolder. Your gaze would catch hers—briefly, long-lens—and the image would autozoom, autofocus, and color correct. There would be a low whirring sound, punctuated by a sharp *clop-clack*. Maximum shutter speed. Full resolution. Magazine quality.

Just kept happening. Virally, as they say. Old girlfriends called out of the blue. Or Face-stalked. Or invited you to drinks in the West

Village. Meantime, some random acquaintance emails. Urges you to meet a friend of hers the next time you're in New York. This sort of thing hadn't happened in two years. Now, the day you book a flight to JFK, boom: It's raining dewy young literistas.

What were the women detecting? Some sort of electrical field? Dr. E would know. Or a pheromone deal? Or some sort of virtual viral-marketing campaign? Hell if you knew. Hell if you cared. Did the male emperor penguin ask, after weeks of solitary egg balancing, "Hey, where'd all the broads come from?" No, he did not. (See also: grizzlies, springtime.)

It occurred to you, while shaking the literista's hand, that you were a walking emporium of sexual dynamism. This was quite a change, following your year-long apprenticeship in advanced eunuchry. Suddenly, every time you came into contact with an attractive woman—or even a half-attractive one, or even a semiambulatory one—your blood boiled. Literally. As if you'd mainlined hot buttered rum. Already Mimi had left you in a state—at one point, you'd requested bread, lest you start kneading the poor girl. Now, as you settled in with this Erin person, and basked in her dewiness, you were vibrating.

She was engaging, chatty, and only as dark as a good-looking person can credibly be. That's pretty much all you took away from the dinner, because it disappeared. Vaporized. At 7:30, you were leaning across the table and saying "You look like the girl who broke my heart . . ." Next thing you knew, it was morning and you were in a cab bound for JFK; you held, in your lap, two items. The first was your wallet, an old black warhorse bursting with crumpled receipts, among them one from a five-star hotel in Lower Manhattan. Check-in date: last night. Total room charges: 950.50 dollars.

Nothing. Zero. But in a refreshing way.

The second item was the iPhone, which bore voicemails from Daniel and Caitlin. Both of them sounded strangely concerned.

"Please call," Daniel said. "I just want to make sure I understand where you are."

"I'm a little unclear about your schedule," Caitlin said.

It was now the middle of the night in Los Angeles. So you turned off the phone. Then something occurred you. It was the middle of the night in Los Angeles.

"Getting on the plane," you told Daniel's machine. "Home this afternoon."

"Where'd you go?" you asked Caitlin's machine. "Dinner tomorrow?"

The mood, upon takeoff, was buoyant. That you retained precious few memories of the night prior—even most of the Mimi stuff was lost in the cushions—was of little consequence. How silly it would be to dwell on events that, for all intents and purposes, hadn't happened. Life, on this sweet spring morning, was about missing the trees for the forest. All you knew, and all you needed to know, was the big-picture theme:

It was October in Alaska, and you were a bear.

The landing could have been softer. You had fallen asleep midway through the flight, thanks to your first-ever morning drunk. (Scotch and Ativan: the thinking man's mimosa.) Everything was black velvet until a sudden commotion—*buh-BUM*P—heralded the beginning of the end.

From the moment the plane touched down in Burbank, and for weeks thereafter, the barometric pressure was variable, moodwise. When it was low, as it had been during the week of treetops and airplanes, you were high; when it was high, as it was once you returned to earth, you were low. And when it was neither high nor low, as it was about a third of the time, you were Nebraska.

But damned if the needle didn't keep bouncing all over the place. That was the real challenge. The electrolife was like riding shotgun in a bush plane over Kodiak, Alaska. One minute you'd be telling the pilot "Hey, look at all the little bears down there!"; the next, you'd be squeezing flotation devices and screaming, "I hope these bears gnaw your fucking face off!"

To wit:

You were, while exiting the plane in Burbank, maybe a shade beneath Nebraska. You were Topeka. Hardly a dream destination. But at least it wasn't Texas. You were comfortable among the cornheads. A native Midwesterner. You came from a place where everyone ate big starchy breakfasts, shunned public displays of emotion, and minded their own fucking business.

But now, the instant you set foot in Los Angeles, the Nosey Parkers sprung from every angle, like jackals to a sleeping gazelle. Daniel drew first blood, after abruptly materializing at the kitchen door. Uninvited.

"So I'm sure I'm being annoying," he said. Accurately. "But I was a little confused about where you were yesterday. And I want to make sure you're okay."

"Thanks," you said. "Very okay."

"Okay, great."

"Okay, then."

He smiled, thrust his hands in his pockets, and nodded. This was a tell. It signaled that he was about to be blunt, but in a Quakery way. Also, it said he was a little fearful that you might stop loving him.

"Okay," he said. "So just bear with me."

"Okay," you said.

"Okay, great. So yesterday you went to . . . ?"

"Boston," you said.

A world without white lies was a world in flames.

"Okay," he said. "And you went to Boston to see . . . ?"

It was almost as if he thought you were an amnesiac or something.

"My doctors," you said. "At McLean."

As you had stated previously. On his voicemail. In the middle of the night.

"Here's the confusion," he said. "When we saw you two days ago, on Sunday night, you didn't mention a trip to Boston the next day."

There was a pause.

"Damn," you said. "Amnesia."

"I understand."

"Thank you—"

"What you *did* say was that you'd be spending the day with Lucy. At her surgery."

There was a pause. A sense of internal strife. The war between your two armies of the night—amnesiac versus liar—had begun.

Lying was difficult enough on the face of it—nobody ever fully appreciated the degree of handiwork that went into your signature brand of dishonesty, with its emphasis on subtleties (hedges, deflections) rather than mass-market whoppers. You rarely lied to anyone, except by omission or measure. Any clown could make shit up. The beauty was in what you *didn't* say (or clarify or emphasize); it was in the antimatter of human communication. There was a killing to be made on the margins of candor.

But the liar who couldn't remember his lies—couldn't even remember why, when, or to whom he'd told them—was in a tight spot. Your impulses, dishonesty-wise, were as sharp as ever: When in doubt, dissemble. But it was pure muscle memory. Dishonesty, in your case, was the means by which you covered tracks, threw people off the scent, or broke their resolve. In order to accomplish any of these goals, however, you first needed the corresponding data points. Amnesia tested this methodology.

The more Daniel pressed, the more you became a liar in search of a lie. There were no bedrocks. At one point, Daniel referenced a prior conversation in which—evidently—you had blamed Cedars-Sinai for postponing the Monday ECT session. "So the ward was closed for the holiday?"

"I guess," you said.

"Well, that's what you told Ben."

"Oh. Right. So . . . ?"

"The holiday was Saint Patrick's Day," he said. "Cedars-Sinai doesn't do ECT on *Saint Patrick's Day*?"

It was nice to know you still had it. Recently.

"I don't make the rules," you said.

Evidently, there were additional inconsistencies in yesterday's stated itinerary. Or itineraries. Evidently, you had told Paula you would be spending Monday with "my shrinks" in Los Angeles. Whereas, to Lizz, you had mentioned a day of "errands" and "exercise." Whereas, to Ben and Daniel, you had mentioned a plan to be with Caitlin and Lucy. "You said Lucy was having surgery on her foot," Daniel said. "You said you wanted to be at the hospital with her."

It occurred to you, at this point, that everyone was way too hung up on small points. Daniel, especially. Whenever the two of you worked together, spitballing story ideas or revising scenes, he just wouldn't move on till he'd Worked Everything Through. He was a slave to logic, structure, process—all that crap. Whereas you, by contrast, were entirely about The Muse. If she was there, great; if she wasn't, nap. This state of grace tended to annoy sweet, naïve Daniel, who had yet to grasp the difference between work and The Work (not to mention talent and The Talent) and who occasionally lashed out, in his smiley, Quakery, Yalie, indie-film way.

"Question," he'd say.

Elliptically. For the tenth time.

There would be silence. The chirping of birds.

"Something wrong?" he'd say.

"Nope," you'd say. "Just waiting for the question."

You didn't care whether "Bus Passenger 4" was male or female, or whether it "made sense" to reference Hurricane Katrina in a movie set in 1999. You transcended knickknacks and trivialities, and who didn't know that by now? Daniel. That's who. He just pushed and pushed. Everyone was a director.

Admittedly, the Lucy excuse fell on the extreme end of discretion. Pushed the envelope. Admittedly, certain people in your life—parents and brothers, friends and colleagues, girlfriend and daughter—might have thought twice before using hobbled toddlers as cover for a party weekend. But you weren't a mind reader. They had their own things going on.

Besides, you had *intended* to accompany the Caitlins. So, given that intent was nine-tenths of the law, you were only 10 percent absent. Also, the "surgery" was really more of a procedure. Outpatient. A tiny snipping of a tiny nodule on a tiny foot. Ninety miles away. And you'd been cautioned about driving. "Don't push it," Caitlin said. "You don't *need* to be there."

Her words. So.

The Boston story arrived organically.

"I'm not feeling great," you said. "I'm having doubts about ECT."

Which was true. In a prescient sort of way. The amnesiac in you was all about the future.

"I should see the doctors at McLean," you said. "Immediately."

A falsehood. Up to a point. Whenever you said "McLean," the déjà vu burbled up. But visions of the place were, by this point, wholly conceptual. Some folks channeled bugling cherubs or alien spacecrafts; you got blue sofas and white orchids. Were they fantasies or flashbacks? Or *flash-forwards*? The prescience add-on made things triply interesting, although not always in a constructive way. Ultimately, it was better to resist dwelling on such matters—a task uniquely suited to the amnesiac skill set.

"Well, then," Caitlin said. "That makes sense."

So. Again.

But now, two days later, you were under suspicion. A Person Of Interest. Suspected but never charged by The Morality-Police Department, whose four volunteer deputies (two males, two females) would soon find themselves woefully ill equipped to handle an adversary of this magnitude. Daniel, in his conspicuously inconspicuous way, surveilled your face and body language, searching for indicators of duplicity or discombobulation. And searching.

"Okay, then," he said.

Throughout the coming week, as ECT Sessions Five through Seven came and went, Lizz, Ben, and Paula probed for information; their MOs were predictable. Lizz played mama bear. "Well, good for you for going to Boston," she said. "How the heck did you manage to work that out?" Ben played papa bear. "I just need to say the Boston thing *is* a little shocking," he said. "I mean, *hello*." Paula played bear cub. "I don't know what I'm asking," she said. "I apologize."

The investigation went nowhere.

You almost felt sorry for them. They were operating under the fatally flawed presumption that a person with impaired cognitive functioning was a person with impaired bullshit functioning (i.e., The *Regarding Henry* Principle). In some ways, amnesia sharpened your god-given aptitude for deception—the way the loss of one sense heightens the others. Also, for a guy whose life had become a perpetual search for car keys, you never forgot how to drive.

Brevity, generalities, and repetition: the watchwords for success. Whenever a member of the truth posse wondered aloud why a Jewish hospital in Hollywood would close for an Irish holiday—while a hospital named McLean remained open for business in the city of a million leprechauns—you stuck to the script.

"Hmm," you'd say. "Dunno."

Most questions could be answered by way of the boilerplate

three-worder: "It was [fine/okay/complicated/nothing/whatever]." Whenever you found yourself in a tight spot, or just kind of bored or hungry, you'd sigh and say you were exhausted/depressed/anxious/freaked/confused/achy/queasy. This was one of two fail-safes. It caused your adversary to die a little, thinking *Holy Christ, I've done it now! What kind monster badgers a poor, bedraggled shock-patient?!*

Your second fail-safe was: "I can't remember."

The gold standard. The Tiffany life raft.

It was a revelation, especially during those first two weeks of electric splendor. To think you'd gone four decades without it—you could only wonder how much easier everything would have been had your arsenal included the ICR card. Three words could stop a locomotive. Or *Ben*. Midsentence. Pause. "Go sit," he'd say. "We're having spaghetti."

But the fail-safes came with a cost. All lies did; every little deception compounded the mounting credibility debt. Scale mattered. All those rationalizations and hip fakes over the years? Pennies. Full-on whoppers? Franklins. Absent fiscal responsibility, you'd better start learning Chinese.

Ever since the New York trip, things had been trending southward. Gradually, in between stretches of rambunctiousness and stability, you grew ever more weary, cranky, anxious. One morning, when Paula drove you to ECT, you didn't speak at all; you dismissed Daniel with curt, monosyllabic replies. Hygiene became optional. On zap days, you looked and smelled as if you'd spent a week at Burning Man. "ECT," you said to Lizz and Caitlin. "I don't think it's working."

There were no credits for bullshit excuses that turned out to be accurate.

You played it straight around Dr. E, expressing only mild doubts and worries. For one thing, you didn't want to come off as some sort of a crazy. For another, his confidence lifted yours. "Takes longer with some patients," Dr. E said. "Just give it time."

———————

Within a week, The Boston Investigation was headed for the cold-case files. On Easter Sunday, you and Caitlin took Lucy to an egg hunt at Lizz's place, then visited Caitlin's family and friends. Caitlin, thank god, had kept her parents in the dark about the current state of affairs. But still. You trod cautiously in their presence, figuring it was only a matter of time before they asked their daughter why you kept saying "So how do you folks know Caitlin?"

You passed easily. The day allowed you to forget, in addition to most things, ECT. You and Caitlin spent hours in the sunshine, eating chocolate rabbits and helping Lucy unscrew plastic eggs filled with jelly beans. Lizz and Paula didn't know what to say, having never seen you and a girlfriend in the same place.

The grandparents took Lucy for the evening, and Caitlin drove you home. There she acquainted you with a daily meal-delivery service she had hired on your behalf. You briefly went upstairs to return a call.

"Everything okay up there?" she asked.

"Absolutely," you said.

Then the two of you studied pictures of a house Caitlin was thinking of moving into: three bedrooms, newly renovated, just around the corner.

"Nice," you said.

One Jamison's later, you fell asleep on the sofa, with Caitlin lying beside you. But when you stirred, a half hour later, the cats had taken Caitlin's place. She was at the dinner table. Just sitting there.

"Hey," you said.

"Hey," she said.

Not in a good way. Her face was flushed. She measured her words—the way she did whenever Lucy misbehaved.

"I feel uncomfortable asking this," she said.

"Don't be," you said.

"I know this is a really hard time for you. And I don't want to add to your stress."

"Thanks. Don't worry."

She gathered herself.

"So I'm just wondering," she said. "Who's Erin?"

"Huh?" you said.

The amnesiac-liar's mantra. Stopgap of champions.

"I *wasn't* snooping," she said. "I just wanted to check my email."

Her eyes led you to the office, where the iMac's screen saver glowed maize and blue—Michigan colors; a keystroke banished the headgear; onto the twenty-inch screen flashed an open email thread, whose most recent exchange read:

You: Thanks for being such a sweetheart. I like you, and hope I get to see you again soonest. xx

Erin: No, thank you! That was super fun.

This clarified the situation.

And yet.

"She's a writer," you said. "Just met her."

"In New York," Caitlin said.

Evidently, the email chain included certain logistical details.

"Well, *yeah*," you said. "When I was there."

This was one of those moments when the liar and the amnesiac became one. Erin, you remembered. Whereas the *experience* of Erin—the date, the emails—was gone. So now the liar in you was fighting a forest fire with a squirt gun. But the amnesiac was in great shape, because he had nothing to hide. Ultimately, then, lying serves a higher purpose.

"I don't understand," she said. "How did Boston become New York?"

This is where you earned your paycheck.

"Okay," you said. "I was in *both*."

Out spilled a lean, mean story about needing a night to "decompress"—get away from it all, see old friends—in between the McLean visit and the return home. "Just something I needed to do," you said. "I knew you guys wouldn't let me. So, I'm sorry."

She studied you the same way Daniel did. Except with less smiling.

"It was nothing," you said. "Quick drink. A friend wanted me to meet her."

"Why?"

"I don't know. Writers."

"Sounded like a date."

"No. Not a date."

"One night in New York and you spend it with a girl you've never met?"

"It was an hour. Between other plans."

"If it was a date, I'd prefer you be honest about it."

"It's the truth."

In a way. By this point, you had no evidence to the contrary. True lies were easy sells.

"I believe in you," she said.

Standing there, looking at her, you had two thoughts. The first was that it took a special person to move beyond petty disappointments. The second was that Caitlin really needed to do the same.

You spent the rest of the night reading all the other emails you'd received from hot, horny women. Two ex-colleagues. Two women you'd dated long ago. One gal you hardly knew, couldn't quite place, and hoped to forget entirely. Her name was Amber. She wrote things like "watcha doin' tonite??? winx!"

And Mimi, of course. The little pistol kept dropping bread crumbs about trips she wanted to take. London, for instance. Frankly, it was a bit much.

Then the Truth Nazis fucked everything up. This was on Tuesday, during the break between zappings eight and nine. Lizz captained the first U-boat.

"Question," she said.

Always a bad sign. The *q*-word, to Lizz, meant "awkward."

"Who is *Erin*?" she continued.

Evidently, your adversaries were more organized than you'd previously thought. They had an intelligence-gathering service. Sig-Int. Hum-int. This you discovered upon turning the tables and breaking into Daniel's email account.

From a chain of back-channel communiqués that circulated one week later:

Daniel wrote:

Guys—I'm worried about him. I have to be honest. He seems slightly delusional to me. This may sound like an overstatement. But, after talking to all of you, here's what I've gathered:

He never had any intention of going to Lucy's surgery on Monday. Yet he told us that he would be going to it, and would therefore be "unreachable." He ignored my follow-up emails. He didn't tell any of us that he was going to Boston.

He told the ECT doctors that he was going to a funeral on Monday. Then he told Caitlin that the doctors said it was okay for him to miss the treatment. In fact, Paula says, the doctors told him that it's unhelpful to miss ECT.

Today he was under the impression that Ben took him to ECT when, in fact, Paula did.

Paula, Caitlin, and I have noticed that he's prone to anger—about small and big issues—and more brusque than usual. He will not allow anyone to spend longer than 4 hours with him, unless he's forced to sleep over.

The last time Caitlin visited him, he told her he was taking a nap. But he went upstairs and repeatedly called someone on the phone.

Part of what worried me is that he has always been honest when confronted about issues that make him uncomfortable. In the last week, however, we've all been hearing different stories.

I think all of us feel that he should have one consistent person to watch him. And I think we should seriously consider (a) asking one of his brothers to stay with him, (b) insisting he otherwise stay full-time with us, and (c) calling his shrink (The last I will do, regardless.) What are your thoughts?

Paula replied:

Well, he *has* told us different things before. He has just been sloppy about it this week. On the other hand . . . He really thought Ben took him today??????? I spent 24 hours with him. I think he is TERRIFIED and feeling out of control.

Ben replied:

I second that his brothers should come. I don't know if I'm more freaked-out that he did it and didn't tell us OR that he lied to all of us, saying Lucy was having surgery.

Lizz replied:

I don't think we can say anything is odd or fucked-up, since we will never understand what it's like to be in the place he is in. His *brain is being fried*. And he is scared. I'm glad he went to talk to those Boston docs. But I just wish we'd known, so we could have supported him.

Daniel replied:

I have no judgment, but my gut tells me he just didn't want to say anything to us. Maybe he was worried we wouldn't let him go, or that it would clue us into how worried he is that ECT isn't working.

Caitlin wrote:

I was hoping that I wasn't overreacting. But now that you have spelled it out, there seems to be reasons for concern. I offered to take time off to stay with him. He didn't respond well at all. I feel very uncomfortable with the fact that his therapist is not a bigger part of the equation. I feel that she should be monitoring his progress—not just the doctor dispensing treatment. There should be more communication, no?

Those poor people. They had no idea what they were up against.

The next two weeks were a clinic in counterintelligence. When Daniel called your shrink, he should have just streamed the conversation on Facebook. Five wouldn't give him a match without your permission. And you signed off knowing that Five was obligated to tell you everything they said. Daniel knew this, too. So, in the end, you heard a replay in stereo.

The conversation had begun predictably, with a banding about the *c*-word. Daniel was "concerned." Also confused and rattled. Also speaking on behalf of a team that felt increasingly ill-equipped. In the beginning, he said, the patient had prepared them for three weeks of Advanced Senior Moments: memory glitches, evening fog. Now it was Week Six. The amnesia had become Amnesia, and the patient had become a Patient. But they could handle that guy. They just didn't know what to do with the cunning, crazy liar.

"It's neither lying nor delusional," Five said. "It's *prevaricating*."

Best word ever.

Standard definition: "to speak or act in an evasive manner; to deviate from the truth."

Amnesiac definition: "to speak the truth."

Granted, you had a knack for evasive tactics. And, yes, your fictions had been born of a fear-based impulse to conceal . . . something. But what? You were an *amnesiac*. You had no past, and therefore none to hide. The history of you began with whatever thought popped into your head, and already revisions were under way.

"Picture a deck of playing cards," Five said. "Three straight times, you throw the cards high in the air, then watch them settle on the ground. Each time, they land in different and unpredictable ways. Likewise, the mind."

That you had spun so many conflicting stories—and had done so with such clear-eyed conviction—went to your credibility (if not your reliability). You believed in the product. Baked fresh daily. From scratch.

Five's analysis made everyone feel better. Daniel, especially. Years earlier, he had befriended a guy who turned out to be a full-on pathological liar, replete with invented jobs, friends, etc. So "prevaricating" was music to his ears.

The idyll lasted three days.

"Question," Lizz said, by phone. "Why would you be getting an email from *Mimi*?"

"Huh?" you said.

Lizz forwarded you the email:

Might you have a quick second to speak asap?
THANKS!
Sent via BlackBerry

"Uh," you said.

"Does Mimi know about ECT?"

"God, no."

"Do you guys even speak?"

"Well, we *speak*."

"*Really*? Since when?"

"I don't know. Are you gonna call her?"

A nightmare scenario.

And yet. Oddly thrilling.

Later that night, Lizz stopped by the house.

"Just got off the phone with Mimi," she said.

"And?"

"She's just a little . . . concerned. About you."

"Why?"

"I know this is none of my business. But are you going through something with Mimi?"

"What? What did she say?"

"She said you're going through something with her."

"Like something bad?"

"Like something *intense*."

"She said that?"

"She said it started two weeks ago. She said you started calling out of the blue."

"Like in a bad way?"

"Like, *a lot*."

Like ten calls a day. Like all hours of the night.

"Jesus," you said. "What else did she say?"

Like a rippling salmon run of emails. Like Lifetime movie-of-the-week territory.

"Jesus," you said. "Why would she tell you that?"

"Because it's not true? Or because she told me?"

"Wait. Do you believe her?"

"No. I don't even like her."

"Sounds like you believe her."

"I don't even know her. We've never met. Which, by the way, is shocking."

"Now you know why. I'll deal with her."

Two scenarios were in play, neither of them good. The first one—a

Third Man/Josef K. Dick scenario—felt a little paranoid (*although* . . .). Dollars to donuts, this crime against honesty fell to The Crazy Ex.

The email read:

Mimi, what the?

Hours passed. Years, in MimiBerry time. So you dropped her another email (or two), plus a voicemail (or two). But the radio silence explained everything. Fucking Verizon. First thing the next morning, having discovered a fresh Post-it note—"Fucking Verizon"—you headed for the phone, determined to give those bumbling incompetents a piece of your mind. You stood there for a couple minutes, trying to remember why the hell you were calling Verizon, when a figure appeared at the door.

"Please don't strangle me," Lizz said.

She had done some additional reporting, buttressing her early reports with hard documentation, specifically email traffic between Mimi and yours truly. The congestion had begun two weeks earlier, and moved fast in the eastbound lanes:

Missing you.
I'd like to talk.
How about London?

Westbound traffic was sparse.

Talk later.
What about?
Don't understand.

Lizz, in her role as Professional Journalist, endeavored to project an air of detached neutrality. Which made the situation doubly galling.

"I don't believe this bullshit," you said.

Textbook nondenial denial. (*All the President's Men,* p. 221.)

And yet. A statement of fact.

Mimi? Hardly the most trusted name in news.

You? Catnip to the ladies.

Period. End of story.

Except it wasn't. This story had legs. Within forty-eight hours, Lizz (with additional reporting by Ben, Daniel, and Paula) cracked the thing wide open. First, in order to conceal a trip to see doctors in Boston, you had manufactured stories about surgical procedures, funerals, and Saint Patrick's Day. Then Boston became Boston and New York, "to see friends." Then friends became a dewy literista. And now, finally, came the real target: Mimi. But the biggest news flash was yet to come.

"Just tell me," Lizz said. "Did you even go to Boston?"

No comment.

Martial law.

That's what it came down to. The curtain of repression fell hard and fast, and endured for three weeks. The junta laid claim over every aspect of your life, i.e.:

Escape seemed impossible. Your car keys were confiscated, your movements restricted to foot travel within the Los Feliz Settlement Zone. Transport beyond the LFSZ was facilitated by the Gang of Four, and generally limited to shock sessions.

Basic civil liberties were stripped. Big Brother was in full effect. Daniel snuck into your office and accessed your email; Paula rifled your iPhone. Naturally, the goons did so under the pretense of "security threats." "We trust you," they'd say. "We just want your safety." They wanted to keep an eye on you (because information is power), and to monitor the Mimi situation (because tyrants fear love).

You would not be denied.

"Good news," you told Mimi. "Love is in the air."

"Sweetie," she said. "I know you don't remember, but we had this conversation."

"I remember."

"You do?"

In a way.

"Meet me in London," you said.

"No," she said.

"That's crazy. Why wouldn't you?"

"For one thing, I'm seeing someone."

"Someone named *Todd*."

"Not funny."

"You know what isn't funny? Anyone named Todd."

"I have to go now."

"To London."

"Listen to me," she'd say. "I'll do anything I can to help you through this, but—"

"We were perfect together."

"We were *not* perfect."

A pause for quiet reflection.

"Well, you were pretty kooky," you said. "But I love you anyway, so . . ."

"I wish I still felt that way, too," she'd say. "But I just don't."

"We can discuss that in London."

"I need to go now."

When the line went dead, you padded around the kitchen, refilled the cat bowls, then hit redial. "Great news!" you said. "Love is in the air!"

Bygones. Amnesia.

Meantime, the thought-control campaign intensified. "Caitlin is the *good witch*," Paula would say. "And Mimi is the *bad witch*."

Just thinking aloud.

"I *love* Caitlin," Daniel said.

"Love her," Lizz said. "Love. Love. Love."

Apropos of nothing.

"Man," Ben said. "That Caitlin is hot."

"Pretty girl," you said.

"The hair. The breasts—"

The awkwardness.

"Caitlin makes me peaceful," you said. "She's just right for me."

"Sounds like Caitlin might be the one, then."

"She might just be."

You'd figured it out on your own. ECT had brought you closer. Now you wanted to share everything with her.

Everything. The new openness developed gradually, during the second week of ECT. There were snippets, teasers. One morning, while Caitlin pulled her hair into a ponytail, your eyes said it all.

"What?" Caitlin said.

"Something Mimi does," you said.

Caitlin would have laughed it off, had the exchange been an isolated one. "Well, that's romantic," she said. "Anything else I can do to remind you of her?"

"Lighten up," you said.

She took a long look, then let it go.

You became a walking audiobook (unabridged, performed by the author). The zap sessions—upwards of ten so far—produced candor in a way the drugs and doctors never had. Caitlin beheld a boyfriend who put it all out there. When you felt low, you asked her to comfort you. When you fell ill, due to the epic one-two punch of ECT and influenza, she nursed and fed you. She even updated your parents, whom she'd never met in person. Her task was made trickier by the fact that you had sold ECT as a kind of psychiatric spa treatment. "Oh, this is my pleasure," Caitlin would tell them.

"Godsend," your dad called her.

"Drama queen," you called her.

Seemed like every time you opened up, laid the soul bare, the Wrath of Caitlin followed. She'd been organizing your kitchen or whatever— just doing her thing—and you'd say something like "I think my hottest girlfriends were . . ." Soon as you listed so-and-so and whoever, she'd go all pink and silent and boohoo.

Early on, at least, Caitlin had the decency to check it at the door. She got over herself. By Week Four, however, it was all me-me-me. The fire starter, in most cases, was Mimi. It was always something. One evening, after spending a few minutes in the office, you ventured the simplest of questions: "Why the hell isn't Mimi calling me back?"

"I wouldn't know," Caitlin said.

"So frustrating. And rude."

"So you've been calling her?"

"No."

Caitlin digressed. Something about the phone in your hand.

"I don't follow," you said.

"Did you brush your teeth with it?" she asked. "You said you were going upstairs to use the bathroom."

The things people remember.

"Call Mimi," Caitlin said. "I'm sure she's an excellent girlfriend."

"Calm down," you said.

"I'm calm. I just think you obviously prefer her."

"Why?"

"Because you can't stop talking about her. Or *to* her."

"That's not true."

"I don't get it. You'd always given me the impression she was kind of a nightmare."

"I did?"

"Um, yeah."

"That's crazy."

"Why?"

"She was remarkable. The best."

Caitlin was impossible. You tried to change the subject to, for example, travel. But no. She didn't want to hear how you and Rachel had found love and magic in Marrakesh.

She left in a huff. Which struck you as selfish. The medical literature was very clear: ECT patients sometimes say things they don't mean. Basically, then Caitlin was blaming a paraplegic for failing to run a four-minute mile.

Finally, she emailed back:

Here are some talking points:
1. How did ECT 'make' you so interested in speaking of ex's like you did? Was it really ECT or some kind of resistance to this relationship?
2. Caitlin means . . . to me. (min. 500 words)
3. In one year, I see us . . .
Humor me.

Lizz talked some sense into Caitlin, reminding her what the doctors had said about ECT. Caitlin returned the following Saturday, Lucy in tow. Normality returned—tension had a way of evaporating when the conversation turned to miniature giraffes. Lucy fell asleep on the couch, while you read aloud from one of her favorite books, *The Velveteen Rabbit*.

But early the next day, as you sat alone in the office, a glottal cry—"*guh!*"—broke the idyll. Caitlin hovered near the doorway, pinkly. Wide-eyed, lost for words, she emitted another "guh" and backed away, assuming the human-shield posture favored by secret service agents and mother grizzlies.

Caitlin's rumpus struck you as, in addition to grandiose and loony, a public-safety hazard. What sort of crazy woman sneak attacks a guy while he's lighting up? A smoker any less prepared, any less *responsible,* would have fumbled the joint, which would have fallen onto a desk strewn with reporter's notepads and sticky memos, which would have exploded into a hellfire, which would have transformed the wooden house into a funeral pyre reeking of Lemon Bubba Kush.

Plus, she was a buzzkill. Marijuana, it turned out, enhanced the sun-salutation experience. Weed entered the picture during Week Three, when a certain band of killjoys and underminers got their hooks into you. An occasional bong hit helped you maintain optimal cruising altitude. But the real value addition came when the "fasten seatbelts" light went on; weed smoothed the turbulence during all those rough takeoffs and landings. Legally, by the way. Medicinally.

Also: helped with memory loss. Made it seem more manageable.

"Unbelievable," Caitlin said.

"Calm down," you said.

"There's a *child* upstairs."

Always a twist.

"Amnesia," you said.

Duh. Hello.

But she remained silent, as she often did when you remembered to blame the memory loss.

"So annoying," you said.

"What?" she said.

"You. You're annoying."

"I apologize for asking you to not smoke marijuana in front of my four-year-old daughter."

"It's not just that."

"So I just generally annoy you?"

"Yes."

Threw up her hands. Literally.

"And Lucy?" she said. "I suppose she does, too?"

"Yes," you said.

But you couldn't reason with a crazy person. Suddenly Caitlin was collecting sippy cups and zipping princess backpacks and guiding Lucy toward the door. Before they drove off, Lucy blew a kiss in presidential fashion.

"Kitties," she said.

The next day, after ECT, Daniel got all directory. Something about how driving was a no-no. Something about you getting lost in the Valley, and endangering this and that. "It's really upsetting," he said. "It's too much."

"I'm sorry," you said. "I didn't remember—"

"No, listen. We've asked your brothers to come help. And that's that."

Silence.

"Wait," you said. "Do they *want* to come?"

This threw him. He got soppy.

"Very much," he said.

Feeling sentimental, he agreed to let you spend a few hours alone at your house. "As long as you promise not to drive," he said.

"Of course," you said.

Four hours later, after you pulled up to LAX, David seemed surprised. "I thought you're not supposed to drive," he said.

"What?" you said.

Long flight. Probably fried his brain. Why else would *he* keep asking *you* "Are you tired?" Some reporter, he was.

Obviously, he'd arrived expecting the worst—god only knew what The Fear-Monger Four had told him. But once you hit the freeway, and displayed your skills as a conversationalist, he'd lighten up.

You were in the passing line, pushing eighty, when David start getting all weird and OCD. He fixated on street signs. "South to Palm

Springs," he said. In that Big Brother way. "Isn't Los Feliz in the other direction?"

An hour later, after you'd given the baby his bottle, David piped up again. The signage fetish, redux.

"Pasadena?" he said. "Isn't that north of Los Feliz?"

Next thing you knew, David was ordering you to pull over and unhand the keys. He drove the rest of the way home, in a white-knuckle sort of way.

It's all about control for these people.

The following day's zap session went quietly, although David did turn pale while transporting you to and from the electric spa. And later, when something slipped your mind—on one or fifteen occasions—you detected a welling in his eyes. Some people, you felt, just couldn't keep it together.

"Your cats," he said, "are satanic."

The next day, a Saturday, promised a respite from your caretaking obligations. Ben and Daniel were hosting an "informal get-together" for you, David, Lizz, and Paula. There would be freshly baked cinnamon buns, you figured. There would be bacon.

You should have seen it coming. All morning, David had been wearing a hinky smile, but you'd attributed it to a series of stealth attacks Scrub had perpetrated on his shins and ankles. But you didn't put it all together until you walked into Ben and Daniel's house. The collaborators sat stiffly in the living room and wore somber half-smiles. A gauntlet of Anderson Coopers.

They assumed their natural roles. Daniel played the director, fetching you water and offering you a comfortable spot on the sofa. But you elected to sit on the floor, near a coffee table strewn with the kids' crayons and drawing pads. "We all just want to be on the same page," he said. "We love you, and we're concerned about your safety . . ." And blah-blah.

Lizz interjected at frequent intervals, in part because she was the mama grizzly, in part because she had the most experience vis-à-vis handling you, in part because she was a control freak. "Just to be clear," she said. "Daniel isn't *angry* at you . . ."

Paula, being codependent with everyone, agreed vigorously—"this isn't about anger"—then apologized for interjecting.

Ben periodically bit his tongue and rolled his eyes—at them, not you—because he found their sops and disclaimers foolish and boring.

And David remained stock-still, because a lot of what he was hearing was news to him, and because seeing his little brother in this position was almost too much to bear.

"The lying cannot happen," Daniel said. "It endangers you and others."

"When Paula signs you out from ECT, you're her responsibility," Lizz said. "If something happens, she's in real trouble."

"This is hard," Ben said. "If we can't trust you, we can't take care of you. And right now . . ."

Ben was more effective, you felt, when he shut up.

"Do you understand this?" David asked. "Anything you want to say?"

That they were a pack of yapping jackals. That you were this close to chewing their faces off. That they had obviously forgotten that you were a Tortured Genius, and that they should be prostrate in gratitude.

"No," you said. "I understand."

Whatever it takes. Just keep your head down. Eyes on the drawing pad. Crayons to paper.

You drew a cat.

"The amnesia," Daniel said. "We know it's severe. But sometimes it feels like it's an excuse."

"The Mimi thing," Lizz said. "It has to stop."

"Caitlin," Paula said. "She's very hurt."

"Okay," you said. And said. And said.

They enumerated a list of grievances, rules, stipulations. Basically, you couldn't do anything. When home alone, you would have to check in with one of them. *Every hour.*

"Okay," you said. "That's a little much."

Ben leaned forward. "I don't mean to sound cold," he said. "But you *cannot* call the shots right now. You're sick. You're going through ECT. You shouldn't be left alone."

"I know, but—"

"And I just need to say this. You're very good at putting distance between people. But that *cannot* happen. I need to hear your voice in order to know what's really going on with you."

There was a chorus of self-righteousness.

"Fine," you said.

"So we're clear on everything?" David said.

"Yep," you said.

"You're sure?" Lizz said.

"Yep."

"Maybe we should review, because you don't seem—"

Wheeling toward her. Finger extended.

"ARE YOU *ENJOYING* THIS!" you said.

Forcefully. With a volume and tone neither she nor the others had ever heard from you.

Worked, too. The remainder of the intervention was muted and businesslike. Somebody told you which person would be looking after you next; somebody else reminded you of upcoming appointments.

"I'm sorry," Lizz said. "I know I can be annoying. If you say you remember the plan, I won't ask again."

"I remember," you said.

It was gone by the time you reached the door.

CHAPTER THIRTEEN

You will never remember the Crash Of 2008.

Not today—more than three years later. Not ever. Kiss those ten weeks goodbye. Likewise the six months that preceded them. Also vast swaths of 2007, save for occasional blips (Caitlin drinking coffee) or snippets (the tunnel en route to McLean). And the picture quality on late 2006 remains spotty at best. In the fall of '06—a year and half prior to ECT—the Detroit Tigers won their first pennant since 1984. You flipped when you heard the news, in January 2009.

Guilt. Shame. Fear.

The heartbreak of amnesia loss always begins with these three classic markers. They arrive gently and gradually, like the first fleeting aches of mad-cow disease. But the memory-infected amnesiac lacks the wherewithal to nip the problem in the bud. He just stands there, mute and frozen, while the viral sponges eat his brain.

That's how you spent the week following your final zapping, in mid-May. Initially, for a day or so, your natural defenses held memory at bay—at one point, having come across a sticky note reading "remember AMNESIA!" you downloaded a British thriller called *Amnesia* (which was sort of like the movie *Memento,* which you likewise found a tad hard to follow).

On day two, certain questions arose: Why's the house so quiet? Where the hell is Caitlin?

On days three and four, you were a clammy mess clutching a plastic frog.

You couldn't remember What Happened.

And yet.

"I'm so sorry."

Just came out. All the time.

The friends shrugged it off. Wouldn't hear of it. Said things like "there's nothing to be sorry for" and "I'm just sorry I couldn't help more."

But nobody is more attuned to nonverbal communications—pauses, inflections—better than a paranoid reporter with a dual diagnosis of social anxiety disorder and avoidant personality disorder.

"What did I do?" you'd say. "Just tell me what I did."

They trod carefully, at first. Broad-brushed it. Used words like *confusing* and *complicated*.

"You just got frustrated," Daniel said. "And sometimes that made things frustrating for us."

"It wasn't easy for Caitlin," Lizz said. "Sometimes you said some things."

You had to weasel the story out of them, in bits and pieces. By that point, your short-term memory had returned to normal functioning. Although you couldn't remember What Happened—and never would—you sure remembered why.

You are bipolar.

"Mania," Five said. "Familiar with the term?"

"Fairly," you said.

"In the clinical sense? As in manic-depressive or—"

"I'm *bipolar*?"

"I'd say you're experiencing a level of mania," she said.

Hypomania. The entry level. Mild to moderate. Characterized by many or most (or all!) of the following:

- persistently elevated mood
- disinhibition
- impulsivity and thrill seeking
- inflated self-esteem or grandiosity
- goal-oriented behaviors
- decreased need for sleep
- increased creativity
- increased exertion and libido
- rapid or repetitive speech patterns (rhyming, alliteration)
- racing thoughts
- reckless driving
- spending sprees
- agitation and anxiety
- obsessions and compulsions
- poor judgment
- substance abuse
- irritability, aggression, or belligerence
- disregard for rules or criticism
- lack of consideration for others
- risky dumbfuck tomfoolery

But no insanity. No delusions or assassination plots or nude sprints down Rodeo Drive. Hypos are sane (more or less); they frequently seem so clear-eyed, so *here,* that their condition goes unnoticed; the mania, to most people, comes off as eccentricity, edge, moxie.

My middle name is Penguin.

One rail couldn't hurt.

I am grizzly.

Darling, we're almost *like other people.*

And there's the rub. The dangers of full-blown mania are, at least, full-blown obvious—the jabbering messiah only gets so far before someone throws a net over him. But the hypomanic flies under the radar. Which is all fine and good until he starts wandering off—to, say, chase birds through blizzards, or snort rails with Chris Farley, or sleep with bears, or plumb dark tunnels to nowhere, equipped only with a flashlight, a pistol, and a rope.

"I'm *bipolar*?" you asked.

Your friends had been right. Your six-week odyssey of magic and lies was, by ECT standards, "atypical."

"ECT made me bipolar?"

"No," Dr. E said. "Hypomania results from a predisposition toward bipolar disorder."

"Well, we can't be *sure* what caused it," Dr. E said. "But probably it was the antidepressants."

Warnings/Precautions

Major depressive episode may be the initial presentation of bipolar disorder. It is generally believed (though not established in controlled trials) that treating such an episode with an antidepressant alone may increase the likelihood of precipitation of a mixed/manic episode in patients at risk for bipolar disorder.

Mania/hypomania occurred in approximately 0.2% (3/1299 patients) of Remeron-treated patients.

In placebo-controlled trials of Lexapro, activation of mania/hypomania was reported in one (0.1%) of 715 patients.

In placebo-controlled trials of Celexa, some of which included patients with bipolar disorder, activation of mania/hypomania was reported in 0.2% of 1063 patients.

In a real-life trial of Lexapro, Celexa and Remeron, which included an ECT patient with amnesia and the wrath of god, activation of hypomania was reported in 100% of 1 patient.

The shrinks nixed the antidepressants. Within three days, the calls to Mimi stopped cold, and the whole drama was forgotten (in every way); by the following week, as the zapping continued apace, the prevarications and midnight runs were in short supply. You'd ascended your last rooftop.

Unfortunately.

Warnings and Precautions

Discontinuation of Treatment

There have been spontaneous reports of adverse events occurring upon discontinuation of these drugs, particularly when abrupt, including the following: dysphoric mood, irritability, agitation, dizziness, sensory disturbances (e.g., paresthesias such as electric shock sensations), anxiety, confusion, headache, lethargy, emotional lability, insomnia.

Or all of the above.

The only person lower than the depressive who abruptly discontinues his antidepressants is the manic who does.

Manics are the last great romantics of the modern world. Because mania is *fantastic*.

Civilians never understand this part. To wit: Your very close friend George Clooney, in *Michael Clayton,* gets schooled by buddy Arthur, a manic lawyer who hordes baguettes, drops his pants during depositions, and channels the Hindu deity Shiva, God Of Destruction and Transformation.

Michael: As good as this feels, you know where it goes.
Arthur: No, you're wrong. What makes this feel good is that I don't know where it goes.

The only person lower than the manic who abruptly discontinues his meds is the one who also discontinues The Treatment Of Last Resort.

This you learned in the immediate aftermath of ECT. Until this point, you'd spent little time deconstructing your misery—amnesiacs don't *de-* things. All you knew was that you'd had it. The decision arrived while Nurse K checked vitals.

"What number is this?" you asked. "Twelve? Thirteen?"

"Twenty," she said.

You cried for the next three weeks, often in the heaving manner normally associated with hysterical third graders. You turned on the Tigers game and cried. You fed the cats and cried. One night you slouched over to Ben and Daniel's, slumped onto the sofa, clutched your forehead, and dissolved. "It didn't work," you said.

"Is it possible that your emotional fragility might turn out to be an okay thing?" Ben said. "Maybe it forces you to look at things you've been haunted by?"

The sun going down. God goes to the other side of the earth and leaves you with the humans.

After a few weeks, Lizz handed over the mother lode: hard copies of every email that passed between her, Paula, Ben, and Daniel during ElectroGate. The transmissions, when printed out, ran in excess of a thousand pages—four phone books, stacked.

Included in the raw data were all transmissions between the group and other major players, among them. Lizz, after your girlfriend problems sunk you into despair, wrote this:

He seems raw, exhausted, and actually quite desperate for honesty. I'd say his overriding emotion is anxiety. He's anxious that it's not working. Anxious that he has to keep doing it. Anxious by how sick and weak he feels. Anxious about what comes next. He's considering checking into Cedars during the process, but worries that would make him more depressed. I think he thought of Cedars so it wouldn't "burden" everyone.

His outbursts and rebellions aside, he is deeply appreciative of what everyone is doing for him. I think he's kind of touched that we started this email chain. But all this attention and scrutiny is (as Jim put it) his worst nightmare. His outburst and rebellions reflect how MORTIFIED he is by the whole situation.

Sometimes the chain included your brothers or Caitlin. Depending.

From Ben:
We need to remove Caitlin from any chains discussing Mimi. We don't want to do anything to scare C off. She is fantastic. We need to plant this in his twisted mind.

Raw meant raw. The emails revealed, in relentless detail, the degree to which your problems had become everyone's problems. Every time Paula dropped you off at ECT, she burst into tears. Increasingly, she felt, ECT was a futile endeavor. "It's bad," she wrote. "I just don't feel like he's gonna wake up and be better." Her child took his first baby steps in a mental ward.

"Here's the Mimi thing," Ben wrote. "He's too scared to go forward with his life, he's going backward."

Every day, during the final few weeks, brought a new flurry of frantic questions, pleas, complaints. They fought among themselves—about who had to do what, or how best to "wrangle" you. They peppered your shrinks with phone calls and letters, then bickered about whether the doctors were competent ("Do we really believe this is 'normal behavior' for an ECT patient?") They were getting pissed—at the doctors, at each other. At you.

From Daniel:
I will do anything for Ned. But right now, though, it's threatening to overwhelm me/us. He's lying and out of control and simply

can't be trusted. We have families to take care of, and cannot shoulder this responsibility alone.

From Paula:
I will do it. But now I'm leaving my husband sitting on the couch while I spend his birthday at a mental hospital. And, of course, I'm acting in a play all week. To be perfectly honest, we need a break. Know that sounds harsh. But this is really tough on all of us.

From Ben:
What the fuck is his problem? I don't mean to be harsh. But I don't care what he wants right now. He wants what he wants when he wants it. He's crazy. He can't make everyone else crazy.

From Lizz:
I keep telling N what he needs to do re us and Mimi. He agrees, then forgets the whole thing. This is all so frustrating, scary, etc for all of us. It's so messy and sad. And exhausting. I've literally got Caitlin crying on line—one, and Mimi complaining on line—two. It's miserable. I just want it to stop.

Every time you came across one of these revelations, your reaction was to slam shut the binder, retreat to the sofa, and glower at Anderson Cooper. That you had been such a nightmare, such a burden, was only half the problem. But what really sucked you dry was the degree to which you had been *exposed*.

From Paula:
He's a fucking fool about Caitlin. What the hell else does he want?

From Daniel:
This goes beyond "prevarication." He has a need to control information. The other day, he logged onto my email account so he could know what we're saying about him. I find it unsettling.

From Ben:
The Mimi thing is happening because he's afraid to move forward. So he moves backward.

From Lizz:
I think his outburst and rebellions reflect how deeply mortified he is by the whole situation. All this attention and scrutiny is (as Jim put it) his worst nightmare.

They knew everything, frequently before you did. Lizz, your original ex-girlfriend, spent her days managing and counseling both Caitlin and Mimi—the Triangle Of Death. Lizz assured Caitlin that "N loves you very much" on the same day she provided Mimi with a list of talking points ("Just say you know he's going through a hard time, then remind him about the rules . . ."). The group reviewed every "private" email you sent, among them this beauty:

Mimi: Since we won't get a chance to talk, I thought I'd memorialize what I was trying to get across. Because I'll be in your neck of the woods, and because we have such a heavy past, I wanted to sit down with you and just put all the cards on the table and start over at the beginning. I had no idea how it would end up, but I was certain it would be, in one way or another, positive. I had no idea you'd never even hear me out. I'd never do that to you. I don't know. Maybe it serves your agenda to receive me as some sort of limping escapee from a mental ward, since that's what you did. "Why can't you shake it?" you actually said. "Why can't you get over me?" Not really the point of it all, but whatever. And had you displayed even a little interest, you would have learned that this has been the healthiest year of my life, and that most people in it have noticed the difference. My experience informed what I wanted to discuss with you, since you were the biggest person in my life for a few years there. I wanted to explain how certain tendencies were amplified by our relationship, and vice versa. I wanted to make sense of our relationship, and perhaps put it in a better place in the future. Alas. Now I remember why it was so difficult to talk something through with you. If you don't like the subject, you shuck and jive, creating chaos, and run the whole thing through your Narcissism funnel. Honestly, I don't think I've ever had anyone talk to me the way you did. Have you forgotten that I'm the nice one? The one who was honest, faithful, loyal to the end? Your track record? Not so much. I wonder if maybe that's why you kind of treat me like garbage these days. Maybe you feel guilty. Or not. Either way, it hardly matters now. I started this week hoping to build something; now I realize I was wasting my time. After all, you never make any effort. So then. Enemies it is.

"This is intense," Daniel wrote to the group.

You appreciated, while reading the emails, why a guy would suddenly drop everything and bomb straight out of town, bound for the farthest state, island, or continent.

"I'm so sorry," you said.

And said. Like hiccups. Tourette's.

You apologized to both brothers. Peter, the eldest, had picked up where David left off. Despite chronic back problems—he'd had six surgeries, with yet another one on the way—he crammed his six-feet-three frame into coach and made the five-hour flight from Detroit. He stayed for a week, patiently enduring your complaints and mini-tantrums. He even met Caitlin. Having cajoled her into joining you for dinner, at a restaurant called the Hungry Cat, you ignored her, then questioned her loyalty, then laughed at her.

"You're a seven-year-old in a man's body," she said, and bolted. For good.

You issued preemptive apologies, especially to female acquaintances. Seemed more efficient that way. "Thanks," a friend said. "I was wondering why you kept asking if I was single."

Radio silence with Mimi had endured for three months, and a large part of you desired a stay of excommunication—until, like, *forever.* But the other part of you wanted to look her in the eyes and say it.

"I'm sane," you said.

"I know," she said.

New York. Same table as usual. Same everything.

Except not.

"It was like a drug allergy," you said.

"I understand," she said.

"But I freaked you out."

She exhaled smoke. Sideways.

"It really wasn't that bad," she said.

A tilt of your head.

"Well," she said. "It was a little obsessive."

"I appreciate the candor," you said.

"And the thing at the Japanese restaurant was weird." There was a pause. "When you showed up at my dinner that night? No?"

Oh, no.

"Did it involve nudity?" you asked. "Was security called?"

"You asked for a hug," she said.

"And then?"

"I gave you one."

"And *then*?"

"You left."

"And that's it?"

"That's it."

"So what's so weird about that?"

"My boyfriend was sitting there."

Her laughter was lovely and infuriating.

"I'm sorry," you said. "I guess my mind went to you because I needed the fairy tale."

And because mania wants mania the way AC wants DC.

"Temporary insanity," she said. "Forgot what a nightmare I am."

"Not a nightmare," you said.

"Neither are you."

A drink.

"To halfsies," you said.

But a bigger fish awaited. Caitlin was to alienated exes as emperors are to penguins, and the journey to see her was long and perilous. Having given up the ghost, you left a package—a birthday gift for Lucy—with the receptionist at Caitlin's office. "Wanted this to arrive on time," read your note. "But I don't expect you to tell her it's from me. I'll forever miss you both."

You were at the door, heading out into the heat, when you heard it.

"Naturally," she said. She was leaning toward a computer screen, using it as a mirror. "Seed in my teeth."

She looked light and surfy—like the pre-ECT Caitlin. "Why so skinny?" she asked.

Your shrinkage—from 188 pounds to 167—seemed ominous to those who hadn't known you pre-Remeron Bloat.

"I'm sorry," you said. "I didn't mean to—"

"Coffee's on you," she said.

Together you drifted along the boardwalk, coffees in hand, tongues tied. You apologized. Pleaded for understanding. Made your case. Just as you had fifty times before. "It was mania," you said. "Manic people act crazy. They say crazy things they don't mean."

"I understand," she said.

"All that shit I did—the real me would *never*—"

"I know. You're a very nice person."

"Well, not to everyone."

She semilaughed.

"Lucy thinks you are," she said.

"Still?" you said.

"She asks about you constantly."

"*Really?* I miss her so—"

"The cats, too."

"Jesus. What do you tell her?"

"I tell her you're out of town."

Just had to ask, didn't you? The Caitlin void had been torturous enough—you had done in The Ideal Girlfriend, whom you missed like a dead wife, and whose absence doomed you to a life of eHarmony win- kettes and mail-order Filipino brides. No romance weighs as heavily as the one you can't remember.

With Caitlin, at least, there was a level of mutual understanding. With Lucy, however, it was zero-sum. No explanations. No horshees. Just one plastic frog.

"Sorry," Caitlin said. "I know it's upsetting."

"I love you guys."

"And we love you."

"So forgive me. Please."

"I do."

"All that crazy, nasty stuff—that wasn't me."

"I know."

"Then why won't you forgive me?"

She stopped. Tossed her coffee in a trash can.

"I forgive you for everything," she said. "But, unlike you, I can't just forget it."

The *just*. That was the dagger. Caitlin felt a bit like the Bride of Freudenstein. The normal you was undeveloped, skittish, a little sickly—but also generally harmless, low-key, companionable. But then things took a turn and the mad scientists created a monster who ran amok. Caitlin knew the normal you didn't run wild or chase exes. But she also knew that seven-year-olds weren't up for big-boy relationships.

"We were dying before this happened," she said.

"Not how I remember it," you said.

She also knew the difference between memory loss and convenient memory loss.

By the time the Summer Remorse Tour wound down, in September, a certain clarity was at hand. Your cognitive functioning was something like normal.

You were stable, sharp, on point. Friends welcomed back the Old You. "All that apologizing was tedious," Jim said. "Once you started mocking me again, I knew you were better."

Meantime, you had the benefit of perspective, i.e., The temptation to herald yet another ECT success story was diminished considerably by the detour into madness. Inasmuch as you continued to believe in the general viability of ECT—and you did—there was no way to view your own experience as anything less than a disaster. And the doctors' explanation for same—a freak drug interaction—reeked of doctor speak. You had been taking the same drug cocktail for months, without incident. Then, a week into ECT, you're king of the jungle. ECT *did* have something to do with The Episode. And it did cause enduring and substantial memory losses.

So it wasn't all bad.

Possibly ECT had simultaneously produced some underlying (or delayed) benefits. But in all likelihood, you felt, normality would have returned no matter what. Most likely, whatever benefits you derived from ECT were of a uniquely indirect nature. Without ECT, the bipolar gene may have remained forever undetected, and therefore untreated.

It was important, you felt, to See The Big Picture and Draw Life Lessons. Because, hey, that's what Major Writers do. Even the good ones. You read and reread the opening lines of David Foster Wallace's fictional story "The Depressed Person"—his own little *Bell Jar*:

The depressed person was in terrible and unceasing emotional pain, and the impossibility of sharing or articulating this pain was itself a component of the pain and a contributing factor in its essential horror.

The mother lode. Oh, the days you spent trying to break that sentence down, expose its fault lines. But no. There it stood, in all its prolixity: the perfect run-on definition of what it was to be One of Us. The sentence was so exemplary, so shaming of your efforts to define *same*, it unlocked new doors of depression. It was the gift that kept on giving. And on top of everything else, the story as a whole had a practical application. Baby steps, Wallace said (in so *many* words): That's where you would make some hay with the happies. Give them, if nothing else, the basic context of the depression—"its shape and texture, as it were"—by relaying information "related to its etiology."

You determined to do likewise. This was in mid-September, after you looked up *etiology* but before you opened *The Times* (Los Angeles and New York, respectively):

David Foster Wallace, the novelist, essayist and humorist best known for his 1996 novel "Infinite Jest," was found dead Friday night at his home in Claremont. He was 46.

Wallace's wife called police at 9:30 P.M. Friday saying she had returned home to find that her husband had hanged himself.

It was National Suicide Prevention Week.

Inevitably, in the days ahead, postmortems referenced the *éminence grise* of modern bipolar writer reporters. In 1961, after ECT stabilized Hemingway's mania, the great man got to wondering: "What is the sense of ruining my head and erasing my memory, which is my capital, and putting me out of business? It was a brilliant cure, but we lost the patient." Then he blew his brains out.

So. Food for thought.

When finally you unclenched the newspaper and glimpsed the world around you, Anderson Cooper was employing his Expression Of Grave Concern™ and every newsman under the sun was wetting his panties about Markets In Crisis and the Dow Under Siege. The timing defied coincidence. Why was it that every time you went crackers, Wall Street collapsed and bond traders jumped to their deaths? Whither the 9/11 Memorial Penguin Pajamas?

That a third of your nest egg had evaporated in a flash was especially disquieting given your current cash-flow issue. Because you had spent a year in the tank, you had failed to satisfy your contractual obligations at *VF*. The contract had lapsed, leaving you without your generous monthly stipend.

Which wouldn't have been quite so scary had the print-media business not gone the way of you and Wall Street, and had Condé Nast's "paradigm shift" not resulted in the death of virtually all writer stipends. Which wouldn't have been the end of the world had you remained a viable screenwriting commodity in Hollywood (which had *not* gone in the tank, but which acted as if it had). Your writing partner and crutch, Daniel, was off directing his brainchild, *Phoebe in Wonderland*: the movie he'd been trying to make since the pre-Bruno days. Which would have been a boon for you, in a reflected-glory sort of way, had your fancy-pants agents not viewed you as Daniel's halfwit-brother-in-the-basement—the guy who hadn't earned a penny, and who had been AWOL forever, owing to "personal issues."

Frankly, what were the odds of finding any form of employment, in this economy, when everyone knew where you'd spent the spring semester? The market for bipolar amnesiac reporters was not an emerging one. You wouldn't hire you. Shortly after ECT ended, Doug offered a toe-in-the-water assignment: a miniprofile of the actress Anna Faris. "Ready to talk about *The House Bunny*?" you asked her.

She talked.

"Terrific," you said. "Ready to talk about *The House Bunny*?"

Trow 2.0. Time to fire off a quick tirade to Graydon, then pack up the cats and head for Alaska, to write a magnum opus about The Death of Media ("Is Anderson Mad?").

But no. The bright, shiny urge to escape was back-burnered, pending the disposition of a development infinitely worse than all the others combined.

It involved your father. It involved the point where "preleukemia" sheds the prefix.

By that winter, the ageless father was an elderly man with advancing leukemia. His shoulders hunched; his gait, which until recently had remained as jaunty as a teenager's, slowed and creaked. Skinny to begin with, he was now frail, gaunt; his weight loss, compared to yours, truly was ominous. The remaining curative options—two experimental drug trials—were major long shots for an eighty-nine-year-old patient. Failing those, he would be dead within months.

For months, throughout the bulk of 2009, you shuttled between California and Michigan. You tended to visit in two-week chunks, especially when your father was in the hospital. The latter occurred with increasing frequency and duration, in accordance with the vagaries of both the disease and the treatment: a "lighter" form of chemotherapy administered as part of a clinical trial at the University of Michigan hospital. The treatment was light only by degree, and had never proven successful on a patient in his eighties. One month, things would look good and he'd be free to go about his normal domestic routines; the next, he'd be back in the hospital, weakened by infection and feeling like a caged animal.

He was too weak to attend a relative's funeral. Michael, a whip-smart seventeen-year-old, had died of a drug overdose. You had barely known Michael, in part because he had seemed almost as standoffish as you were. In fact, though, shyness wasn't his major issue. The issue was his manic depression. The shared characteristic was purely symbolic. He was a step-relative, born of a different gene pool. The funeral, you felt, was not about you. You held it together right up until a friend of Michael's recalled how he would periodically vanish, only to return a half hour later. "Sorry," Michael would say. "I was in my car. I needed a place to scream."

Every day you and Mom made the sleety forty-five-minute drive to and from Ann Arbor. Days were spent fetching Dad's sandwiches from Zingerman's Deli—he dismissed hospital food with a wave of the hand and a curt "feh"—and bemoaning the football team's wretched defense, and peppering doctors with unanswerable questions.

It was crushing.

And yet.

Notwithstanding the unavoidable hazards—squalls of anger, a thousand moments of quiet grief—The Great Bust-up never came to pass. Never got a clean shot at you. There were too many things to do and people to look after. Depression, panic attacks, self-abuse: they simply had no place here. You didn't even worry about them, because *you didn't worry about them*.

Rumination and isolation. The evil twins. The princes of darkness.

They remained at bay until the end, which arrived on February 7, 2010. You were on a plane, en route to Detroit, when he died; it was Super Bowl Sunday—a fact Dad would have found funny; the whole family did, up to a point. That day, as you arrived at the house, you expected an emotional bloodbath. As it turned out, though, your mother and brothers were something like tranquil (as opposed to tranquilized). They were grief-stricken. But nobody felt cheated. He was a man who had lived a full, and fully *connected,* life.

The last time you'd spoken to him, a few days earlier, he was brittle but true to form. "Enough about me," he said. "Tell me how you are."

You attempted the same gambit.

"Knock it off," he said. "Tell me."

"I'm just fine," you said. "Really—"

He cleared his throat. Conspicuously.

"Listen to me," he said. "I don't like the way you live. I know you don't like talking about it, but too bad. I'm an old man. So you need to *promise me* you're taking care of yourself, getting out, living life."

"I promise."

"I'm *serious.*" He paused. "*Promise me.*"

So there's that.

Certain changes were immediate, starting in the shrink department. Five was competent and well-intentioned, but no match for an equivocator of your caliber. Plus, once she lost the confidence of your friends, she was cooked. In came a new psychiatrist (for meds) and a separate therapist (for whining), whom you see frequently and eagerly. That both seem to "get" you—whatever that means—is a function of (a) their skill and (b) your realization that, for nearly a decade, you had paid doctors to not understand you.

Also, both shrinks agreed on one basic point:

You are not bipolar.

Not necessarily, anyway. And certainly not to the degree that Bruno, Jay, and George were. And Tim. Possibly. Probably. Not long ago, while browsing animal books, you came across a book called *Death in the Grizzly Maze: The Timothy Treadwell Story*; the author, a wildlife writer named Mike Lapinski, persuasively theorized that Tim was a member of the B-squad. Your first reaction was one of shame—of all things, that's the detail you miss?

You went four decades before anyone detected slightest trace of manic depression. Most people who know you—the ones who missed the big show—still seem skeptical. The Episode was prompted by, lo and behold, "an adverse reaction to prescription pain medication." A freak one at that. During the three years since then, you've had only one minor scare: engine running a little hot, thoughts turning to mischief. Five tweaked your carbamazepine, a gentler alternative to lithium. A day later, you returned to a life of quiet moderation.

Hardcore manic-depressives were classified as bipolar I's or II's. You were "Bipolar Not Otherwise Specified."

"It's what doctors say when they don't know everything," said the new psychiatrist, Dr. Six. "And there's a lot we don't know about bipolar disorder."

"So it means I'm 'Bipolar Maybe'?"

"It means you're someone with symptoms consistent with bipolar spectrum. It's a broad diagnostic spectrum. Like autism to Asperger's."

"So I'm 'Bipolar Maybe A Little'?"

He half smiled.

"Close enough," he said. "I guess."

"I just need to know what I am," you said.

Six thought about that.

"Okay," he said. "You have a case of Ned Zeman."

The nerve.

You paced the night away, wondering where some highfalutin Harvard headshrinker got off disrespecting your status as a Doomed Bipolar Literary Genius. Would he have told Hemingway "You have a case of Ernest Hemingway"?

A beeline back to Six's office. "I feel like you're saying it's all in my imagination," you said.

"Glad you didn't just ruminate about this," he said. "What you've had is real and serious," he said. "And it's unique to you—that's what I was trying to stress. *Bipolar* doesn't explain everything. Your mind is more complex than that. It's a mix of things. Some you're stuck with—maybe you've just got a naturally melancholic demeanor. Some will respond to meds and therapy." He nodded. "And lifestyle choices."

There it was again. The dirty little phrase you'd rejected for years (along with "environmental factors" and "personal inventory"). The one that put the onus on you, The Victim. The one you should have embraced years ago, while you were still alive.

You could have nipped this thing in bud. You, like most moodies, had a say in your fate. For the better part of a decade, you said "Fuck off and fix me." Sometimes you still say it. Sometimes you still go underground. But then you remember what happened not too long ago. Even though you can't.

The sign in the hallway outside Six's office reads: YOU ARE HERE.

Keep waiting around for some super-pill to save the day, you're fucked. Keep waiting for Things To Turn Around, you're fucked.

Psych wards and ECT save lives. But they don't create new ones.

Stay on the meds and off the Bolivian flake. Find the right shrink, go routinely, and tell him the icky parts first. Fight the urge to slap the next Health-Care Professional Baring Life Skills or Coping Tips For A Better Tomorrow.

Get up. Get the blood flowing. Go somewhere. Anywhere. Except to the shooting range or Ohio.

Stop tearing paper.

Call someone, anyone. Some fifty-five million Americans have a mood disorder, and every one of them feels a little less alone when they meet a fellow traveler.

Distinguish those friends and relatives who ask "How are you?" from the ones who ask "How *are* you?" The latter should be avoided at all costs. But the former will save your ass every time. You say this on good authority.

Resistance is futile.

Adapt or die.

The future is yours.

These are the rules of the tunnel.

ACKNOWLEDGMENTS

This book, like its author, would be a blank white void—literally—were it not for the minds and hearts of Ben and Daniel Barnz, Jim Boyd, Lizz Leonard, Paula Lisbe, and David and Peter Zeman.

And two Caitlins.

Blessings also to Barry Battia, Matt Brune, Mark Leibovich, Mike Lisbe, Michael Mahon, David Pitofsky, Carrie Rosenbloom, and Naomi Wax.

I'm beyond grateful to the editor of this book, Lauren Marino, a person of uncommon gifts, grace, and patience. Gotham's publisher, William Shinker, gave me this opportunity. My literary agent, Richard Abate, made it happen. And Lizz, editor-without-portfolio, did everything else.

As ever, I owe a huge debt to Graydon Carter and the staff of *Vanity Fair*, most notably Doug Stumpf and Evgenia Peretz.

And, not least, godspeed to four mad fools—Bruno Zehnder, Jay Moloney, Tim Treadwell, and George Trow—who saw the light.